A Very Industrious People

Production & Operations Management
with a Latter-day Saint Twist

Fifth Edition
Michael G. Clark

Fifth Edition

Contents

PREFACE

On 10 December 1974 President Ezra Taft Benson, then President of the Quorum of the Twelve Apostles of The Church of Jesus Christ of Latter-day Saints, gave a BYU Devotional address in which he said the following:

> Only a Zion people can bring in a Zion society. And as the Zion people increase, so we will be able to incorporate more of the principles of Zion until we have a people prepared to receive the Lord.

> This means that on this campus, in due time, there will be an increasing number of textbooks written by inspired men of the Church. There will be less and less a tendency to subscribe to the false teachings of men. There will be more and more a tendency first to lay the groundwork of the gospel truth in every subject and then, if necessary, to show where the world may fall short of that standard. In due time there will be increased teaching by the Spirit of God, but that can take place only if there is a decreased promotion of the precepts of men.

This book, *A Very Industrious People*—so named in honor of the converted Lamanites who abandoned their profession of plunder and became "a very industrious people" (see Alma 23:18, 24:17-18)—represents my best efforts to follow President Benson's inspired injunction, that is, to write a textbook that will "first...lay the groundwork of the gospel truth in [production and operations management]." My **primary purpose** in doing so is to "[increase] **teaching by the Spirit of God**" by **making more accessible and familiar** a subject that many students find difficult. This purpose supports the first imperative for BYU-Idaho, outlined by former President Kim B. Clark at his 2005 inauguration, that is, to "raise substantially the quality of every aspect of the student experience."

As BYU-Idaho "[serves] more students" (President Clark's second imperative), especially those from developing countries, it becomes increasingly important "to lower the cost of education" (President Clark's third imperative). Hence, my **secondary purpose** in writing this book is to **help lower the cost** of education for students taking a production and operations management course from BYU-Idaho, either in a traditional setting (on campus) or online. Note that a traditional operations management textbook can cost more than $200 while this book costs less than $15, or, if students desire, they can forego this purchase and simply use the PDF version of this book for free.

Writing this book has been a labor of love—a love of the subject matter and my career in this field, a love of students, a love of latter-day teachings, and a love of our Father and His Son, the ultimate Creators and Masters of production and operations management.

Michael G. Clark

Chapter 1

TRUE WEALTH

*A man may possess all the gold, silver and precious stones in the world, which are called wealth and yet starve to death. Wealth does not give true greatness. It will purchase medical aid in case of sickness; it will purchase food, clothing and shelter; but **true wealth consists in the skill to produce those conveniences and comforts from the elements**."*

Brigham Young[1]

Production, the act of creating or manufacturing something, is as old as the earth. Indeed, the first verse in the Bible tells us: "In the beginning God *created*[2] the heaven and the earth."[3] Furthermore, the book of Abraham clarifies that the Gods took materials[4] and with them "organized and formed the heavens and the earth."[5] This process of creating the earth could be depicted as follows:

If we translate these scriptures and basic process into business-speak we would say that raw materials were transformed into value-added outputs:

Such a transformational or value-adding process is at the core of any business, be it a manufacturer or service provider. Yes, at the heart of any business is its ability to produce something of value for which customers will give their hard-earned money. Accepting this knowledge as fact helps us more fully understand and appreciate Brigham Young's statement that "true wealth consists in the skill to produce...conveniences and comforts from the elements."

---

[1] Brigham Young, *Man's Agency*, 1889 (emphasis added).
[2] The Hebrew tells us that created could also mean shaped, fashioned, organized or formed.
[3] Genesis 1:1.
[4] Abraham 3:24.
[5] Abraham 4:1.

Not only do the scriptures give us valuable insights into the basic process of production, they also shed light on the practice of production and operations *management*—the planning and directing of such activities. For example, we know that God created all things, "spiritually, before they were naturally upon the face of the earth."[6] This spiritual creation was an essential planning activity that helped ensure the success of the enterprise.

Moreover, this management extends beyond the one-time endeavor of creation and reaches into recurring, ongoing processes such as procreation. The grass, herbs and fruit trees were designed to "[yield] seed after his kind" in a never-ending process of production, where seeds (an input) would be transformed into plants (value-added outputs).[7] Likewise, great whales, every winged foul, cattle, creeping things and all other forms of animal life were instructed to "be fruitful, and multiply" and fill the earth"[8] as part of their ongoing existence or mode of operation.

Adam, the firstborn man,[9] engaged in production activities when he "began to till the earth, and to have dominion over all the beasts of the field, and to eat his bread by the sweat of his brow, as I the Lord had commanded him. And Eve, also, his wife, did labor with him."[10] We can confidently assume that this work required skilled hands *and* enlightened minds in order for our great parents, Adam and Eve, to be successful. The associated brainwork elevated their efforts from mere manual labor into the more challenging practice of production and operations management.

Even though we now live in very different times, where few work on farms or in factories, many of the same principles that applied to Adam and Eve also apply to us. Hence, we should not be surprised by this statement from President Ezra Taft Benson:

> There are blessings in being close to the soil, in raising your own food, even it if is only a garden in your yard and a fruit tree or two. Man's material wealth basically springs from the land and other natural resources. Combined with his human energy and multiplied by his tools, this wealth is assured and expanded through freedom and righteousness. Those families will be fortunate who, in the last days, have an adequate supply of each of these particulars."[11]

No matter our chosen career or our level of prosperity, there are benefits that come from always acknowledging that "true wealth consists in the skill to *produce* those conveniences and comforts from the elements" and that our "material wealth basically stems from the land and other natural resources." The Book of Mormon corroborates these ideas by including many verses where great men led by example, "laboring with [their] own hands" for their support,[12] and where the people were instructed to be industrious and to labor with their hands.[13] Learning about

---

[6] Moses 3:5.

[7] Moses 2:11-12.

[8] Moses 2:22.

[9] Abraham 1:3.

[10] Moses 5:1.

[11] *Teachings of Ezra Taft Benson*, pg. 474.

[12] See Mosiah 2:14 and Alma 30:32 (or the opposite case in Alma 1:3; 17:14).

[13] See 2 Nephi 5:17, Mosiah 18:24; 24:4-5 and Alma 24:18.

production and operations management helps us remember these truths because its basic planning activities[14] are inextricably connected to the value-creating activities of sourcing, making and delivering.

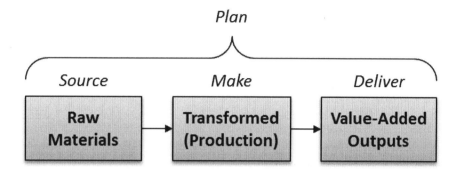

Just as "there are blessings in being close to the soil," as President Benson stated, there are blessings available to those professionals who remain close to "the gemba"[15] or, in other words, "the actual place" within a firm where value creation takes place. Whether in a manufacturer or service provider, and whether you work in Finance, Marketing, Operations and Supply Chain Management or some other function, the degree to which you are able to add value to the company—in terms of solving problems and seizing opportunities—will largely flow from your working knowledge of its core value-adding activities.

Preview of Book Structure

The subsequent chapters of this book are divided into three sections: (1) Competing with Operations, (2) Planning and Controlling Operations, and (3) Linking Supply Chains.

- Chapters 2 through 6 deal with the three key components of value—responsiveness, cost, and quality—and how they contribute to successful operations strategies.
- Chapters 7 through 11 cover the processes that are part of a typical production and operations planning and control system.
- Finally, chapters 12 and 13 discuss how to effectively manage upstream and downstream supply chain relationships.

---

[14] Plan, Source, Make and Deliver (along with Return) are the basic macro processes within the supply-chain operations reference (SCOR) model, a standard diagnostics tool for supply chain management.
[15] In lean manufacturing, the Japanese term gemba refers to "the actual place" where value is created.

COMPETING

WITH

OPERATIONS

Chapter 2

PROCESS STRATEGY

The scriptures speak of "the shield of faith wherewith," the Lord said, "ye shall be able to quench all the fiery darts of the wicked" (D&C 27:17).

This shield of faith is best fabricated in a cottage industry. While the shield can be polished in classes in the Church and in activities, it is meant to be handcrafted in the home and fitted to each individual.

President Boyd K. Packer[16]

The Bible Dictionary tells us that "faith is kindled by hearing the testimony of those who have faith" whereas "strong faith is developed by obedience to the gospel of Jesus Christ."[17] If we looked at "kindled faith" and "strong faith" as two separate, but related products, we would recognize that the processes for creating these two "products" are different. Consistent with the Bible Dictionary, the quote above from President Packer shows how different processes can be used to fabricate, fit, and polish the shield of faith.

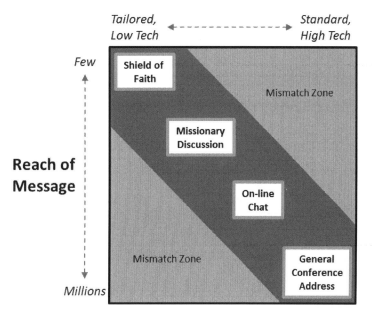

Nature of Message and Required Technology

---

[16] Boyd. K. Packer, "Do Not Fear," General Conference, April 2004.
[17] Bible Dictionary, pg. 669.

Faith can be kindled from hearing the good word in lessons, conversations, and even mass media. The sharing of testimonies through mass media can reach countless individuals at once—think of General Conference. On the other hand, the process of building strong faith requires answering gospel-related questions and encouraging and committing an individual to obey the commandments. This is typically much more personal than merely hearing the good word, but rather requires more effort on the part of the hearer. (Think of a parent teaching a child or of a missionary teaching a discussion to an investigator.)

Delivering and listening to General Conference requires sophisticated, specialized technology that simultaneously delivers the same message to millions (although the Holy Ghost can and does customize the messages through individualized promptings), but requires very little skill to turn on the radio or the television or the computer to receive those messages. Teaching a child, however, can be delivered and received with virtually no technology, but requires highly-skilled teachers (parents) who can adjust lessons according to spiritual promptings and the needs of the learner (the child).

These two process examples of building faith represent the polar extremes along a continuum of process options that can be selected. Without a doubt, many in-between process options can be found or designed along this continuum. For example, the Church uses internet chats as a means of introducing individuals to and building faith in the restored gospel. The "Chat About Faith" graphic comes from an internet ad that was placed on the Yahoo! Sports website covering the 2010 World Cup in South Africa.

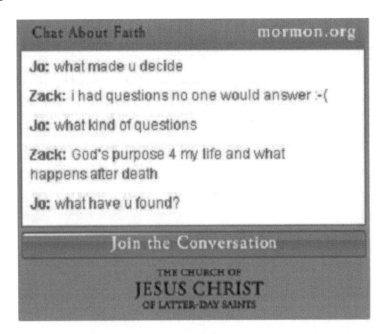

This in-between process requires more technology than a parent teaching a child or a missionary discussion but less than a General Conference broadcast. Moreover, the technology used to send out these online messages is more general purpose and accessible than the equipment used to broadcast General Conference (an internet browser and internet connection versus television cameras and broadcast equipment). On the other hand, the chat requires much more human interaction than watching General Conference but less than teaching missionary discussions. It can deliver messages that are more customized than a General Conference address but less customized than a face-to-face parent-child or missionary discussion.

In summary, missionary discussions and online chats are in-between solutions—in terms of audience size, customizability, and technology. The online chat is designed to reach a broader audience than a missionary discussion but not as big as General Conference; deliver messages that are more customized than General Conference but less than a missionary discussion; use technology that is more sophisticated than a missionary discussion but less sophisticated than a General Conference broadcast.

In like manner, production and service delivery processes can exhibit great variety in their efforts to meet the variety in product and service needs and wants demanded by customer. Here are two examples:

- Production: When comparing the production process for a Ford Focus to that of a NASCAR racecar, the Focus' process will feature highly specialized and automated equipment (robotics) which can produce high volumes of standard products as opposed to the NASCAR production team, which will feature less automation but higher-skilled workers who produce fewer, more customized vehicles.
- Services: Frequent standard banking transactions (like deposits and withdrawals) can be handled with highly-specialized technology—an ATM—and no human intervention whereas infrequent, but customized transactions (like investment portfolio changes) often require a skilled specialist and less-specialized technology (a telephone call, email, or face-to-face meeting).

Chapter Objectives

All the examples above show that seemingly similar products or services often require vastly different processes. One of the key challenges and opportunities in operations and supply chain management is learning to identify or design processes that support the company's strategy, that are appropriate for the given products or services to be made and delivered. In this chapter you will learn how to make such decisions. Specifically, after studying this chapter you should be able to:

1. Describe how a firm's operations strategy can support a company's strategy.
2. Describe the flow, equipment selection, personnel skill requirements, and main priority of each of the main process types.
3. Match a given product or service to the most appropriate process type.
4. Perform line balancing and process layout analyses.
5. Describe the five focusing steps within the Theory of Constraints.
6. Perform a break-even analysis to select an appropriate process or equipment option given different output volumes.

Process Selection and Operations Strategy

<u>Question</u>: What are the ways in which a company can secure a competitive advantage, and how do they relate to process strategy?

A company can secure a competitive advantage by putting its primary focus into one of three areas: (1) **responsiveness**, (2) **cost leadership**, or (3) **differentiation**. These three areas can be mapped into a framework that we will call the "value triangle."

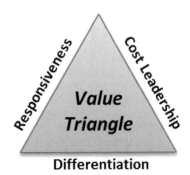

In order to develop an effective operations strategy a company should clearly understand its value proposition. In other words, it should clearly know which side of the value triangle it will focus on, as seen in the company examples below:

- When a firm competes on **responsiveness,** its processes focus on flexibility and service so that it can quickly respond to customer needs and desires. **Dell's** assemble-to-order, direct shipment model is an example of this.
- A **cost leadership strategy** means a company will compete on price and will endeavor to lower its costs in order to compete profitably. **Wal-Mart** provides a great example of a company that competes on price and has made cost cutting a hallmark of its operations strategy.
- A **differentiation strategy** means the firm focuses on making its offerings truly unique (features, quality, etc.), where there is that extra "something" to the offerings that cannot be easily imitated. To the extent it can do this, it will have the ability to charge a premium for its offerings. As part of its successful differentiation strategy, **Apple** has invested in its own retail operations (Apple Store, iTunes Store) and has focused heavily on integrated hardware and software product design. Manufacturing, not seen as an operations differentiator, has been outsourced.

<u>Question</u>: What is the Product-Process Matrix?

The product-process matrix was developed by Robert H. Hayes and Steven C. Wheelwright (President of BYU-Hawaii) to explain the appropriate relationship between product characteristics and processes characteristics. The graphic below is an adaptation of the original product-process matrix[18] and highlights the basic product and process structures typically found within manufacturing and service organizations.

<u>Question</u>: How can the product-process matrix help organizations properly align production processes with corporate strategy?

This conceptual framework can be used to help organizations determine if their product and process characteristics are properly aligned, and if not, lead them to

---

[18] See Robert H. Hayes and Steven C. Wheelwright, "Link Manufacturing Process and Product Life Cycles," Harvard Business Review, January-February, 1979.

identify what changes should be made. We need look no further than fast food giant McDonalds to see how their processes evolved over time to more appropriately meet the demands of the product offerings.

For several decades McDonalds had a very simple menu (standard products) and primarily employed a make-to-stock build strategy. Appropriately, their equipment was highly specialized and they placed a premium on process efficiency and repeatability. This product and process strategy served McDonalds very well for decades, as they were able to offer highly consistent food at affordable prices.

Adaptation of the Product-Process Matrix

As competition intensified in the fast food industry during the 1970s and into the 1990s, McDonalds responded by adding more items to its menu. However, they did not adjust their processes accordingly. In the 1990s they found themselves in the lower left-hand "mismatch zone" of the product-process matrix, trying to offer a variety of products with inflexible, efficient processes. As product variety increased it became more difficult to forecast demand for each individual item, and since they were making inventory to stock, their inventory costs exploded because they were scrapping (throwing out) more and more finished goods that were not sold within the products' shelf life.

Realizing this mismatch, McDonalds adapted their processes and build strategies. All the short-shelf life items (burgers) would be supplied using a two-step process. Hot hamburger patties are now made-to-stock and are stored hot in special drawers (with longer shelf life than a finished burger) until they become part of an assemble-to-order burger. By employing this more flexible assemble-to-order process for their burgers, McDonalds can offer a wider variety of fresher products (as demanded by customers). At the same time, they have been able to greatly reduce inventory costs by reducing scrap of finished goods.

The McDonalds example is very indicative of firms who, in response to customer demands, expand their product lines without making appropriate adjustments to supporting processes; where they continue to bow at the altar of efficiency when more flexibility or responsiveness may be appropriate.

Facility Layout

The layout of a production facility should tightly correspond to its process strategy and should flow from the business strategy. For example, McDonald's made several layout changes to support their more flexible process—which supported its new strategy of providing a greater variety of fresher products.

Question: What are the basic types of facility layouts used in production and service operations?

There are four basic facility layouts that are employed in production processes. Each is typically best suited to a particular process type, designed to meet the needs of the product or service being delivered. The four basic options are:

1. Fixed-position layout (project)
2. Process layout (functional)
3. Product layout (line)
4. Cellular layout (plus a number of other hybrids)

Question: What is a fixed-position layout and when is it used?

A **fixed-position layout** brings labor, material, and equipment to the work site. It is most often used for one-of-a-kind and very large product and service offerings.

- **Examples** of fixed-position layouts include ship building, construction, operating rooms.

Question: What is a process layout and when is it used?

Process or functional layouts group together workers and equipment that perform similar functions. They are well suited to batch production environments with low-volume, high-mix make-to-order products and services. By employing highly skilled workers and general-purpose equipment, output can be easily tailored to meet exacting customer-specific requirements. Work flow is intermittent and can take different routes through the various departments.

- **Examples** of process layouts include machine shops, offices (grouped by department), emergency rooms, and gourmet restaurants.

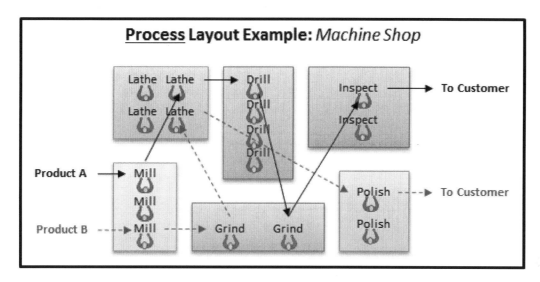

Question: What is a product layout and when is it used?

Product or line layouts are highly structured arrangements of specialized equipment and low-skill workers who often perform mundane and repetitive tasks. Product layouts are most appropriate for high-volume, low-mix production of standard products in a make-to-stock or assemble-to-order production environment. This layout is the traditional assembly line layout.

- **Examples** of product layouts include computer assembly, automobile assembly, and snack food production.

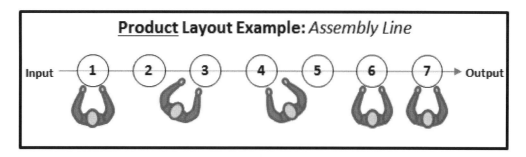

Question: What is a cellular layout and when is it used?

A **cellular layout** or **manufacturing cell** is a hybrid layout (cross between process layout and product layout), which groups 3 to 10 machines and cross-trained workers to produce a family of products as opposed to just one product. It is an alternative to traditional batch production and is very supportive of just-in-time principles (discussed in the JIT and Lean Production chapter). It is more efficient than a process layout and more flexible than a product layout.

- **Examples** of cellular layout include sewn products, mechanical assembly, and distribution.

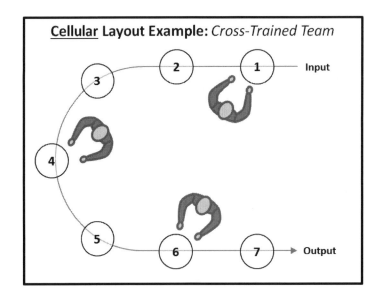

Question: What are the advantages and disadvantages of each layout?

The advantages and disadvantages of these basic layouts are in the table below:

Layout	Advantages	Disadvantages
Process	• Supports customized products • Flexible equipment and personnel • Fewer breakdowns (from low-cost, general-purpose equipment) • Enhanced job satisfaction from greater work variety	• High materials-handling cost • High work-in-process inventory • Long set-up times, lead times • Low equipment utilization • Complex production scheduling • High-cost skilled labor
Product	• Low materials-handling cost • Low work-in-process inventory • High utilization of equipment and personnel • Simplified production scheduling • Low-cost unskilled labor	• Supports little product variety • High-cost specialized equipment, vulnerable to breakdowns • Interdependent tasks (difficult to balance work across stations) • Decreased job satisfaction
Cellular	• Economical to produce small batches (lower work-in-process) • Low WIP (work in process) = short lead times, better quality • Easier to balance tasks with fewer, cross-trained employees • Enhanced jobs satisfaction from teamwork and communication	• Requires sufficiently similar processing steps among products within a family • Requires sufficiently high volumes to be cost effective • Vulnerable to equipment breakdowns

Process (Functional) Layout Method: Load-Distance Minimization

The most common method for locating departments or functions within a process layout is to minimize the interdepartmental movement of material. This reduces costs and can create synergies when highly interactive departments are located next to each other. The **load-distance method** can be employed to minimize inter-departmental movement. Here are the steps to this method:

1. Identify the distances between department locations (or potential locations).
2. For each department estimate the expected number of trips to and from each of the other departments.
3. Calculate the total load-distance for the layout. This is done by multiplying the load (number of interdepartmental trips) by the distance for each department-to-department combination.
4. Through trial and error,[19] see if you can reduce the load-distance by rearranging department locations.

Let's follow these steps within an example to see how they work. *Picture Perfect Designs* is an IBC company that produces customized wood-mounted photos. All production activities currently take place at BYU-Idaho's wood shop. The company operations manager would like to see how much total distance they travel during one week of production. To do so we'll follow the steps outlined above.

1. Identify the distances between work centers (departments).

    ➤ Action Taken: The graphic below contains given distances for this problem.

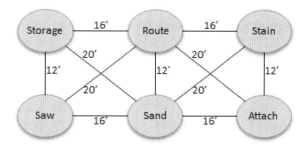

2. Estimate the expected number of trips to and from each work center.

    ➤ Action Taken: The estimated number of trips is given in the table below.

"Load" Between Work Centers (step 2)						
From ＼ To	Storage	Saw	Route	Sand	Stain	Attach
Storage	-	70	65	40	30	60
Saw	55	-	40	10	0	0
Route	45	0	-	80	25	0
Sand	50	5	15	-	75	10
Stain	35	0	5	25	-	75
Attach	0	0	5	20	15	-

---

[19] Trial and error is sufficient to help you learn the basics of the load-distance method. In large, complex, real-life situations, sophisticated computer software is employed to help in the design of process layouts.

3. Calculate the load-distance for the layout.

> Action Taken: To help with this step we will create another table which contains the distances to and from each work center (to go along with the graphic in step 1). Now we will multiply the numbers in this new distance table by the corresponding numbers in the load table (from step 2) to get the total distance traveled between each work center, shown in the third table below. (The formula for cell C23 is in the formula bar so you can see this equation for computing the load-distance from the saw to storage.) The grand total for this layout configuration is an estimated 15,620 feet traveled per week.

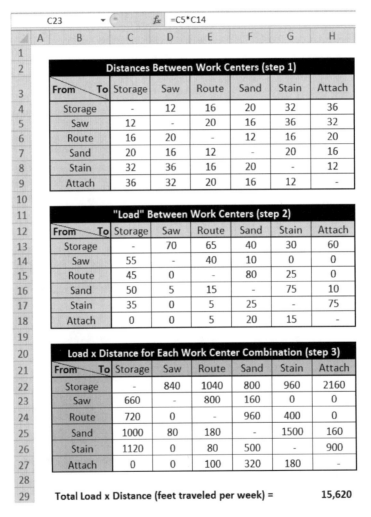

C23 f_x =C5*C14

Distances Between Work Centers (step 1)

From\To	Storage	Saw	Route	Sand	Stain	Attach
Storage	-	12	16	20	32	36
Saw	12	-	20	16	36	32
Route	16	20	-	12	16	20
Sand	20	16	12	-	20	16
Stain	32	36	16	20	-	12
Attach	36	32	20	16	12	-

"Load" Between Work Centers (step 2)

From\To	Storage	Saw	Route	Sand	Stain	Attach
Storage	-	70	65	40	30	60
Saw	55	-	40	10	0	0
Route	45	0	-	80	25	0
Sand	50	5	15	-	75	10
Stain	35	0	5	25	-	75
Attach	0	0	5	20	15	-

Load x Distance for Each Work Center Combination (step 3)

From\To	Storage	Saw	Route	Sand	Stain	Attach
Storage	-	840	1040	800	960	2160
Saw	660	-	800	160	0	0
Route	720	0	-	960	400	0
Sand	1000	80	180	-	1500	160
Stain	1120	0	80	500	-	900
Attach	0	0	100	320	180	-

Total Load x Distance (feet traveled per week) =   15,620

4. Try to reduce the load-distance by rearranging the location of work centers.

> Action Taken: Nothing. We will not take this step in this example as the primary focus is to show how to calculate load x distance. If we were to take this step we would see if it was possible to centrally locate those work centers which are highly interactive (as shown in the step-3 table above).

Product (Line) Layout Method: Line Balancing

Product or line layouts are designed to sequence the required production activities in such a way as to *maximize equipment and worker utilization* and therefore *minimize cost*. The method for achieving these objectives is called **line balancing,** which is done by following these steps.

1. Identify all the separable tasks for assembling the product, including the time required for each task and each task's immediate predecessor(s).
2. Draw a **precedence diagram** based on the information gathered in step 1. (This will look much like network diagrams that are drawn for projects.)
3. Compute the **total time** required to complete all the tasks.
4. Compute the takt time for the line. **Takt time** is the available production time divided by the required output rate. It is the maximum allowable time between the completion of successive units.

$$\boldsymbol{Takt\ time} = \frac{available\ production\ time}{required\ output\ rate}$$

5. Compute the **theoretical minimum** number of workstations required for the line. This is the total time required to complete one unit of production (step 3) divided by the takt time (step 4), *rounded up to the nearest whole number* (because there is no such thing as a fractional workstation).

$$\boldsymbol{Theoretical\ minimum\ number\ of\ workstations} = \frac{req'd\ time\ for\ one\ unit}{takt\ time}$$

6. Assign each task to a workstation. Make sure that (a) all precedence relationships are strictly honored and (b) the total time for the tasks assigned to any workstation does not exceed the takt time.
7. Evaluate the performance of the proposed line by calculating cycle time (CT), idle time (IT), and efficiency.

Let's follow these steps within an example to see how they work. *Lenny's Lawnmowers* is a small but successful manufacturer of simple lawnmowers. In fact, they have a very simple operation because they produce and sell just one model. Their current manufacturing process utilizes individual workers who assemble entire lawnmowers on their own. They work one 8-hour shift and are required to produce 80 units a day.

Lenny noticed that some workers are better at certain tasks than others, but under the current process each worker must perform each assembly task. He would like to see if the process would be more efficient if they changed the production facility into a product layout, enabling his workers to focus on those tasks which they perform best. To explore this possibility we'll follow the steps outlined above.

1. Identify all the separable tasks for assembling the product, including the time required for each task and each task's immediate predecessor(s).

> ➤ Action Taken: The table below contains all of the information required for this step.

Task	Description	Duration	Predecessors
A	Mount chassis for assembly	2	-
B	Attach wheel assemblies	4	A
C	Attach handle	4	A
D	Install engine	5	B
E	Attach safety release handle	2	C
F	Attach throttle control	3	E
G	Connect throttle cable	2	D, F
H	Attach blade	4	D
I	Install trailing shield assembly	3	C
J	Install mulch plug assembly	2	H
K	Assemble and attach bag	2	G, I, J
Total time required for all tasks		**33**	**minutes**

2. Draw a precedence diagram based on the information gathered in step 1. (A precedence diagram is a graphical method of depicting the sequence of the tasks within a process or project.)

> ➤ Action Taken: See the diagram below.

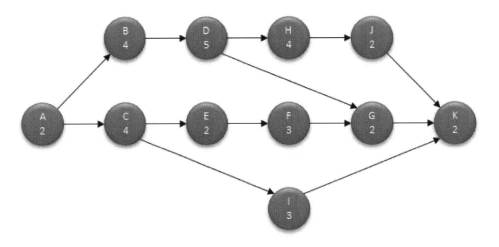

3. Compute the total time required to complete all the tasks.

> ➤ Action Taken: Total time = T = 33 minutes (as seen in the table above).

4. Compute the takt time for the line.

> ➤ Action Taken: 6 minutes (as seen in the equation below).

$$Takt\ time = \frac{8\ hours \times 60\ minutes\ per\ hour}{80\ units\ per\ day} = \frac{480\ minutes\ per\ day}{80\ units\ per\ day}$$

$$Takt\ time = 6\ minutes$$

5. Compute the theoretical minimum number of workstations.

> ➤ <u>Action Taken</u>: 6 workstations (5.5 rounded up to 6).

$$Theoretical\ minimum = \frac{33\ minutes\ total\ task\ time\ to\ produce\ one\ unit}{6\ minutes\ (takt\ time)}$$

6. Assign each task to a workstation.

> ➤ <u>Action Taken</u>: Assigned each task to a workstation as shown in the diagram below. (**Note** that there is more than one way this could have been done. For example, an **alternative assignment of tasks** could have put tasks F and I in workstation 4, G and H in workstation 5, and J and K together in workstation 6. **Also note** that the assigned task time for each workstation must not exceed six minutes, the takt time.)

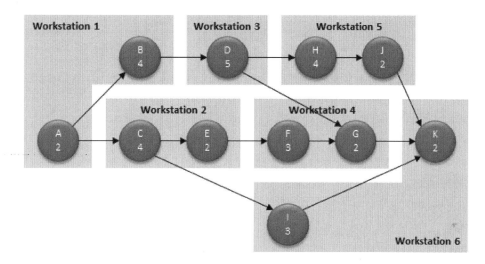

The diagram above is helpful to show precedence relationships and how the tasks could be assigned to workstations. However, it does not show the final line sequence of tasks within the assembly line. This is shown in the graphic below.

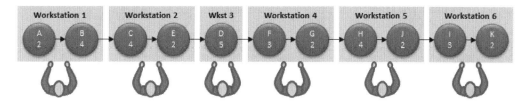

Notice that there is only one worker assigned to each workstation and that time required at each workstation is similar, hence the term "line balancing."

7. Evaluate the performance of the proposed line by calculating cycle time (CT), idle time (IT), and efficiency.

> ➤ <u>Cycle time calculation</u>: 6 minutes

Cycle time = CT = maximum amount of time spent on any workstation

> ➤ Percent idle time calculation: 8.33%

$$Idle\ time = Actual\ No.\ of\ workstations\ (W)\ \times CT - total\ task\ time\ (T)$$

$$Idle\ Time = 6 \times 6 - 33 = 3\ minutes$$

$$Percent\ idle\ time = \frac{idle\ time}{W \times CT}$$

$$Percent\ idle\ time = \frac{3}{36} = 8.33\%$$

> ➤ Efficiency calculation: 91.67%

$$Efficiency = \frac{total\ task\ time\ (T)}{actual\ no.\ of\ workstations \times cycle\ time\ (CT)}$$

$$Efficiency = \frac{33}{6 \times 6} = 91.67\%$$

From these calculations we can see that this line layout is quite efficient with less than 10 percent idle time. Still, there is room for improvement with cellular layouts and the application of JIT principles.

The Theory of Constraints

Question: What is the Theory of Constraints?

The Theory of Constraints is a holistic management philosophy developed by Dr. Eliyahu M. Goldratt (author of *The Goal*). The five focusing steps of this philosophy include: 1) identify the constraint, 2) exploit the constraint, 3) subordinate all processes to the constraint, 4) elevate the performance of the constraint, and 5) return to step 1. Let's use the diagram below to better understand this process.

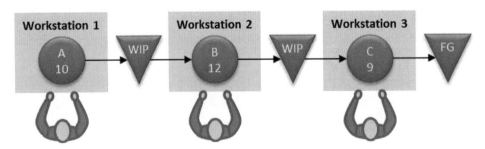

Suppose we have a three-step assembly process where each task is assigned to a separate workstation, and let's further suppose that we want to increase the process output above its current capacity. To achieve this objective we would apply the five focusing steps as follows:

1. Identify the constraint or "bottleneck" (the workstation or task, within a series of connected tasks, which takes the longest to perform).

    > ➤ Action Taken: Identify Workstation 2 as the constraint.

2. Exploit the constraint.

> ➢ <u>Action Taken</u>: Make sure Workstation 2 is always running (for example, never let it sit idle waiting for material from Workstation 1).

3. Subordinate all processes to the constraint.

> ➢ <u>Action Taken</u>: Make sure output on Workstations 1 and 3 matches, but does not exceed, the output of Workstation 2, whose capacity is five units per hour ($60 \div 12 = 5$). This will prevent a buildup of excess WIP (work-in-process inventory).

4. Elevate the performance of the constraint.

> ➢ <u>Action Taken</u>: Let's assume we find a way to shorten Task B to eight minutes, thereby "elevating" the constraint.

5. Return to step 1.

> ➢ <u>Action Taken</u>: Identify Workstation 1 as the new constraint with a capacity of six units per hour ($60 \div 10 = 6$). From here we again work through the remaining five focusing steps.

As can be seen from the example above, the Theory of Constraints is a never-ending process of improvement. By adopting such a mindset and by methodically following these steps, dramatic process improvements can be achieved, not only in manufacturing environments, but any setting where multi-step processes exist.

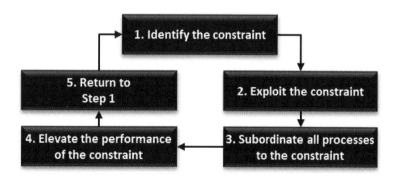

Break-Even Analysis

<u>Question</u>: What is a break-even analysis and how can it be used when selecting a process type?

A break-even analysis shows the unit volume required to recoup an investment or to identify the point at which two options have the same total cost. It can also be used to identify which process type is most appropriate given projected unit volumes.

Consistent with the product-process matrix, spending more on highly-specialized (dedicated) equipment will typically result in greater efficiency. Hence, you have high fixed costs (for the equipment) and low variable costs (for the units produced). Conversely, lower fixed costs (for general-purpose equipment) will result in higher variable costs. Using a break-even analysis can therefore help us determine the optimal process type (mix of fixed costs and variable costs) for a given unit volume.

Break-Even Example

Let's suppose we want to manufacture large bolts and that we have three process options available to us:

1. Purchase a standard lathe for $1,000, resulting in a $3 per bolt variable cost
2. Purchase a computer numerical control (CNC) lathe for $2,000, resulting in a $2 per bolt variable cost
3. Purchase a highly-specialized, high-volume lathe for $4,000, resulting in a $1.50 per bolt variable cost

If we compute the total cost for each option at various volume points—from zero units to 5,000 units in 1000-unit increments—we get the following table of total costs. Notice how at a volume of 1,000 units we get the same total cost for the first two options, namely, $4,000. Likewise, at a unit volume of 4,000 units, we get the same total cost of $10,000 for the second and third options.

| Machine Type | Cost Type | | Total Cost at Different Unit Volumes | | | | | |
	Fixed	Variable	0	1000	2000	3000	4000	5000
Standard Lathe	$ 1,000	$ 3.00	$ 1,000	$ 4,000	$ 7,000	$ 10,000	$ 13,000	$ 16,000
CNC Lathe	$ 2,000	$ 2.00	$ 2,000	$ 4,000	$ 6,000	$ 8,000	$ 10,000	$ 12,000
Dedicated Lathe	$ 4,000	$ 1.50	$ 4,000	$ 5,500	$ 7,000	$ 8,500	$ 10,000	$ 11,500

Graphing these results helps us conceptualize break-even points.

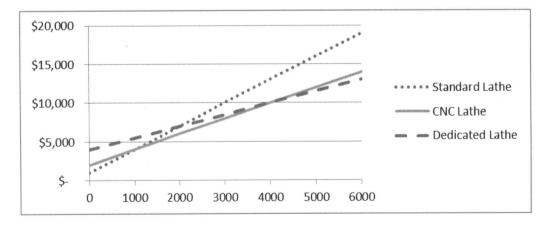

We should always select *the lowest line in the graph*, and this line changes depending upon the unit volume. For volumes up to 1,000 units, we are best served by buying a lower cost machine (dotted red line) and paying a little more for labor (hence, a higher variable cost) because we don't have enough unit volume to justify the purchase of a more expensive machine. If unit volume is greater than 1,000 units but less than 4,000, then the middle option (solid green line) is best. For volumes above 4,000, then the third option is best as the higher number of units makes it possible for us to recoup the higher fixed costs of the dedicated lathe (dashed purple line).

Question: How do you compute break-even point (especially when you don't have nice round numbers)?

Below we will show you two ways to compute the break-even point. The first will be done with a break-even equation. The second will use the "Goal Seek" function in Excel. Below is the equation for computing the break-even point between two process options.

$$Break-even\ point = \frac{FC_1 - FC_2}{VC_2 - VC_1}$$

Where

FC_1 = fixed costs for the first process option
FC_2 = fixed costs for the second process option
VC_1 = variable costs for the first process option
VC_2 = variable costs for the second process option

Note: in this equation the denominator variables are reversed ($VC_2 - VC_1$).

If we plug the numbers from the example above into this equation we will come up with the same answers for the break-even point between process 1 and process 2.

$$Break-even\ point\ (Standard\ vs.\ CNC) = \frac{1000 - 2000}{2.00 - 3.00} = \frac{-1000}{-1} = 1000\ units$$

And, as expected, doing the same for the difference with process 2 and process 3 will give us the same answer as the example above.

$$Break-even\ point\ (CNC\ vs.\ Dedicated) = \frac{2000 - 4000}{1.50 - 2.00} = \frac{-2000}{-0.50} = 4000\ units$$

G4		f_x =(C4-C5)/(D5-D4)				
A	B	C	D	E	F	G
1						
2		Cost Type		Volume & TC		
3	Machine Type	Fixed	Variable	4000		B-E Point
4	Standard Lathe	$ 1,000	$ 3.00	$ 13,000		1,000
5	CNC Lathe	$ 2,000	$ 2.00	$ 10,000		
6	Dedicated Lathe	$ 4,000	$ 1.50	$ 10,000		4,000

The graphic above shows the break-even formula in Excel with cell G4 containing the break-even point between the Standard Lathe and the CNC Lathe.

We can also compute the break-even point in Excel using a handy tool called "Goal Seek." However, to do so we must first create a formula for the total cost of each option, making sure that each option's formula refers to the same unit volume cell. Algebraically, here's the equation for total cost.

$$\textbf{\textit{Total cost}} = FC + (VC \times \textit{unit volume})$$

Next, we create a cell (C8 in the example below) that subtracts the total cost for one option from the total cost of another ($TC_{Standard\ Lathe} - TC_{CNC\ Lathe}$). With this cell in place we are ready to invoke Goal Seek, which is found in the "What-If Analysis" drop-down menu within the "Data" tab of Excel.

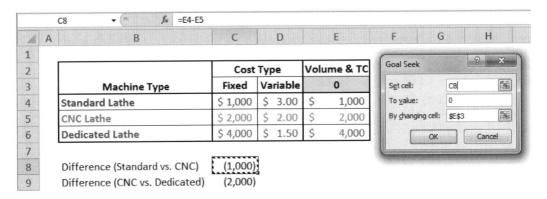

After we click "OK" the volume cell (E3) is changed such that the total cost between the Standard Lathe and CNC Lathe are the same (and the difference is zero as seen in cell C8). Hence, the break-even point for these two processes is 1000 units.

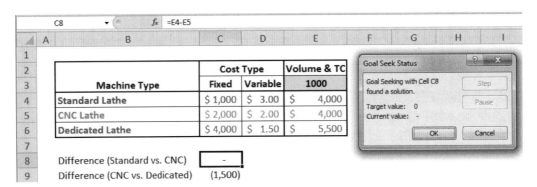

To get the break-even point between the CNC Lathe and the Dedicated Lathe we would simply do Goal Seek again, but this time the target cell would be C9 instead of C8.[20]

Chapter Summary

Below are some of the main points you should have garnered from the study of this chapter:

- **Process strategy is an indispensable element of corporate strategy.** Firms should be careful to make sure their processes are appropriately

---

[20] This is just one simple example of how Goal Seek can help you quickly find answers when variables are involved.

matched to the needs and characteristics of the products and services delivered.

- **A key tradeoff** in process design is having a primary focus on **efficiency versus** a primary focus on **responsiveness**.
- **Facilities layout** should be aligned to support the primary process focus.
- **Process layout** calculations and **line balancing** are quantitative methods to help firms optimize physical layout.
- **Break-even analysis** is a flexible and powerful general-purpose tool to help make capital equipment decisions.

Chapter 3

PRODUCTIVITY

Hearken; Behold, there went out a sower to sow:

And it came to pass, as he sowed, some fell by the way side, and the fowls of the air came and devoured it up.

And some fell on stony ground, where it had not much earth; and immediately it sprang up, because it had no depth of earth.

But when the sun was up, it was scorched; and because it had no root, it withered away.

And some fell among thorns, and the thorns grew up, and choked it, and it yielded no fruit.

And other fell on good ground, and did yield fruit that sprang up and increased; and brought forth, some thirty, and some sixty, and some an hundred.

Mark 4:3-8

As we examine the parable of the sower we learn that there was a great variety in each plot of ground's output or yield. Most of the inputs were the same irrespective of where the seeds were planted—seeds, sunshine, and perhaps water or rainfall. One input was different—the ground—where some was stony, other was among thorns, and finally, there was good ground. Clearly we would expect to see different yields of fruit (in other words, productivity) depending on where the seeds were planted. And such is the case. However, what's particularly interesting, is the differences in productivity when the inputs are seemingly the same as is the case with the "good ground," where the yield varies from thirty, sixty, to an hundred. What could account for these differences when all the inputs appeared to be the same?

Chapter Objectives

Production and operations personnel hold various titles and work in a wide variety of industries, but among these differences is a common thread: productivity—trying to get as much output as possible (of acceptable quality) from a given set of inputs. In this chapter you will learn about factors that affect productivity within a production system. Specifically, after studying this chapter you should be able to:

1. Compute single-factor and multi-factor productivity.
2. Define and compute design capacity, effective capacity, utilization, efficiency, and expected output for a given process.

3. Describe the main categories of inputs and outputs of a production system.
4. Identify some of the key individuals, events, and organizations in the development of operations management.

Overview of Productivity

From its inception, Brigham Young University-Idaho—with its motto of "rethinking education"—was intended to be a model of high and ever-increasing educational productivity. In his landmark address, "A Steady Upward Course," then Elder Henry B. Eyring prophesied many things related to the productivity of BYU-Idaho and its graduates, such as:

- Finding ways to bless more students at a lower cost per student.
- Attaining academic excellence by putting faith in the Lord Jesus Christ and obeying His commandments.
- Blessing the lives of others by innovating with scarce resources.

In summary, President Eyring prophesied that BYU-Idaho graduates would be "natural leaders" with an ability to "innovate and improve" without needing more money to do so, ultimately becoming "legendary for their capacity to build the people around them and to add value wherever they serve."[21]

President Eyring's comments make clear a few essential ingredients or inputs required to bring about the miraculous results being prophesied. Faith in the Lord Jesus Christ and obedience to His commandments[22] lead the list. Such actions result in an increase of the Spirit which "quickens" our understandings so that you—the students—can comprehend "all things"[23] (and "all things" means just that—any subject you may study). Sacrifice[24] is another ingredient, an example of which could be the three-track schedule where some students sacrifice to attend school at a time other than their preferred track. Faculty members are also asked to sacrifice as they work a longer school year than is required at most universities. Such sacrifices increase the number of students that can be served at a lower relative cost. The school's productivity increases because the growth rate in the number of students (the output) does not require a proportionate growth in inputs like the number of buildings or the number of faculty.

Question: How is single-factor productivity calculated?

The above discussion on productivity focuses on the gospel-related inputs (faith, obedience, sacrifice) whereas the world typically measures productivity in terms of labor, materials, and capital. Productivity is measured by simply dividing the

[21] Henry B. Eyring, "A Steady Upward Course," Brigham Young University–Idaho Devotional, September 18, 2001.
[22] See Leviticus 26:2-6. In particular, it seems that Sabbath observance greatly helps us be more productive with the other six days of the week.
[23] See Doctrine and Covenants 88:11, 67
[24] See Doctrine and Covenants 97:8-9 for how obedience "by sacrifice" results in a very productive land which "yieldeth much precious fruit."

outputs of a given process by the inputs. (Note that the units of measure for the outputs and inputs may change, depending on the circumstances.)

$$Productivity = \frac{outputs}{inputs}$$

Single factor productivity involves only one input. For example, let's compute the productivity for the number of students taught in a given school year by the number of faculty.

$$Productivity\ (in\ 2005) = \frac{18,000\ students}{720\ faculty} = 25\ students\ per\ faculty$$

Let's now fast forward five years and assume the school has gone to a 3-semester track system, added a number of on-line courses (many of which being taught by remote faculty), and can now handle many more students per year.

$$Productivity\ (in\ 2010) = \frac{26,000\ students}{800\ faculty} = 32.5\ students\ per\ faculty$$

With these two data points—productivity in 2005 and 2010—we can calculate the change or growth (improvement) in productivity over this period.

$$Change\ in\ productivity = \frac{new\ productivity}{old\ productivity} - 1$$

$$Change\ in\ productivity = \frac{32.5}{25} - 1 = 30\%\ improvement$$

If we take the above example of single-factor productivity and use Excel to make the calculations, we would get something that looks like this.

B4		f_x	=B3/B2
	A	B	C	D
1	Assumptions	2005	2010	% Change
2	Faculty	720	800	11%
3	Students	18,000	26,000	44%
4	Productivity	25.0	32.5	30%

D4		f_x	=(C4/B4)-1
	A	B	C	D
1	Assumptions	2005	2010	% Change
2	Faculty	720	800	11%
3	Students	18,000	26,000	44%
4	Productivity	25.0	32.5	30%

The two snapshots above show (1) the formula for calculating the single-factor productivity in 2005 (cell B4) and (2) the formula for calculating the percentage change in productivity from 2005 to 2010 (cell D4).

Question: How is multi-factor productivity calculated?

Multi-factor productivity is calculated in the same way as single-factor productivity except that the total costs of all the inputs are added before being divided into the value of the outputs. With multi-factor productivity, the same unit of measure should be used when combining the costs of the inputs.

$$Multi-Factor\ Productivity = \frac{value\ of\ outputs}{cost\ of\ (labor + capital + mat'ls + etc.)}$$

For this example, let's look at Performance Apparel, a company that designs and produces custom t-shirts. Let's suppose that they produce 1000 shirts a month and that to do so costs them $2,000 in labor, $3,000 in materials, and $1,500 in overhead expenses.

$$MF\ Productivity = \frac{1,000\ shirts}{(\$2,000\ labor + \$3,000\ mat'ls + \$1,500\ overhead)} = 0.154$$

This means that Performance Apparel produces 0.154 shirts with every dollar of inputs. Below is an example of how this is calculated in Excel (cell B6).

	B6	f_x =B2/(SUM(B3:B5))	
	A		B
1	**Given Data**		
2	Output (shirts)		1,000
3	Labor		$ 2,000
4	Materials		$ 3,000
5	Overhead		$ 1,500
6	**Productivity (shirts per dollar of input)**		0.154

If Performance Apparel were to become more productive and drop their labor costs to $1,500 per month, then they could produce 0.167 shirts for every dollar of inputs for an 8.3% increase in productivity. Again, turning to Excel, we get the following (cell D6).

	D6		f_x =(C6/B6)-1		
	A		B	C	D
1	**Given Data**		**Base Case**	**Lower Labor**	**% Change**
2	Output (shirts)		1,000	1,000	
3	Labor		$ 2,000	$ 1,500	
4	Materials		$ 3,000	$ 3,000	
5	Overhead		$ 1,500	$ 1,500	
6	**Productivity (shirts per dollar of input)**		0.154	0.167	8.3%

A Different Twist on Multi-Factor Productivity

In the multi-factor productivity example above the value of the outputs is simply the units produced and productivity merely states the number of shirts produced for every dollar of input. We can also measure productivity in terms of the number of dollars of revenue (output) for every dollar of inputs.

Suppose each shirt produced sold for $15 each. Instead of putting 1,000 in the numerator of the productivity equation, we'll now put $15,000 (1,000 units X $15 per unit). The results of this change can be seen in the spreadsheet below.

B6		f_x	=B2/(SUM(B3:B5))		
	A		B	C	D
1	Given Data		Base Case	Lower Labor	% Change
2	Output (shirts)		$ 15,000	$ 15,000	
3	Labor		$ 2,000	$ 1,500	
4	Materials		$ 3,000	$ 3,000	
5	Overhead		$ 1,500	$ 1,500	
6	Productivity (shirts per dollar of input)		2.308	2.500	8.3%

The results now tell us that in the base case we get $2.308 dollars of output for every dollar of input. Lowering labor increases the output to $2.50 for every dollar of input, still an 8.3% improvement (whether measured in units or dollars of output).

Establishing the right productivity measures can provide valuable insights into an organization's performance. It should go without saying that effective managers, regardless of functional area, constantly search for ways to increase productivity.

Capacity Management

Question: What is capacity?

Capacity is the capability of a system, worker, machine, work center, plant, or organization to produce output per time period. Planning for capacity is typically done in three timeframes identified as follows:

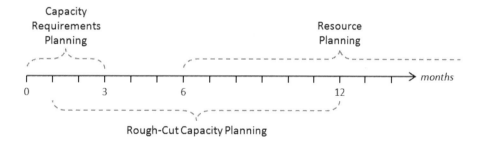

Each of these planning activities is differentiated by (1) how long it takes to secure the required capacity resources and (2) the level of management or organization that is tasked with driving the planning process.

- **Capacity Requirements Planning** is typically driven by first-level supervisors and planners and focuses on how to best meet capacity demands with *existing* human and equipment resources. Working overtime is the primary option for increasing capacity in this timeframe.
- **Rough-Cut Capacity Planning** extends far enough into the future to consider adding *new resources*—personnel, materials, suppliers, equipment, leased property—to meet capacity requirements. Middle management typically takes the lead with these decisions.
- **Resource Planning** focuses on those capacity resources that take a long time to secure such as land, new facilities, the development of new, highly specialized equipment, etc. These activities are usually in the realm of senior managers.

Question: When is the best time to expand capacity?

When looking at increasing capacity to meet growing demand, it's important to recognize that unlike demand—which can and often will grow gradually and almost linearly—capacity expansions take place in large incremental steps. Hence, given these differences in the growth of demand and in the growth capacity, businesses must employ one of three basic internal capacity expansion strategies and one external.

Strategy	Description	Advantages	Disadvantages
Lead the Demand	Expansion stays ahead of the requirements	Supports a first-mover strategy; less disruptive than other strategies	Risk of overbuilding; requires more money up front; resource utilization is lower
Lag the Demand	Expansion takes place only after the demand materializes	Less risk of overbuilding; easier to finance; higher resource utilization	May hinder business growth; expansion can be more disruptive
Straddle the Demand	Capacity alternates from leading and lagging the demand	Middle of the road solution	Middle of the road solution
Outsource	Contract production to outside company	Low fixed costs and potentially low variable costs	May require high contracted volumes; lack of control, quality; long lead times

These three strategies are depicted in the graphic below.

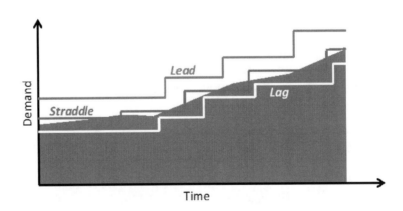

Question: What are the main terms and measures related to capacity, and how are they calculated?

- **Design capacity** is the theoretical maximum output of a system to perform its expected function.

- **<u>Effective capacity</u>** is the capacity a firm can expect to achieve from a given system when factoring scheduling, maintenance, and product mix, etc. For example, performing a "changeover" or setup on a machine to run a different product reduces the effective capacity of that machine.
- **<u>Output</u>** is the measure of a product being completed by a process or facility.

Given these terms as defined above, we are now ready to present the formulas for two important measures of capacity: utilization and efficiency.

Utilization

$$Utilization = \frac{Output}{Design\ Capacity}$$

Efficiency

$$Efficiency = \frac{Output}{Effective\ Capacity}$$

<u>Question</u>: What are the optimal utilization targets for a business?

Theoretically it would be great if a business could operate at 100 percent utilization and make the most of its capacity resources. Of course, this ideal is not practical given the realities of running that business. This is where efficiency comes in. Whereas utilization compares output to the design capacity (the capacity in a perfect world), efficiency measures how well a company makes use of its effective capacity, allowing for the operational realities of maintenance, breaks, product mix, and so forth.

Utilization will tend to vary by industry and company. If we refer again to the product-process matrix we would expect to find the highest utilization in continuous flow environments and the lowest where jumbled flows dominate. Skillful operations managers are able to identify the salient characteristics of their product and service offerings and select and measure process performance accordingly.

Production Systems

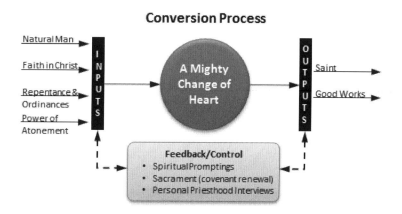

In *True to the Faith* we read that "Conversion is a process, not an event. You become converted as a result of your righteous efforts to follow the Savior. These efforts include exercising faith in Jesus Christ, repenting of sin, being baptized, receiving the gift of the Holy Ghost, and enduring to the end in faith."[25] This conversion process might be represented in the diagram above. At the heart of any production system is a "conversion process" where inputs are transformed or "converted" into higher value outputs. In the case of the "production system" that makes a saint, the inputs are described in the preceding paragraph (as well as in Mosiah 3:19).

Question: What is a production system?

Just like the conversion process described above, a production system is a functionally related group of elements that accepts inputs and converts them into desired outputs.

The drawing below[26] provides a conceptual framework for a typical production system. Notice that three main components—inputs, transformation activities, and outputs—correspond to the conversion process above and to the components in the simple diagram in the True Wealth chapter, namely elements (inputs), production (transformation or conversion), and true wealth (outputs). This detailed drawing of a typical production system will serve as a guide for much of the topics covered in this book and in our production and operations management course.

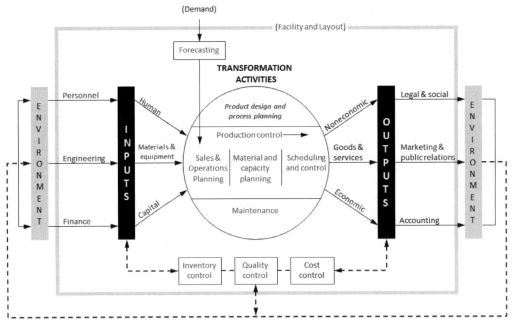

Schematic Model of a Production/Operations System

[25] *True to the Faith*, 41.
[26] Modified from Joseph G. Monks, Schaum's Outline of Operations Management, Second Edition [New York: McGraw-Hill, 1996], 6.

Question: How do service systems differ from production systems?

Healthcare, retail, transportation, consulting, teaching, advertising, and financial services are examples of service industries. In such industries the supporting service systems differ from production systems in that they are primarily concerned with attaching intangible value to the flow of customers (humans) rather than adding tangible value to the flow of materials.

For example, a teacher may imbue a student with an eternal principle or a financial advisor may provide stock recommendations (both examples of intangible value) whereas a production process may add an upgrade (ex., more memory, leather seats, etc.) to a tangible product. While the basic flow of inputs and outputs may be similar between a service system and a production system, there are some important differences that typically differentiate service systems from production systems:

- Variable demand patterns
- High labor content (which enables customization)
- Extensive interaction with customers
- Intangible output delivered just-in-time (no accumulation of inventory)

In reality, most organizations provide a mix of tangible goods and service. This mix varies by industry and by company. For example, you can buy tires from a warehouse store like Costco or you can buy from a local family-owned tire retailer. In both cases you will be purchasing goods (the tires) but with differing degrees of service. Costco will provide a little service—tire installation—while the family-owned retailer may provide additional services like free tire repair, tire rotation and rebalancing, oil changes, minor repairs and loaner vehicles.

Development of Production and Operations Management

It should come as no surprise that the world has seen dramatic increases in agricultural, mining, manufacturing and service productivity due to the discovery and development of new technologies concurrent with the restoration of the gospel.

President Joseph Fielding Smith stated that since the time of the restoration there have been many labor-saving discoveries to aid in furthering the Lord's work in the latter-days. "The inspiration of the Lord has gone out and taken hold of the minds of men, though they know it not, and they are directed by the Lord. In this manner he brings them into his service that his purposes and his righteousness, in due time, may be supreme on the earth."[27]

President Smith's grandson, Joseph Fielding McConkie, reiterated these truths by saying, "In short, the Spirit of God—meaning the light of Christ—has been behind the rapid intellectual, scientific, and technological developments from the time of

---

[27] Joseph Fielding Smith, *Doctrines of Salvation*, 3 Volumes [Salt Lake City: Bookcraft, 1954-1956], 1: 179-181.

the Industrial Revolution to our own Information Age. The Modern Seer (Joseph Smith) presides over this age of enlightenment and expansion."[28]

More recently, at the May 22, 2007 BYU-Idaho Devotion, Elder Merrill J. Bateman of the Seventy stated, "It is apparent that secular knowledge has flowered since the time of Joseph Smith, that the Lord has been flooding the earth with temporal knowledge as well as spiritual." Elder Bateman also cited the work of Angus Maddison, a British economist who spent "20 years [to develop] a model of world economic growth for the last 2000 years. The results were both stunning and unexpected."[29] The graphic below attempts to show these stunning results by (1) charting selected data from Maddison's findings,[30] (2) superimposing the growth of Church membership,[31] and (3) juxtaposing a timeline of basic human inventions.[32]

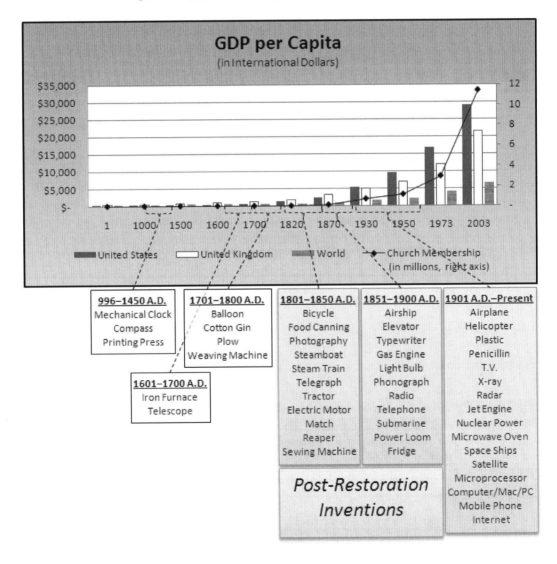

---

[28] Joseph Fielding McConkie, *Joseph Smith: The Choice Seer* [Salt Lake City: Bookcraft, 1996].

[29] Merrill J. Bateman, "Nothing Shall Be Withheld," BYU-Idaho Devotional address, 22 May 2007.

[30] Angus Maddison, *Contours of the World Economy, 1–2003 AD* (cited from Wikipedia).

[31] Liahona, October 2006 and Ensign, May 2010.

[32] Adapted from http://www.dawnbible.com/booklets/kingdom.htm.

With this testimony-building foundation in place, let us return our focus to those persons and technologies that have led to dramatic productivity gains in the area of production and operations management.

Question: Who are the key individuals in the development of production systems that appeared prior to the Industrial Revolution?

- **James Watt** was a Scottish inventor and mechanical engineer who made dramatic improvements to steam engine design (circa 1764) and promoted the use of *mechanical power*.
- **Adam Smith** (1776) publicized the advantages of *division of labor* in a high-volume production setting.
- **Eli Whitney** (circa 1800) was the inventor of the cotton gin who also advocated the use of *interchangeable parts*—a practice which revolutionized manufacturing in the North and greatly contributed to its Civil War victory.

The dramatic increases in manufacturing productivity during the Industrial Revolution came from combining the innovations of (1) mechanical power, (2) division of labor, and (3) interchangeable parts.

Question: Who are the key individuals that appeared in the early 1900s to further refine production systems?

- **Frederick Taylor** was an American mechanical engineer and is regarded as the father of *scientific management*, which promoted the use of training, time studies and work standards for discrete tasks.
- **Frank and Lillian Gilbreth** were pioneers in *motion study* as they sought ways to increase worker output while making jobs easier. They also authored *Cheaper by the Dozen*.
- **Henry Gantt** developed *visual aids (Gantt charts)* that are useful in the loading and scheduling of work.
- **Henry Ford** developed the *assembly line*, where workers stand still and material moves.
- **F.W. Harris** developed the *economic order quantity* (EOQ) model.
- **Walter Shewhart** developed methods for *statistical process control* and sampling.

Question: What are some of the computer-based technologies which have enabled recent productivity gains?

- **Material Requirements Planning** (MRP) is a computer-based, time-phased method which makes fast and accurate planning of complex material requirements (well beyond what is possible with manual or spreadsheet calculations).
- **Computer-Aided Design** (CAD) provides a highly interactive environment for rapid design of manufactured items and systems.
- **Computer-Aided Manufacturing** (CAM) is the use of computers to program, direct, and control production equipment in the fabrication of manufactured items.

- **Flexible Manufacturing Systems** (FMS) are groups of numerically controlled machine tools with the ability to automatically execute all manufacturing tasks on many product designs, thus enabling production in small quantities and fast delivery times.
- **Automated Guided Vehicle Systems** (AGVS) automatically route and position material handling devices (carts, pallet trucks, etc.) without operator intervention.
- **Automated Storage/Retrieval Systems** (AS/RS) are high-density, rack inventory storage systems with vehicles automatically loading and unloading the racks.
- **Automatic Identification Systems** (AIS) use various means, including bar code scanning and radio frequencies, to sense and load data in a computer.
- **Electronic Data Interchange** (EDI) is the paperless (electronic) exchange of trading documents, such as purchase orders, shipment authorizations, advanced shipment notices, and invoices, using standardized document formats.
- **The Internet** has enabled dramatic improvements to international and cross-company collaboration on product designs, marketing campaigns, and the streamlining of business transactions.
- **Radio Frequency Identification** (RFID) systems make use of electronic tags and tag readers to store and retrieve information about items without the need for line-of-sight access for data retrieval.

Chapter Summary

Below are some of the main points you should have garnered from the study of this chapter:

- **A production system consists in converting inputs into higher value outputs.** A "conversion process" is at the heart of all production systems (whether for producing goods or providing services). Most companies offer a combination of goods and services.
- **Productivity is calculated by simply dividing the outputs of a process by the inputs of that process.** (Make sure to clearly describe the units of measure when making such calculations.) Calculating multi-factor productivity requires that all inputs (in the denominator) use the same unit of measure (typically dollars).
- **Measures of utilization and efficiency help a firm make proper use of its resources**.
- Since the time of the Restoration, many labor-saving inventions have driven dramatic productivity improvements, resulting in higher standards of living. Productivity has soared in the past few decades due to the introduction of many computer-based technologies.

Chapter 4

QUALITY MANAGEMENT

I have been quoted as saying, 'Do the best you can.' But I want to emphasize that it be the very best. We are too prone to be satisfied with mediocre performance. We are capable of doing so much better.

President Gordon B. Hinckley[33]

Within the first year of service as President of The Church of Jesus Christ of Latter-day Saints, President Spencer W. Kimball made the following remarks in a devotional address at Brigham Young University.

> Perfection is a long, hard journey with many pitfalls. It's not attainable overnight. Eternal vigilance is the price of victory. Eternal vigilance is required in the subduing of enemies and in becoming the master of oneself. It cannot be accomplished in little spurts and disconnected efforts. There must be constant and valiant, purposeful living—righteous living. [34]

The words of President Hinckley and President Kimball make it abundantly clear that achieving the highest level of personal, individual quality—even perfection—requires consistent, vigorous effort over a long period of time. Fortunately, as we face this seemingly impossible task, great hope is extended to us in the perfect example and enabling power of the Savior. Indeed, we are told in Ether 12:27 that if we come unto the Lord He will show us our weakness, and if we are humble, He will make those weak things become strong.

Chapter Objectives

Striving for individual perfection or working to improve quality in a business setting requires similar ingredients. Among them are *humility*—a willingness to look for and acknowledge weaknesses—and *resolve*—the fire and drive to face and overcome those weaknesses. This process is not for the proud or the faint of heart, as our nature leads most of us to seek a specious safety in our comfort zones. But such complacency is a recipe for long-term mediocrity or worse, both individually and in business.

In this chapter you will become familiar with some of the thought leaders in quality management who helped organizations develop the humility and resolve to

---

[33] Gordon B. Hinckley, "Standing Strong and Immovable," Worldwide Leadership Training Meeting, January 2004.
[34] Spencer W. Kimball, "Be Ye Therefore Perfect," BYU Devotional, 17 September, 1974.

successfully address quality-related matters and consequently reap great rewards. Moreover, you should be able to see, in many cases, how their techniques are similar to many Gospel principles and practices in place within the Church. Specifically, after studying this chapter you should be able to

1. Understand and articulate the many dimensions of quality, including the costs of quality.
2. Describe the main concepts and tools of Total Quality Management (TQM).
3. Identify the key thought leaders in the quality movement, as well as their respective contributions to quality management.
4. Describe Quality Function Deployment (QFD) and the House of Quality.
5. Describe Six Sigma and its methodologies.
6. Describe the roles of the International Standards Organization and the Malcolm Baldrige Awards in promoting quality.

Introduction to Quality

Quality is an important aspect of product or service differentiation. Along with product price and product availability (or supply responsiveness), it is one of the key pillars upon which companies can and do compete.

Question: What is Quality?

Each of us might think we know what "quality" means, but the reality is that quality can mean different things to different people. One reputable definition states that "Quality means user satisfaction: that goods or services satisfy the needs and expectations of the user."[35] This definition is helpful, but it still leaves room for individual interpretation.

While it may be unrealistic to pen a simple universally-accepted definition of quality, here are several widely accepted dimensions of quality that can be identified.[36]

- **Performance**. Refers to a product's primary operating characteristics. For instance, with an economy car this would be miles per gallon.
- **Features**. This is a secondary dimension of performance, often referring to the "bells and whistles" of a product.
- **Reliability**. The probability of a product malfunctioning or failing within a specific time period. This is usually measured in terms of MTBF (mean time between failure).
- **Conformance**. The degree to which the product's design and performance meet established standards. Meeting this dimension is typically manufacturing's responsibility.
- **Durability**. A measure of the product's life, after which it can no longer be repaired.

---

[35] J.R. Tony Arnold, *Introduction to Materials Management* (Prentice Hall, Upper Saddle River, NJ, 2008), pg. 466.
[36] "Competing on the Eight Dimensions of Quality," David A. Garvin, *Harvard Business Review*, November-December 1987.

- **Serviceability**. The speed and ease of product repair.
- **Aesthetics**. A subjective measure of how a product looks, feels, tastes, or smells.
- **Perceived Quality**. Largely based on reputation, an indirect measure of a product's quality.

Question: What are the costs of poor quality?

The costs of poor quality fall into four categories.

1. *Prevention costs* or costs incurred to minimize appraisal and failure costs.
2. *Appraisal costs* or costs incurred to determine the degree of conformance to quality standards.
3. *Internal failure costs* or costs associated with defects that are found *before* the customer receives the product or service.
4. *External failure costs* or costs associated with defects that are found *after* the customer receives the product or service.

The first three categories can be reasonably estimated, but external failure costs can far exceed the actual costs of repair or of fixing the problem. The highly-publicized 2010 recall of several Toyota automobile models with faulty accelerator pedals is as an example of where the external costs of failure (the loss of sales from a tarnished reputation, lawsuits, and so forth) far exceed the actual costs to repair the vehicles.

Total Quality Management (TQM)

Question: What is Total Quality Management (TQM)?

Total quality management is a customer-focused, process-oriented management system that involves all employees in organizational efforts to improve "processes, goods, services, and the culture in which they work."[37] Very simply, TQM is a management approach that promotes long-term success through customer satisfaction. TQM philosophies and tools come from the teachings of quality leaders like W. Edwards Deming and others.

Question: What are the main **concepts** of TQM?

While there is no single list of universally accepted TQM concepts, most lists will include the following:

- **Customer focus**. Listening to customers and conforming the design of products and services to meet customer-driven standards. Customers ultimately determine—with their wallet—whether products and services meet their quality needs and wants.
- **Management commitment and systematic efforts**. Setting the tone for the organization through word and deed. This means integrating quality into the organization's vision, mission, and goals and personally following up on progress toward those goals.

---

[37] http://asq.org/learn-about-quality/total-quality-management/overview/overview.html

- **Total employee involvement and empowerment**. Training employees in quality methods and pushing decision making as low as possible in the organization (often through the use of **quality circles**, where small groups of employees meet to identify, analyze, and solve quality-related problems).
- **Process-centered continuous improvement**. Establishing stable, repeatable processes and then relentlessly seeking and finding ways to improve those processes.
- **Benchmarking**. Comparing company performance in key processes to that of a company thought to have superior performance and then incorporating what was learned in order to make improvements.
- **Supplier partnering**. Minimizing total cost (not just acquisition costs) by partnering with single-source suppliers.
- **Fact-based decision making**. Gathering required data, using appropriate tools and statistical methods to measure process performance and identify opportunities for improvement.
- **Communications**. Ensuring open communication flows freely in all directions. Successful quality implementations depend on effective communication within the organization and with customers and suppliers.

Question: What are the main tools of TQM?

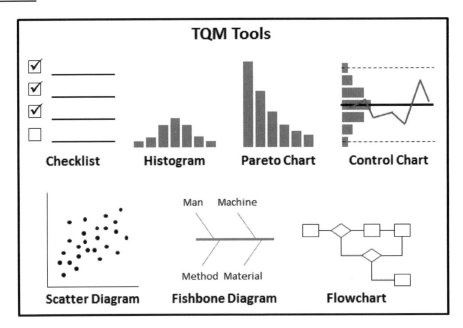

Checklist—A simple data-recording device. Check sheets and simple surveys are effective methods, easy to design and implement. They provide a snapshot of the process being studied and reveal underlying patterns including the frequency of an event or activity. Frequently, check sheet results are turned into Pareto charts.

Histogram—A graphic summary of a set of data that reveals the amount of variation that a process has within it. The pictorial nature of the histogram lets people see patterns that are difficult to detect in a simple table of numbers. Control charts are actually a series of histograms laid on their side with acceptable variation levels indicated in the form of upper and lower statistical control limits.

Pareto Chart—A graphical tool for ranking causes from most significant to least significant. A Pareto chart is a series of vertical bars lined up in a descending order—from high to low—to reflect frequency, importance, or impact. Pareto charts quickly draw everyone's attention to the most important factor—providing an at-a-glance snapshot of priorities.

Control Chart—A run chart with upper and lower control limits on which values of some statistical measure for a series of samples or subgroups are plotted. The chart frequently shows a central line to help detect a trend of plotted values. It helps determine whether a process is experiencing common variation (natural and acceptable) or abnormal variation (assignable to some special cause) that would require further investigation and action.

Scatter Diagram—A graphical technique to analyze the relationship between two variables. Two sets of data are plotted on a graph, with the y-axis being used for the variable to be predicted and the x-axis being used for the variable to make the prediction. The graph will show possible relationships among variables: those who know most about the variables must evaluate whether they are actually related or only appear to be related.

Fishbone Diagram—A fishbone or cause-and-effect diagram is a tool for analyzing and illustrating a process by showing the main causes and sub-causes leading to an effect (symptom). It is sometimes referred to as an "Ishikawa diagram," because Kaoru Ishikawa developed it. A fishbone diagram is easy to construct and invites interactive participation. In order to identify the root cause of a particular problem, a team will repeatedly ask "why" the problem exists (see **five why's** in the glossary) and will assign the causes to one of "**four Ms**" or categories which correspond to the main "bones" or branches in the diagram: (1) man, (2) machine, (3) method, and (4) materials.

Flowchart/Process Map—Graphical tools that show the major steps in a process. Developing a flowchart requires identifying key process steps and inventory points and the dominant flow among them. Flowcharts are useful for examining how various steps are related to each other. By studying these charts individuals and teams can often uncover potential sources of trouble or identify steps to be taken to improve or error-proof a process.

W. Edwards Deming

Question: Who was Deming, and what are his 14 points?

Dr. W. Edwards Deming is known as the father of the industrial revival that took place in Japan after World War II. In 1950 he trained hundreds of Japanese engineers in statistical process control (or "SPC," covered in the next chapter) and concepts of quality. He encouraged industrial leaders to improve quality, saying it was the key to lower costs and higher productivity.

In 1982 Deming published *Quality, Productivity, and Competitive Position* (renamed to **Out of the Crisis** in 1986) which challenged many of the management practices found in US companies. *Out of the Crisis* contains Deming's famous "14 Points" (**listed below**, with *additional comments from this author*).[38] Contemplate how these points challenge beliefs that might be prevalent in the workplace, and how things might be improved by following them.

1. **Create constancy of purpose for improving products and services**. *(Resources should primarily be allocated to meet long-term needs rather than merely focusing on short-term profitability.)*

2. **Adopt the new philosophy**. *(The post-war era of American dominance is long past and the United States should abandon the traditional Western management approach and adopt a new way of managing business, with a long-term focus, if it is going to compete in the global marketplace.)*

3. **Cease dependence on inspection to achieve quality**. *(Quality should be built into the product in the first place, evidenced by statistical measures, rather than depend on end-of-the-line mass quality checks.)*

4. **End the practice of awarding business on price alone; instead, minimize total cost by working with a single supplier**. *(The goal is to minimize total cost, not just initial cost. Working with a single supplier for any one item increases loyalty and trust, ultimately leading to higher quality and lower total costs.)*

5. **Improve constantly and forever every process for planning, production and service**. *(Management should focus on improving the processes and systems within a business—design, innovation, incoming materials, maintenance, equipment, supervision, training, retraining, etc.)*

6. **Institute training on the job**. *(Institute modern training methods for all employees, including management. New skills are required to compete globally and to keep up with changing developments in materials, equipment, information technology, and service innovation.)*

7. **Adopt and institute leadership**. *(Institute leadership that focuses on improving processes and systems, thus making it easier for employees to do their job. Focus more on quality, not merely on numbers. Make sure that immediate action is taken on defects and conditions detrimental to quality.)*

8. **Drive out fear**. *(Encourage two-way communication and other means to eliminate fear so that employees will be more productive and effective.)*

9. **Break down barriers between staff areas**. *(Use cross-functional teams to increase focus on and improve products and services, as most business processes run across departmental boundaries.)*

10. **Eliminate slogans, exhortations and targets for the workforce**. *(The right employees don't respond to a lot of hoopla but rather are intrinsically and naturally motivated when they are part of logical efforts and plans that confront the "brutal facts" of their workplace reality.[39] Managerial slogans without managerial focus on the system—fixing processes—do not improve productivity, but often foster an adversarial relationship.)*

11. **Eliminate numerical quotas for the workforce and numerical goals for management**. *(Arbitrary goals, set solely by management, can be demotivating to the workforce. Perhaps it is better to let those closest to the*

---

[38] Modified from the list on the American Society for Quality (ASQ) website at http://asq.org/learn-about-quality/total-quality-management/overview/deming-points.html.

[39] See Jim Collins, *Good to Great* (New York: HarperCollins Press, 2001), pp. 177-78.

processes set goals, or provide input on goals, and have management focus on fixing the system or processes so that such goals can be met.)

12. **Remove barriers that rob people of pride of workmanship, and eliminate the annual rating or merit system**. *(Perhaps this point, like the previous one, is a bit too idealistic. Nevertheless, it again highlights the view that management should be more focused on improving quality—by improving the system—than on pushing and micromanaging employees.)*

13. **Institute a vigorous program of education and self-improvement for everyone**. *(Employee knowledge improves competitive position.)*

14. **Put everybody in the company to work accomplishing the transformation**. *(Action is required by all employees. Top management must set the tone by clearly defining their permanent commitment to improve quality and productivity. This commitment should include a structure to implement the 13 preceding points. All employees should feel the pride of ownership for quality—and be empowered to make a difference.)*

Question: What is the Deming Cycle or PDCA?

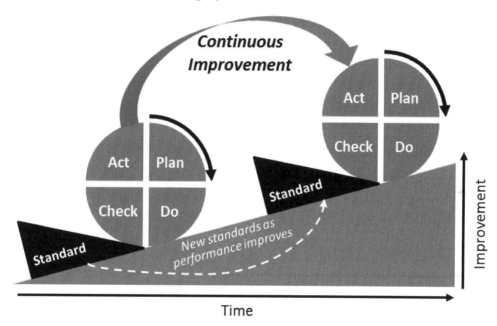

PDCA ("Plan-Do-Check-Act") is an iterative four-step problem-solving process typically used in quality control. A fundamental principle of the scientific method and PDCA is iteration—once a hypothesis is confirmed (or negated), executing the cycle again will extend the knowledge further. Repeating the PDCA cycle can bring us closer to the goal, usually a perfect operation and output. The PDCA cycle is one way we can implement these words from President Thomas S. Monson.

A cardinal principle of industrial management teaches: "When performance is measured, performance improves. When performance is measured and reported, the rate of improvement accelerates."[40]

---

[40] Thomas S. Monson, General Conference Report, October 1970.

Other Leaders and Pioneers in Quality Management

Question: Besides Deming, who are other key figures in quality management?

In addition to W. Edwards Deming, the following individuals have made significant contributions to the field of quality management.

- **Philip B. Crosby** was a corporate quality manager and consultant who published *Quality is Free* in 1979. This was his first business book and it came out when American companies were facing a quality crisis and losing business to Japanese companies who had higher quality products. The book's premise is that it is better to do the job right the first time and that doing so would save more than the cost of the effort, hence "quality is free." He also coined the phrase *zero defects*.
- **Armand V. Feigenbaum** is an American businessman and quality expert who devised the concept known as Total Quality Control, later to be known as *Total Quality Management* (TQM).
- **Kaoru Ishikawa** was a Japanese university professor and quality innovator who was instrumental in the transformation of Japan's post-war industrial sector. He is credited with the introduction of *quality circles* and with the development of the *Ishikawa diagram* (fishbone/cause-and-effect diagram).
- **Joseph M. Juran** was an American management consultant and evangelist for quality. Among his contributions are the application of the Pareto principle (the 80/20 rule of "the vital few and the useful many") and the human element in quality management. He made 10 trips to Japan starting in the 1950s and focused on training senior and middle managers, with his work paying off by the 1970s when Japanese products started to be recognized for high quality. (Also interesting to note are his marriage of 81 years and living to nearly 104!)
- **Genichi Taguchi** is a Japanese engineer who developed methods for applying statistics to improve the quality of manufactured goods. His key contributions are in the areas of (1) measuring the financial loss from poor quality—the "quality loss function," (2) promoting robust product design where high quality is less affected by adverse process conditions, and (3) target-oriented quality.

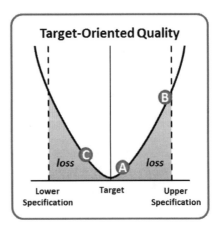

More on Target-Oriented Quality

Genichi Taguchi contends that conformance-oriented quality is not good enough (where products A, B, and C, as seen below left, each fall within the upper and lower design specifications. Rather, there is an increasing cost (loss in value to the company, customer, and society) the further products stray from the design target (above right). The difference between conformance-oriented and target-oriented quality is illustrated in the following anecdote.

> Ford Motor Company was simultaneously manufacturing a car model with transmissions made in Japan and the United States. Soon after the car model was on the market, Ford customers were requesting the model with Japanese transmission over the US-made transmission, and they were willing to wait for the Japanese model. As both transmissions were made to the same specifications, Ford engineers could not understand the customer preference for the model with the Japanese transmission. Finally, Ford engineers decided to take apart the two different transmissions. The American-made car parts were all within specified tolerance levels. On the other hand, the Japanese car parts were virtually identical to each other, and much closer to the nominal values for the parts—e.g., if a part was supposed to be one foot long, plus or minus 1/8 of an inch—then the Japanese parts were all within 1/16 of an inch, less variation. This made the Japanese cars run more smoothly and customers experienced fewer problems.[41]

An outstanding discussion on how target-oriented quality applies in our personal lives can be found in a BYU Devotional address entitled "Looking Toward the Mark," by BYU Engineering professor Val D. Hanks.[42] Brother Hanks proposes that looking at and barely staying within boundaries of personal conduct ("lower" or "upper" specifications") is a far inferior mindset and approach to living the gospel than looking toward the perfect mark of the Savior and striving to live like Him.

Quality Function Deployment (QFD) and the House of Quality (HOQ)

<u>Question</u>: What is Quality Function Deployment?

Quality Function Deployment (QFD) is a method for (1) determining customer needs and wants (the voice of the customer [VOC]) and (2) translating those desires into a product or service design. A thorough discussion of QFD is beyond the scope of this book; however, a brief overview of the House of Quality, QFD's main tool, is in order.

The House of Quality (HOQ) is a house-shaped diagram or tool that helps firms implement QFD. It is used iteratively to help define and refine the relationship between customer requirements and technical requirements so that firms may more effectively design and implement product and service offerings. To further assist in this design process, HOQ diagrams can also provide a structured way to assess competitor offerings, understand the relationship between specific firm capabilities or offerings, and document product or service specifications or target values.

---

[41] Aguayo, Rafael (1991). Dr. Deming: The American Who Taught the Japanese about Quality. Fireside, pp. 40–41, quoted from http://en.wikipedia.org/wiki/W._Edwards_Deming.
[42] http://speeches.byu.edu/reader/reader.php?id=8499.

Let's suppose we run a small diner named "Breakfast at Home." The HOQ diagram below right shows how our offerings or capabilities stack up to what customers are asking for. (The "HOQ Structure" diagram is merely for reference purposes so that you can clearly see this tool's basic structure.)

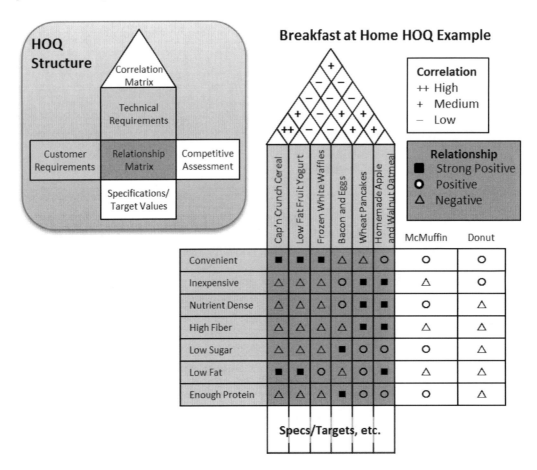

Of course this example is quite simple, but it does show how well our technical requirements or current capabilities (the various breakfast items we can make) stack up to our list of customer requirements. The relationship matrix gives us a clear picture of where our capabilities fall short of the voice of the customer (VOC), and this knowledge should guide us to promote those offerings that match customer requirements and modify or swap out those that don't. In most cases, responding to the VOC would require several iterations or versions of the HOQ until our technical requirements are adequately defined with targets and detailed specifications—down to the exact ingredients to be used in our offerings as well as all process steps for making those items.

Overview of Six Sigma

Question: What is Six Sigma?

Six Sigma is a business management strategy, originally developed by Motorola, which today enjoys widespread application in many sectors of industry. Six Sigma seeks to identify and remove the causes of defects and errors in manufacturing and business processes. It uses a set of quality management methods, including statistical methods, and creates a special infrastructure of people within the organization who are experts in these methods. Each Six Sigma project carried out within an organization follows a defined sequence of steps and has quantified financial targets.

The statistical definition of a six sigma process is one that produces 3.4 defective parts per million opportunities (DPMO). This is based on the fact that a process that is normally distributed will have 3.4 parts per million beyond a point that is 4.5[43] standard deviations above or below the mean.

Question: What are the Six Sigma certifications? How do you get certified?

Individuals can become certified in the different levels of Six Sigma expertise (Green Belt, Black Belt, Master Black Belt, etc.). Note that there is no single sanctioning body or organization that awards Six Sigma certifications. Rather, certifications can be obtained from four different types of providers: (1) employers, (2) professional associations, (3) colleges and universities, and (4) certification service provider institutions.

The process for obtaining a Six Sigma certification can vary greatly given the number and variety of granting organizations. Certification typically requires two to four weeks of training, the passing of a qualifying exam, and the participation in or the leading of one or more relevant projects.

Question: What are the main methodologies used in Six Sigma?

Six Sigma has two key methodologies: **DMAIC** and **DMADV**, both inspired by Deming's Plan-Do-Check-Act Cycle. DMAIC is used to improve an *existing* business process; DMADV is used to create *new product or process* designs.

DMAIC – The basic methodology consists of the following five steps:
- **Define** process improvement goals that are consistent with customer demands and the enterprise strategy.
- **Measure** key aspects of the current process and collect relevant data.
- **Analyze** the data to verify cause-and-effect relationships. Determine what the relationships are, and attempt to ensure that all factors have been considered.
- **Improve** or optimize the process based upon data analysis using techniques like Design of Experiments.
- **Control** to ensure that any deviations from target are corrected before they result in defects. Set up pilot runs to establish process capability, move on to production, set up control mechanisms and continuously monitor the process.

---

[43] The number 4.5 is derived by taking 6 sigma or standard deviations minus the 1.5 sigma shift introduced to account for long-term variation. Hence, "six sigma" is technically 4.5 sigma, but the name "six sigma" is the standard name for these types of programs.

DMADV – The basic methodology consists of the following five steps:

- **Define** design goals that are consistent with customer demands and the enterprise strategy.
- **Measure** and identify CTQs (characteristics that are Critical To Quality), product capabilities, production process capability, and risks.
- **Analyze** to develop and design alternatives, create a high-level design and evaluate design capability to select the best design.
- **Design** details, optimize the design, and plan for design verification. This phase may require simulations.
- **Verify** the design, set up pilot runs, implement the production process and hand it over to the process owners.

ISO and the Malcom Baldrige National Quality Award

Question: What is ISO?

The International Organization for Standardization, also known as ISO, is an international-standard-setting body with over 150 cooperating institutes representing nearly 100 countries. It was founded in 1947 and acts as a bridge between public and private (industrial) sectors. In many cases, an ISO certification can be a deal qualifier for establishing a business relationship.

ISO 9000 is the most widely known set of international standards on quality. They were developed to help companies document and maintain their quality procedures. These standards were published in 1987 and are not particular to any industry, product, or service. ISO 9000 focuses more on quality practices than on quality outcomes. Companies who follow these standards will periodically bring in independent auditors to certify that their company is indeed ISO 9000 compliant.

With the recent push for environmentally friendly business practices, ISO has developed the ISO 14000 set of standards (environmental management standards) and ISO 24700 (standard for reusing recovered components).

Question: What is the Malcom Baldrige National Quality Award?

This award is named after the late Secretary of Commerce, Malcom Baldrige, who was a great proponent of quality management. It was established in 1987 to raise awareness of quality management within American companies. It is awarded annually, by the President of the United States, to companies who are judged to be outstanding in their practices and outcomes related to quality management.

Chapter Summary

Below are some of the main points you should have garnered from the study of this chapter.

- **The term "quality" can mean different things to different people**. Eight dimensions of quality were identified earlier in this chapter. At a basic level, quality should focus on meeting or satisfying customer needs. Poor quality can be very costly to a company.

- **TQM** (total quality management) is a management approach to long-term success through customer satisfaction. TQM consists of many concepts and tools to help organizations strive for consistent high quality.

- **The chief pioneers** in the quality movement include Deming, Crosby, Feigenbaum, Ishikawa, Juran, Taguchi, and others. Their teachings helped Japan develop its post-war manufacturing prowess and later found their way into American industry.

- **Quality Function Deployment** (QFD) and the **House of Quality** (HOQ) provide a structured process for understanding customer requirements or the **Voice of the Customer** (VOC) and designing appropriate product and service offerings.

- The **Six Sigma** management strategy was started by Motorola and has become the quality rage in recent years. Six Sigma's methodologies are similar to Deming's PDCA cycle. Six Sigma practitioners can achieve "green belt" or "black belt" status or certification. Despite its widespread popularity, there is no single sanctioning body for Six Sigma certifications.

- **Free-flowing communication is essential to establishing and maintaining high levels of quality**. As Elder M. Russell Ballard states, "**An effective leader encourages free expression**"[44] or, in other words, open two-way communication. This is how quality problems are identified, and once identified, they can be addressed. On the other hand, failing to discuss problems destroys working relationships and organizations.[45]

---

[44] M. Russell Ballard, *Counseling with Our Councils* (Deseret Book, Salt Lake City, UT, 1997), pg. 24.

[45] In a February 2014 *Ensign* magazine article entitled, "Speak, Listen, and Love," the author states, "If couples tiptoe around deeper issues that should be discussed, they will never learn to resolve conflict or connect with each other. Couples bond as they discuss things that matter—not things that don't. I have seen many couples in my practice who have tried to preserve their relationship by keeping their communication at the superficial level. By avoiding the 'weightier matters' (Matthew 23:23), they have actually destroyed their marriage."

Chapter 5

QUALITY CONTROL

Early warning signals are evident in many aspects of our lives. For example, a fever can be a first symptom of sickness or disease....And depending upon the area of the world in which we live, we may receive flood, avalanche, hurricane, tsunami, tornado, or winter storm warnings.

[A] spiritual early warning system...can help parents...recognize early signals of spiritual growth in or challenges with their children and be better prepared to receive inspiration to strengthen and help those children.

Elder David A Bednar[46]

Chapter Objectives

Much like the spiritual early warning system mentioned by Elder Bednar, statistical process control is an indispensable informational tool that often warns of *potential* process-related problems before they become *real* problems. Such early warnings can enable timely low-cost preventive adjustments instead of more costly, major corrective actions at a later time.

In this chapter you will learn about quality control, especially statistical quality control. Specifically, after studying this chapter you should be able to

1.   Describe the main methods used in quality control.
2.   Explain acceptance sampling, including producer's and consumer's risk.
3.   Identify and explain the purpose of control charts, build control charts.
4.   Explain process capability and compute Cp and Cpk.

Overview of Quality Control

Quality control is the "process of measuring quality conformance by comparing the actual [measurement] with a standard for the characteristic and acting on the difference."[47] **Statistical quality control** is central to quality control and includes **two major approaches**: (1) *acceptance sampling* and (2) *statistical process control (SPC)*.

---

[46] David A. Bednar, "Watching with All Perseverance," April 2010 General Conference.
[47] John H. Blackstone Jr., editor, *APICS Dictionary*, 13th edition (Falls Church, VA: APICS, 2010).

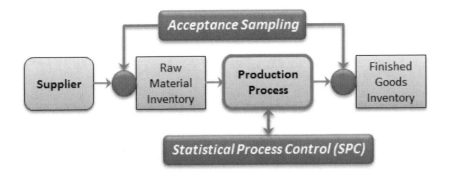

Acceptance sampling is used to determine whether to accept or reject an entire incoming supplier shipment or an entire outgoing production lot. **Statistical process control**, on the other hand, is used *during* the production process to ensure processes are performing within specified control limits. Both acceptance sampling and statistical process control observe and make use of two types of quality characteristics: *attributes* and *variables*.

- **Attributes** are quality control values that are either a "yes" or "no" value. Examples of attributes would include a product being either good or defective; an airline flight being either on time or late. There is no middle ground, only a binary "yes" or "no" type of answer can be given.
- **Variables** are characteristics that are manifest in varying degrees. Examples include dimensions, weights, and time, where differences can be measured. Continuous distributions (like the normal distribution) are used to measure variables.

Acceptance Sampling

Whether inspecting incoming shipments from suppliers or outgoing lots from production, few organizations have enough time or money to inspect every incoming or outgoing item to ensure 100 percent acceptable quality of each unit in the lot. Hence, sampling of a subset of a lot's entire population is used to help make this "accept" or "reject" decision with a high probability of being right. However, since any given sample might not be an accurate representation of the entire population, there is a risk of rejecting good lots and a risk of accepting bad lots.

- **Producer's risk** (α) is the risk that a *good* lot of acceptable quality will be rejected by the consumer. This can happen when the sample has a *higher* proportion of defectives than the population (the entire lot) as a whole, thus leading the consumer (receiver of the lot) to erroneously reject the entire (good) lot. Such an event is called a **type I error**.
- **Consumer's risk** (β) is the risk that a *bad* lot will be accepted. This can happen when the sample has a *lower* proportion of defectives than the population as a whole, thus leading the consumer to erroneously accept the entire (bad) lot. This is known as a **type II error**.

Sophisticated statistical models have been developed to help producers and consumers create sampling plans that balance the tradeoff between their respective risks while minimizing the costs of sampling.

Question: What is an operating characteristic curve (OC curve)?

An operating characteristic curve is a graph which represents a **sampling plan** based on a specific sample size and reject threshold combination. It shows the probability of accepting lots of varying quality levels.

For example, let's suppose we have an incoming lot of 1000 units and that we can afford a sampling plan which (1) calls for 100 percent inspection (sample size, n = 1000, or the entire lot) and (2) sets a defective threshold at 3 ½% (critical value, $c ≤$ 35) for the lot. For this sampling plan our OC curve would appear as follows:

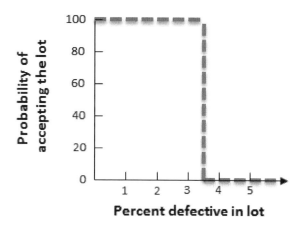

How do we read or interpret this OC curve? This curve tells us that we would inspect and accept the entire lot so long as there are no more than 35 defective units in the lot (remember, the critical value is 35). It further shows that there is absolutely no risk for either the producer or the consumer because we are inspecting the entire lot. In other words, we know with complete certainty that the lot is either good or bad (fewer or more defects than the critical value of 35) because we have inspected each unit. However, such a sampling plan is impractical given the exceedingly high costs of 100 percent inspection. Ideally, we should aim to devise a more cost-effective plan that keeps risks at an acceptable level.

Question: What are AQL and LTPD, and what role do they play in the construction of sampling plans?

- The acceptable quality level (AQL) is the maximum defect level at which a consumer will always accept the lot.
- The lot tolerance percent defective (LTPD) is the highest defect level of an individual lot that a consumer will "tolerate" or accept.

Let's suppose we wanted to devise a sampling plan for AQL = 1.37% and LTPD = 6.55%. To limit producer's risk to around 5% and consumer's risk to around 10% we would need a sample size of $n = 100$ units and a critical value of $c \le 3$. These variables or sampling plan would result in the operating characteristic curve below.

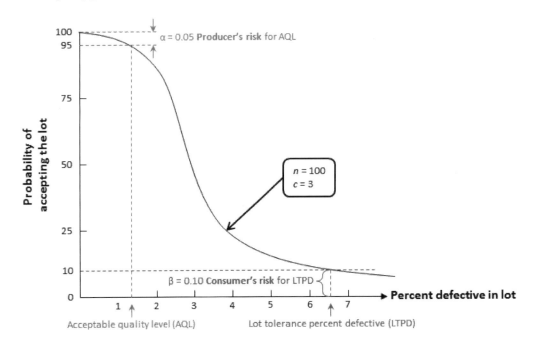

What would happen if we proportionally increased and decreased the sample size (n) and the critical value (c) while holding AQL and LTPD constant? As shown below, we would see dramatic increases and decreases to producer and consumer's risk. (Larger sample size and critical value result in lower risk to both producer and consumer.)

Question: Are there optimal levels for producer's risk and consumer's risk? If so, what are they?

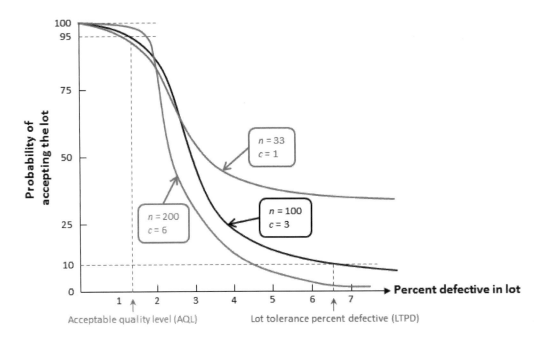

As a general rule sampling plans strive to keep producer's risk near $\alpha = 0.05$, or 5% and consumer's risk around $\beta = 0.10$, or 10%. In the example above, where we have three different OC curves, the producer's risk ranges from 2.12% (blue line) to 7.49% (red line), with the black line being most appropriate at 4.92%. The consumer's risk ranges from 2.11% (blue line) to 35.43% (red line), with the black line at 10.01%. It's great that the blue line ($n = 200$, $c = 6$) gives us low producer's and consumer's risk, but achieving these low risk levels requires doubling the sample size. Hence, the benefits of decreased risk must be balanced against the increased costs of larger sample sizes.

Question: What happens to rejected lots?

Rejected lots will typically go through 100 percent inspection in order to weed out and replace all defective units within those lots. This replacement technique will therefore increase the average outgoing quality (AOQ) of the lots.

Statistical Process Control (SPC)

Statistical process control is the application of statistical techniques to monitor the variability within a process. Variability is inherent in all processes and comes from two basic sources.

- Variation from **natural causes** is expected and requires no corrective action as it is present even in properly functioning processes. (Variation within 3 standard deviations of the mean or center line is considered normal.)
- Variation from **assignable causes** is abnormal and the result of some identifiable or "assignable" cause that should be (1) eliminated if it decreases process performance or (2) incorporated if it improves performance.

Question: What is a control chart and what is its purpose?

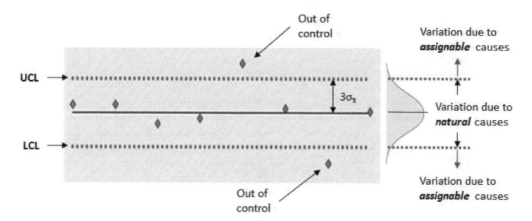

A control chart is a run chart, with upper and lower control limits (or boundaries), and its purpose is to detect *assignable* causes of variation within a process. When sample data falls above a control chart's upper control limit (UCL) or below its lower control limit (LCL) we say that the process is [likely] "out of control" and should be investigated further to find the "assignable" cause of this variation. In this way control charts provide early warning signals to process problems or significant changes.

Construction of Statistical Process Control Charts

Question: What are the steps required to build, use, and maintain a control chart?

The computation of sample statistics and calculation of control limits for control charts will vary by chart type, however, the basic steps for building, using, and maintaining control charts are similar and outlined as follows:

1. Take samples from the population and compute the appropriate sample statistic.
2. Use the sample statistic to calculate control limits and draw the control chart.
3. Plot sample results on the control chart and determine the state of the process (in or out of control).
4. Investigate possible assignable causes and take any indicated actions.
5. Continue sampling from the process and reset the control limits when necessary.

Question: How are control limits calculated?

Calculating upper and lower control limits varies by chart type and will be explained in detail below. Regardless of chart type, control charts typically set control limits at plus or minus 3σ (3 sigma or standard deviations) from the central line (process target or process mean). This means that in such processes, sample observations should fall between the upper and lower control limits 99.73% of the time resulting in 2,700 defects per million.

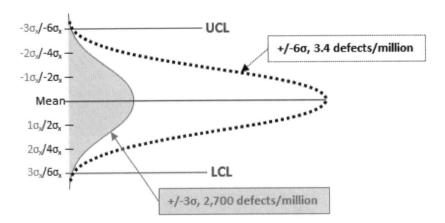

You should note that the Six Sigma management strategy (discussed in the previous chapter) has its roots in statistical process control. Statistically speaking, the idea of Six Sigma is to have exceedingly high-quality processes that can squeeze in plus or minus 6σ from the mean and still be in control. In these processes, sample means fall within a very narrow distribution and the observations within the samples should fall between the upper and lower control limits 99.9997% of the time, resulting in only 3.4 defects per million. The graphic above depicts the differences between 3-sigma and 6-sigma capable processes.

With this conception discussion behind us, we are now ready to provide specific examples on the construction of the various control charts mentioned above.

Question: What are the primary control charts used in statistical process control?

The primary control charts used in SPC fall into two basic categories: (1) control charts for variables and (2) control charts for attributes. **Variables control charts**, such as **x-bar charts** or **R-charts**, monitor continuous measurable data (weight, height, length, time, etc.). **Attributes control charts**, such as **p-charts** and **c-charts**, monitor discrete countable data. In other words, the data is more "yes/no" or "go/no-go" or "binary" in nature. For example, a part is either good or not; the student either passed or failed the exam. There is no measuring how good the part was or what score the student received, only a binary designation (one way or the other, no in-between answers).

Variables Control Charts
- **x-bar charts** (also known as "average" charts or "mean" charts) are used to evaluate the stability of process sample averages.
- **R-charts** (also known as "range" charts) are used to evaluate the stability of the process sample ranges.
- Note that these two charts **must <u>always</u> be used together** to verify that a variables-measured process is "in control" (which will be discussed further below).

Attributes Control Charts
- **p-charts** (or "proportion" charts) are used to monitor the proportion of defective units within a group. For example, a p-chart could be used to monitor the number or proportion of defective jump drives found in each batch of 1,000 produced.
- **c-charts** (or "numbers" charts) are used to monitor the count of defects within one unit of production or service. For example, a c-chart could be used to monitor the number of defects (blemishes or knots) found in each single roll of carpet produced.

A More Detailed Look at x-bar charts and R-charts
Suppose we want to monitor the packaging operation of a skin care product to ensure the proper amount of product is being inserted into each tube (container). Our goal is to insert 4 ounces of product into each container.

Based on historical data, we have computed an upper control limit of 4.049 ounces and a lower control limit of 3.951 ounces (about +/- 5 hundredths of an ounce from our target of 4 ounces). Our sampling plan calls for us to sample the process each hour of every shift with a sample size of 5 units. In other words, when we sample the process we take the mean (or average) weight of the 5 observations (within each sample) and plot each sample mean in our control chart (as seen below where 8 sample means have been plotted).

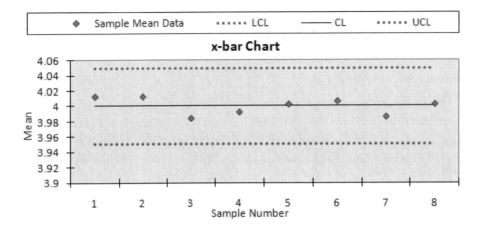

Given that each of the sample means falls within the control limits (the dotted red lines), we would say that this skin care product's packaging process appears to be "in control." But before we can make this assertion we must also examine the *R*-chart for this same process.

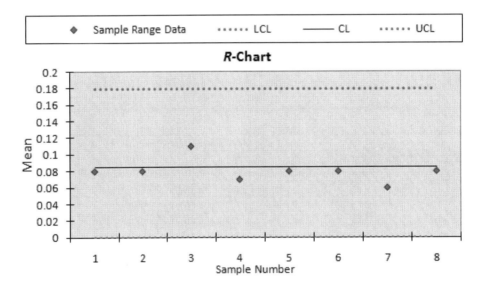

Using data from the same process we have constructed the corresponding *R*-chart below. Based on this data, we have computed an upper control limit of 0.18 ounces and a lower control limit of zero (0) ounces for this process. This means that within any given sample (of 5 observations), the difference in weight between the heaviest and lightest observations should not exceed 0.18 ounces. Our average range (the center line) for this data is 0.085 ounces. As can be seen in the chart below, each sample's range is fairly close to the center line and well within the upper and lower control limits (dotted green lines).

Now that we have verified that the sample means and sample ranges fit within the upper and lower control limits of *both* the x-bar chart and the *R*-chart, we can definitely state that the process is "in control."

Question: Why must an x-bar chart and an *R*-chart be used together to verify that a variables-measured process is in control?

Simply put, there can be cases where one chart will look perfectly normal while the other is out of control. Consider these hypothetical scenarios with our tube-filling process.

- **Scenario 1**: The sample ranges (the dispersion or distribution) remain constant but the sample means increase (the average weight of each sample progressively increases). The *R*-chart would not reveal any problems while the x-bar chart will show sample means that climb out of control (exceed the upper control limit).
- **Scenario 2**: The sample means (average weights) remain constant but the sample ranges increase. In this case, the x-bar chart will not show any problems while the *R*-chart will reveal the increasing dispersion with each sample.

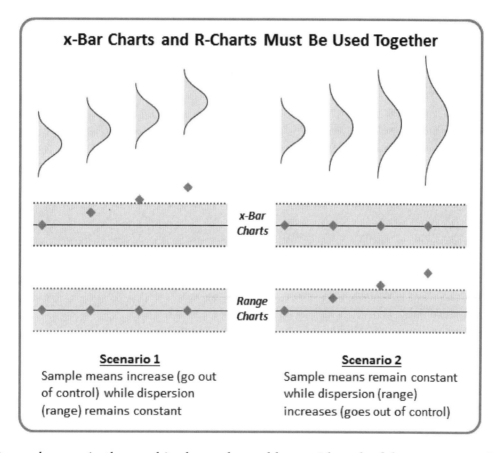

As can be seen in the graphic above, the problems with each of these two scenarios become readily apparent and make it very clear that both x-bar charts and R-charts are required to provide a complete assessment of process variability.

x-bar charts (where standard deviation *is* known)

When we know, from historical data, the standard deviation for a process, then we can use the following formulas to determine the upper control limit (UCL) and lower control limit (LCL) for a mean chart (x-bar chart).

$$UCL_{\bar{x}} = \bar{\bar{x}} + Z\sigma_{\bar{x}}$$

$$LCL_{\bar{x}} = \bar{\bar{x}} - Z\sigma_{\bar{x}}$$

Where

$\bar{\bar{x}}$ = average of the sample means or the target value for the process

Z = number of normal standard deviations (Z = 3 for 99.73% confidence)

$\sigma_{\bar{x}}$ = standard deviation of the sample means = $\sigma/\sqrt{n}$

σ = standard deviation of the population (or of the observations)

n = sample size (made up of n observations)

Example 1: A 1-hour photo service aims for a 55-minute turnaround for all orders received. Each day they sample the process nine times to make sure it is in control. They found that the standard deviation of the population (observations) to be six (6) minutes. What are the upper and lower control limits for this process?

$$UCL_{\bar{x}} = \bar{\bar{x}} + Z\sigma_{\bar{x}} = 55 + 3\left(\frac{6}{\sqrt{9}}\right) = 55 + 3\left(\frac{6}{3}\right) = 55 + 6 = 61$$

$$LCL_{\bar{x}} = \bar{\bar{x}} - Z\sigma_{\bar{x}} = 55 - 3\left(\frac{6}{\sqrt{9}}\right) = 55 - 3\left(\frac{6}{3}\right) = 55 - 6 = 49$$

Note that in this example the standard deviation was given for population (σ = 6) and not for the sample means ($\sigma_{\bar{x}}$). This meant that in order to find the standard deviation for the sample means—which is required in these equations—we had to divide the standard deviation of the population (σ = 6)by the square root of the sample size (in this case, n = 9).

With the control limits established above, we would continue to monitor the process to make sure it is "in control." If, after establishing these control limits, we were to get a sample where the sample mean falls above the UCL or below the LCL, we should then investigate to identify the "assignable" cause of this variation and take corrective action to eliminate it.

R-charts and x-bar charts (where standard deviation *is not* known)

When historical data is not available to compute the standard deviation for a process we must use different equations to compute upper and lower control limits. The table below contains factors that are used in the computation of upper and lower control limits for both x-bar charts and R-charts.

The equations are as follows for the x-bar chart's control limits.

$$UCL_{\bar{x}} = \bar{\bar{x}} + A_2\bar{R}$$

$$LCL_{\bar{x}} = \bar{\bar{x}} - A_2\bar{R}$$

Where

$\bar{R}$ = the average range of the samples

A_2 = the factor for $\bar{x}$-charts (as seen in the table below)

Here are the equations for the upper and lower control limits of the R-chart.

$$UCL_R = D_4\bar{R}$$

$$LCL_R = D_3\bar{R}$$

The values for D_3 and D_4, used in the above formulas for range-chart control limits, come from the table below.

Observations (sample size)	$\bar{x}$-charts Factor: A_2	R-chart LCL Factor: D_3	R-Chart UCL Factor: D_4
2	1.880	0	3.268
3	1.023	0	2.574
4	0.729	0	2.282
5	0.577	0	2.115
6	0.483	0	2.004
7	0.419	0.076	1.924
8	0.373	0.136	1.864
9	0.337	0.184	1.816
10	0.308	0.223	1.777
11	0.285	0.256	1.744
12	0.266	0.284	1.716
13	0.249	0.308	1.692
14	0.235	0.329	1.671
15	0.223	0.348	1.652
20	0.180	0.414	1.586

Factors for Control Charts

Example 2: Let's return to our 1-hour photo service example, except in this case let's suppose that we do not have enough historical data to accurately compute the standard deviation, however; we do know that the average range (R-bar) has been 11. Our target turnaround time remains 55 minutes and our sample size is still nine. With this data we are able to compute the following upper and lower control limits.

$$UCL_{\bar{x}} = \bar{\bar{x}} + A_2\bar{R} = 55 + 0.337(11) = 55 + 3.707 = 58.707$$

$$LCL_{\bar{x}} = \bar{\bar{x}} - A_2\bar{R} = 55 - 0.337(11) = 55 - 3.707 = 51.293$$

The upper and lower control limits for the range chart are computed as follows:

$$UCL_R = D_4\bar{R} = 1.816(11) = 19.976$$

$$LCL_R = D_3\bar{R} = 0.184(11) = 2.024$$

The control limits for this range chart tell us that we should expect the range for any given sample—the difference between the longest and shortest observation within the sample—to be no lower than 2.024 minutes and no greater than 19.976 minutes, otherwise we would say the process is likely out of control.

p-charts

As mentioned earlier, *p*-charts are used to track the proportion of defective units found within a batch of units being produced. Upper and lower control limits for *p*-charts are computed as follows:

$$UCL_p = \bar{p} + Z\sigma_{\hat{p}}$$

$$LCL_p = \bar{p} - Z\sigma_{\hat{p}}$$

Where

$\bar{P}$ = proportion of defectives
Z = number of normal standard deviations ($Z = 3$ for 99.73% confidence)
n = sample size (made up of *n* observations)
$\sigma_{\hat{p}}$ = standard deviation of the sampling distribution, calculated as follows

$$\sigma_{\hat{p}} = \sqrt{\frac{\bar{p}(1-\bar{p})}{n}}$$

Note that for p-charts the standard deviation of the sampling distribution must be estimated by using the formula above. **You _may not_ use one of Excel's standard deviation functions** *in this case.*

Example 3: Let's return again to our 1-hour photo service to establish control limits for a *p*-chart. In this case we will not be setting up control limits to measure the variability of the process, as in the previous two examples; rather, we will set up control limits to monitor the attributes of the process. In this case, with a *p*-chart, we want to know the percentage of on-time completed orders and whether our performance in this regard is acceptable.

Day (sample number)	1	2	3	4	5	6	7	8	9	10	11	12	13	14	15
No. of defective/late orders	1	4	2	1	2	0	5	1	0	2	6	1	0	2	0
% defective orders	2%	8%	4%	2%	4%	0%	10%	2%	0%	4%	12%	2%	0%	4%	0%

Table 7.2: Defective Items/Orders in 15 Samples of *n* = 50 Orders

This 1-hour photo service is extremely busy and processes well over one hundred jobs or orders per day. Each month they sample 50 orders on 15 different days to see what percentage of orders are completed late (take more than 60 minutes). Above is the sample data from last month.

In this example, we have 27 defectives out of 750 total orders sampled. Thus, our average proportion defective is 0.036 or 3.6%. Our upper and lower control limits for this *p*-chart are as follows:

$$UCL_p = \bar{p} + Z\sigma_{\hat{p}} = \bar{p} + Z\sqrt{\frac{\bar{p}(1-\bar{p})}{n}} = 0.036 + 3\sqrt{\frac{0.036(1-0.036)}{50}} = 0.115$$

$$LCL_p = \bar{p} - Z\sigma_{\hat{p}} = \bar{p} - Z\sqrt{\frac{\bar{p}(1-\bar{p})}{n}} = 0.036 - 3\sqrt{\frac{0.036(1-0.036)}{50}} = -0.043 \ (or \ 0)$$

Since the lower control limit is less than zero (a negative number) we will simply set the lower control limit equal to zero. These limits tell us that if more than 11.5% of the orders exceed 60 minutes, then the process is out of control.

c-charts

As mentioned earlier, c-charts are used to monitor the count of defects within one unit of production or service. Upper and lower control limits for c-charts or numbers charts are computed with the following equations.

$$UCL_c = \bar{c} + Z\sigma_c$$

$$LCL_c = \bar{c} - Z\sigma_c$$

Where

$\bar{c}$ = average number of defectives per unit

Z = number of normal standard deviations (Z = 3 for 99.73% confidence)

σ_c = standard deviation of the sampling distribution, calculated as follows

$$\sigma_c = \sqrt{\bar{c}}$$

Note that for c-charts the standard deviation of the sampling distribution must be estimated by using the formula above. **You _may not_ use one of Excel's standard deviation functions in this case.**

Example 4: Let's return one last time to our 1-hour photo service to establish control limits for our c-chart. In this case, given the performance of 3.6% late orders from the previous example, we want to find out if the number of customer complaints is getting out of control. The table below provides data on the number of complaints during the past 10 weeks.

Week (sample number)	1	2	3	4	5	6	7	8	9	10
No. of complaints per week	8	4	5	6	2	0	5	7	4	2

Table 7.3: Complaints Received by Week

Based on this data they receive an average of 4.3 complaints per week. The upper and lower control limits for the c-chart are computed as follows:

$$UCL_c = \bar{c} + Z\sigma_c = \bar{c} + Z\sqrt{\bar{c}} = 4.3 + 3\sqrt{4.3} = 10.521$$

$$LCL_c = \bar{c} - Z\sigma_c = \bar{c} - Z\sqrt{\bar{c}} = 4.3 - 3\sqrt{4.3} = -1.921 \ (or \ 0)$$

As was the case with our *p*-chart, the lower control limit is less than zero (a negative number), so we will simply set the lower control limit equal to zero ($LCL_c = 0$). These limits tell us that if they receive more than 10.521 complaints in a week, the process is out of control.

Process Capability

Whereas Statistical Process Control (SPC) primarily uses historical process data to establish process control limits, process capability looks at how well a stable process performs against the design specifications of that process. In other words, a stable process may be "in control" according to SPC control limits and still not meet the design specifications for that process. Process capability tells us whether a process is capable of meeting design specifications.

Question: How can we know a process is capable of delivering acceptable performance (or the designed performance)?

There are two popular measures for determining if a process is capable of delivering acceptable performance: (1) process capability ratio and (2) process capability index.

Process capability ratio (C_p) compares process variation to design specifications to determine if a process meets those specifications. A $C_p \geq 1$ means the process is capable of meeting the performance requirements. C_p is computed as follows:

$$C_p = \frac{USL - LSL}{6\sigma}$$

Where

      USL = upper specification limit (of the design)
      LSL = lower specification limit (of the design)
      σ = standard deviation of the population

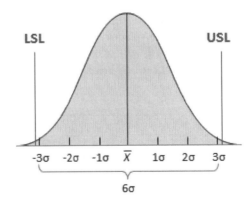

The graphic above attempts to conceptually explain what it means to have a $C_p \geq 1$. If the difference between the upper and lower specifications (USL – LSL) is greater than 6σ, then the process capability ratio will be greater than one (1) and more than 99.73% of the observations will fall within the specification limits, thus indicating that the process is capable of meeting the design specifications. Notice that the distance between the two red lines is slightly greater than 6σ. If you divide the distance between these red lines by 6σ, you will get a number slightly greater than 1, again indicating that the process is capable of meeting the design specifications.

Example 5: Let's suppose that the 1-hour photo service sells a variety of inexpensive plastic picture frames. The design specification calls for a diagonal dimension upper limit of 8.77 inches and a lower limit of 8.72 inches. The supplier has a process standard deviation of 0.008 inches. Is the supplier's manufacturing process capable of meeting the design specifications?

$$C_p = \frac{USL - LSL}{6\sigma} = \frac{8.77 - 8.72}{6(0.008)} = 1.042$$

In this case we would say that our process is capable of meeting the design specification because six standard deviations (6 x 0.008 = 0.048 inches) is less than the difference between the USL and LSL (8.77 – 8.72 = 0.05 inches).

In this example we have assumed that the process mean $(\bar{X})$ is centered between the USL and LSL. And since Cp = 1.042 ≥ 1, we know that the process is sufficiently stable (has low enough variability) to meet the design specifications. What we do not know, however, is whether the process mean is indeed centered between the design limits. This is where the process capability index comes into play.

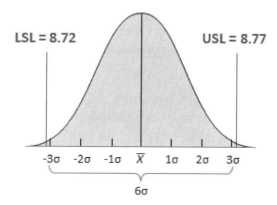

Process capability index (C_{pk}) measures the proportion of variation between the process center and the nearest specification limit. A $C_{pk} ≥ 1$ means the process is sufficiently centered to meet the design specification. C_{pk} is computed as follows:

$$C_{pk} = Minimum\ of \left[\frac{USL - \bar{X}}{3\sigma}, \frac{\bar{X} - LSL}{3\sigma}\right]$$

Where

$\bar{X}$ = process mean
σ = standard deviation

Example 6: Continuing with our picture frame example, let's suppose that our process mean was 8.75 inches rather than being perfectly centered (8.745 inches) between the USL and LSL. C_{pk} would be computed as follows:

$$C_{pk} = Min.\, of\, \left[\frac{USL - \bar{X}}{3\sigma}, \frac{\bar{X} - LSL}{3\sigma}\right] = Min.\, of\, \left[\frac{8.77 - 8.75}{3(0.008)}, \frac{8.75 - 8.72}{3(0.008)}\right] = 0.83$$

Since $C_{pk} < 1$, we can conclude that the process, while adequately stable (as shown by C_p), is not sufficiently *centered* to consistently meet the design specifications.

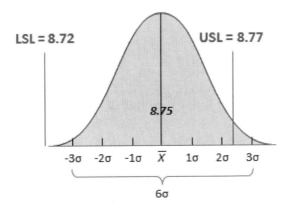

The above graphic, based on the data in this example, shows that the process mean (8.75) is not centered between the USL and LSL. (Note that if our process was perfectly centered, then C_p and C_{pk} would be equal.) Should an observation fall 3σ to the left there would be no problem; 3σ to the right and the observation would fall outside the USL, therefore showing that this process—due to its off-center position—is not capable of consistently meeting the design specifications. The process capability ration (C_p) only tells us about the dispersion of the process but says nothing of its centering. Hence, there is a need for the process capability index (C_{pk}) in addition to C_p.

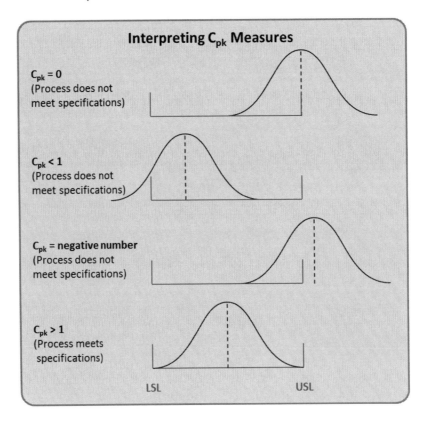

The graphic examples above show a number of scenarios that bear this out. In each case the process' dispersion is sufficiently narrow to support the specifications' variability requirements, yet only the bottom process is properly centered and truly capable of meeting the design specifications.

Chapter Summary

Below are some of the main points you should have garnered from the study of this chapter.

- **Quality control is the process of measuring quality**. Statistical quality control includes both acceptance sampling and statistical process control (SPC).
- **Acceptance sampling typically happens upon receipt of materials** from a supplier (before being used in production) or upon completion of a production lot (receipt into finished goods, for instance). Sampling plans strive to strike an appropriate balance between producer's risk and consumer's risk. The OC (operating characteristic) curve represents a sampling plan.
- **SPC is an early warning signal** whose purpose is to detect assignable causes of variation (as opposed to natural causes of variation). It takes place **during the production process**.
- **Control charts come in two basic varieties**: (1) control charts for variables and (2) control charts for attributes.
- **Process capability** goes beyond SPC and **determines if a process is capable of meeting design specifications**.

Chapter 6

PROJECT MANAGEMENT

And there stood one among them that was like unto God, and he said unto those who were with him: ***We will go down, for there is space there, and we will take of these materials, and we will make an earth whereon these may dwell;***

Abraham 3:24

Thus we have the great **project charter** of the Creation of our earth. This charter describes the project scope and objectives as well as the key roles of the participants involved.

- **Scope and Objectives**: "we will take of these materials, and we will make an earth whereon these may dwell;"
- **Key Roles**: "We" included "the Gods, who organized and formed the heavens and the earth"[48] and "these" comprised "the intelligences that were organized before the world was"[49] who would dwell upon the earth.

Chapter Objectives

A project charter is just one of the tools that are required to effectively manage projects. In this chapter you will learn about project management and the main concepts, tools, and techniques that will help you effectively manage projects. Specifically, after studying this chapter you should be able to

1. Explain the difference between business operations and projects.
2. Describe the major project phases.
3. Describe the organization options for projects and the role of a project manager.
4. Construct a project network diagram, calculate the project duration, and identify the activities in the project's critical path.
5. Calculate the earliest start and finish times for each activity (forward pass), calculate the latest finish and start times for each activity (backward pass), and calculate each activity's slack time.
6. Crash a project.

---

[48] Abraham 4:1
[49] Abraham 3:22

Overview of Project Management

Question: What is a project?

A project is a temporary, organized effort with a set of activities designed to meet specific objectives such as the creation of the earth, the development and introduction of a new product or service, the construction of a new building or highway, or the implementation of a new business process and related systems.

Question: What is project management?

Project management is the use of skills and knowledge to initiate, plan, execute, and close out the activities associated with a project.

Question: How do projects differ from daily business operations?

Projects differ from operations in that they typically have a temporary, one-time focus whereas day-to-day business operations are generally more repetitive in nature. For example, constructing and launching a new restaurant would be a project whereas running the restaurant once it is opened would require a different set of operations management tools and techniques.

Returning to our example of the Creation, the forming of the earth could be viewed as a "project" that has made it possible for God to pursue the day-to-day "business operation" or work of "[proving us] herewith, to see if [we] will do all things whatsoever" He shall command us.[50] This project and operation are consistent with our Father's overall mission or vision "to bring to pass the immortality and eternal life of man."[51]

Question: What is the project management triangle?

The basic constraints of (1) time, (2) cost, and (3) quality (or scope) represent the three sides of a "triangle" of tradeoffs known as the "project management triangle" (similar to the "value triangle" introduced in chapter 2). Like any endeavor, projects have constraints within which the team must work. Hence, the saying goes that you can choose to make improvements on one or two of these three constraints but you cannot improve all three simultaneously. Therefore, tradeoffs are required.

---

[50] Abraham 3:25
[51] Moses 1:39

For example, let's say you're building a house and you want it to be done quickly (time constraint), at low cost (cost constraint), and with many labor-intensive extras like custom tile work, extensive wallpaper, real wood floors, in-house vacuum, and so forth (quality or scope constraint). Well, it's pretty obvious that you can't have all three—done quickly, at low cost, and with lots of extras—at the same time. You can choose up to two. If you want the house

- Quickly and at low cost → it cannot have lots of extras (reduce scope).
- Quickly and with lots of extras → it cannot be low cost (increase cost).
- Low cost with lots of extras → it cannot be done quickly (more time).

We should note, however, that at times, with the inspiration of the Light of Christ or the Holy Ghost, it is possible for individuals and organizations to make simultaneous improvements across these three dimensions. President Kim B. Clark's inaugural response in 2005 included such a bold endeavor when he outlined the "three imperatives" for BYU-Idaho.

1. "Raise substantially the quality of every aspect of the experience our students have" (improve the quality, or in other words, the scope of the student experience).
2. "Make a BYU-Idaho education available to many more of the young people of the Church" (increase the university's capacity, or in other words, get more done with the university's available time).
3. "Lower the relative cost of education"[52] (self-evident, the cost dimension).

As we saw in the Productivity chapter, it has been prophesied that a hallmark of a BYU-Idaho education and an increasing trademark of its graduates will be the ability to do more with less—in a sense, to summon the faith and marshal the good works necessary to overcome man's conventional wisdom as represented in the project management triangle. *(Author's note: I pray that this will be your heritage!)*

Question: What are the phases in a project?

There are four basic phases to most any project: (I) Initiation, (II) Planning, (III) Execution, and (IV) Close Out. (Sometimes "monitoring" a project is considered a separate phase, thus making a total of five phases.) Below are more detailed, though not comprehensive, explanations of each project phase as well as some examples of each that are drawn from the creation of the earth.

- **PHASE I: Initiation or Concept** – In this phase, a project idea or opportunity is explored to determine the feasibility of proceeding. As the Savior taught, "For which of you, intending to build a tower, sitteth not down first, and counteth the cost, whether he have sufficient to finish it?"[53] The output of this phase is formally documented in a project charter—a

---

[52] www.byui.edu
[53] Luke 14:28

statement that lists the project's goals (financial and otherwise), objectives, scope, and key resources.

> Charter Example: "We will go down, for there is space there, and we will take of these materials, and we will make an earth whereon these may dwell."[54]

- **PHASE II: Planning** – The key deliverables of this phase include breaking down the work into assignable tasks or activities, sequencing these activities by honoring predecessor relationships, and assigning and scheduling resources (people) to do this work.

> Plan Example: "And every plant of the field before it was in the earth, and every herb of the field before it grew. For I, the Lord God, created all things, of which I have spoken, spiritually, before they were naturally upon the face of the earth."[55] (Of course, this quote is a highly simplified version of pre-creation planning and does not contain all the detail that would normally be covered in this phase. But we can safely assume that there was adequate detail in these plans for them to perfectly perform the work.)

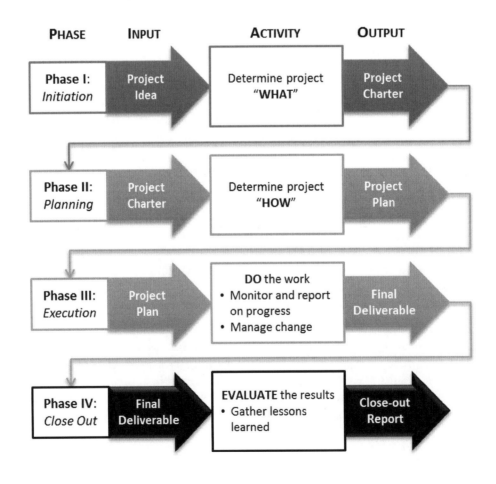

---

54 Abraham 3:24
55 Moses 3:5

- **PHASE III: Execution** – The focus of this phase is to monitor and control or adjust the project's activities as work progresses.

  ➢ <u>Execution and Monitoring Example</u>: Read Moses 2:2-30 for a day-by-day narrative of all the detailed work that was done in the execution phase of the creation. Each completed activity was declared as being "good" upon completion. We gain further insights on this phase from Elder M. Russell Ballard who tells us that "a council of Gods, operating under the direction of God our Heavenly Father, worked together to physically create the world on which we live....Throughout the entire creative period this council worked closely together, receiving specific instructions from God, carefully carrying out these instructions, and then returning and reporting their progress while awaiting further instructions."[56]

- **PHASE IV: Close Out** – This phase typically includes a final evaluation by the project's customer and key stakeholders. The project team would also perform a "post-mortem" to gather "lessons learned" that could be applied to future projects.

  ➢ <u>Final Deliverable and Close-out Report Example</u>: Upon completion of all the project work we read, "And I, God, saw everything that I had made, and, behold, all things which I had made were very good;"[57]

Project Leadership and Organization

<u>Question</u>:   What makes a good project manager (or project leader)?

According to Elder Ballard, an important lesson that we "can learn from the Creation council is that Heavenly Father didn't do all of the work Himself—even though He certainly could have. As God, He had all of the authority and power He needed to create the world, and He clearly was the one who had the full vision of the project. Still He chose to delegate responsibilities, always asking for a follow-up report to make sure that the work had been done correctly."[58]

Thus we learn that good project managers should have proper organizational **authority**, understand and be able to **articulate the full vision** of the project, know how to **effectively delegate**, and skillfully **follow up** to make sure the work is done correctly. However, we should note that as non-omniscient beings, it is nearly impossible for a single project manager to have deep knowledge of and the skills required for all the work to be done across a complex cross-functional project. Hence, it is critical that project managers be **skillful "investigators"** who ask lots of questions of the functional experts in order to breakdown the work to assignable

---

[56] M. Russell Ballard, *Counseling with Our Councils: Learning to Minister Together in the Church and in the Family* [Salt Lake City: Deseret Book Co., 1997], 25 - 26.

[57] Moses 2:31

[58] M. Russell Ballard, *Counseling with Our Councils: Learning to Minister Together in the Church and in the Family* (Salt Lake City: Deseret Book Co., 1997), 29.

activities and to identify all of the interdependencies of those activities when in the planning phase of a project.

Question: What organization designs are used for managing projects?

As depicted in the graphic below[59] there are three basic ways to structure cross-functional organizations to work on projects: (1) project organization, (2) lightweight project matrix organization, and (3) heavyweight project matrix organization. The cross-functional nature of many projects often poses organizational challenges, especially in large organizations. The two basic approaches to project organizational structure are a project organization or a matrix or hybrid organization, of which there are two varieties. The most appropriate organizational structure depends on the goals and objectives of the given project.

- In a **project organization**, all team members report directly to the project manager, thus creating clear allegiance and enabling rapid coordination among team members.
- **Lightweight project matrix organizations** preserve project team members' "solid line" or direct reporting relationships to their functional managers, thus helping them maintain their deep functional expertise while still having a "dotted line" or matrix reporting relationship to the "lightweight" project manager.
- **Heavyweight project matrix organizations** reverse the lightweight reporting relationships so that there is a direct reporting relationship to the "heavyweight" project manager and a matrix relationship to the functional manager—thus placing a stronger allegiance to the project team while still encouraging access to deep functional expertise through the matrix relationship to the functional group.

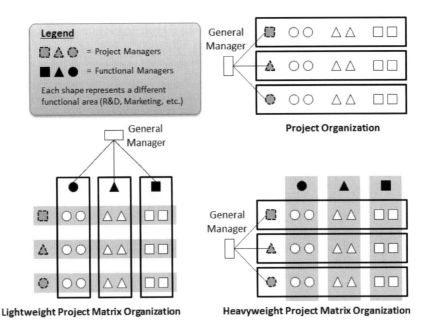

59 Adapted from Robert H. Hayes, Steven C. Wheelwright, and Kim B. Clark, Dynamic Manufacturing: Creating the Learning Organization (New York: The Free Press, 1988).

Project Scheduling: Network Diagrams

Question: What are the steps to scheduling a project?

Scheduling a project is part of the planning phase and includes the following steps.

1. Break down the major tasks of the project into a list of assignable activities.
2. Estimate the time required to complete each activity and determine the precedent relationships among these activities.
3. Construct a network diagram for the project.
4. Determine the project duration and identify the project's critical path.
5. Calculate the earliest start and finish times for each activity (forward pass), calculate the latest finish and start times for each activity (backward pass), and calculate each activity's slack time.

Over the next several pages we will walk through many of these steps to help you become familiar with them. While much of this work in the workplace is typically done with the assistance of specialized software, going through these scheduling mechanics will further your knowledge of project management and prepare you to participate more effectively as a project team member or even a project manager.

Question: What is a network diagram?

A network diagram is a drawing or graph that (1) uses small circles (or nodes) to represent project activities and (2) uses lines (or arcs) to show the precedent relationships among these activities. Before examining these diagrams further, however, we need to understand a bit more about a key predecessor to this process: the **work breakdown structure**.

Let's say we want to host a hamburger barbecue. At a very high level we would say the main task would simply be to "barbecue hamburgers." But this seemingly simple task is too general for us to assign work and be confident that everything would be taken care of. Okay, so let's break down this single task to the next level, into two parts: (1) grill the meat and (2) prepare the hamburger buns. Does this next level of additional information give us enough confidence to end the planning at this point? Probably not. We need more details. These tasks need to be broken down further. If we were to continue the work breakdown process we would finally end up with a list of assignable activities that would look something like this.

Activity	Description	Duration	Predecessors
A	Heat charcoal	20	-
B	Prepare patties	11	-
C	Slice tomatoes and onions	9	-
D	Grill patties	6	A, B
E	Set out condiments	4	C
F	Prepare burger buns	8	E
G	Assemble hamburgers	4	D, F
H	Ask a blessing	2	D

Creating the work breakdown structure requires that project managers be effective questioners, who don't assume "everything is under control" or that "so and so will take care of all of that." Rather, effective project managers assume nothing and "leave no stone unturned" in their quest to understand all the work that must be done as part of their projects. With this work breakdown structure in place—which includes activity names, descriptions, durations (in minutes), and predecessor relationships—we can now draw our network diagram (below).

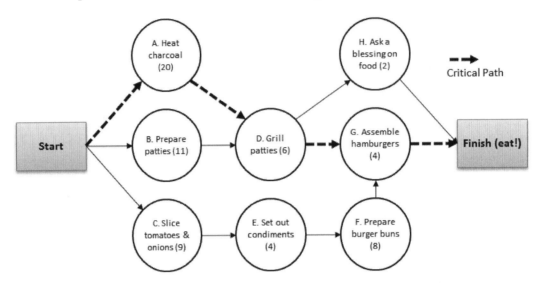

Notice how all the nodes and arrows in the network diagram comply with the predecessor relationships as outlined in the work breakdown structure (table above). For example, activity D (Grill patties) cannot begin until after both activity A (Heat charcoal) and activity B (Prepare patties) are completed. In other words, even though it will only take 11 minutes before we have formed the patties and they are ready to be grilled, we must also wait until the charcoal is ready (20 minutes) before we can place them on the grill.

In a nutshell, this is how a project network diagram is constructed.

Question: How do you determine the project's duration?

To determine the project's duration we must (1) calculate the duration of each path through the project and (2) identify the longest path to determine the overall duration of the project. In our example above

- Path A-D-H   = 20 + 6 +2   = 28 minutes
- Path A-D-G   = 20 + 6 + 4   = 30 minutes ←the longest path!
- Path B-D-H   = 11 + 6 + 2   = 19 minutes
- Path B-D-G   = 11 + 6 + 4   = 21 minutes
- Path C-E-F-G = 9 + 4 + 8 +4 = 25 minutes

In this case, the project's **duration** is 30 minutes. Path A-D-G—the longest path through the project—is also known as the project's **critical path,** which means that any delay to any activity on this path (A, D, or G) will result in an increase to the overall project duration.

Question: What is the critical path method (CPM) and how does it differ from PERT (program evaluation and review technique)?

The critical path method—which comprises creating a project network diagram, calculating the project duration, and identifying the critical path—is a technique for planning and controlling the activities in a project.

PERT is similar to CPM in that it also makes use of network diagrams to plan project durations. However, PERT requires that each activity be assigned an optimistic, most likely, and pessimistic estimate of duration from which a weighted average duration for each activity is then derived. This estimation process allows for probabilistic project durations to be calculated. (Yes, this sounds a bit complex, and it is rarely used except for in the most complex, uncertain project management environments. Therefore, the mechanics of PERT calculations are beyond the scope of this book.)

Question: What is slack time, how is it calculated, and why is it important?

Slack time is the amount of time an activity can be delayed without increasing the overall project duration. Its importance will be more easily understood after we show how it is calculated. To calculate slack time

1.   Calculate the earliest start time (ES) and earliest finish time (EF) for each activity. This is done by doing a "forward pass" through each path in the network diagram, working only in the top half of each activity node.
2.   Calculate the latest start time (LS) and latest finish time (LF) for each activity with a "backward pass" through each path in the network diagram, working only in the bottom half of each node.
3.   Calculate the slack time for each activity by subtracting its earliest start time from its latest start time or by subtracting its earliest finish time from its latest finish time. Slack time = LS – ES or LF – EF.

When calculating ES, EF, LS, LF, and slack times, it's best to draw the network diagram with detailed nodes like the one below.

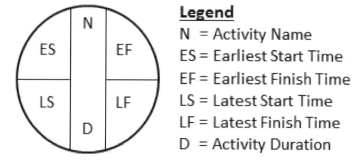

Legend
N = Activity Name
ES = Earliest Start Time
EF = Earliest Finish Time
LS = Latest Start Time
LF = Latest Finish Time
D = Activity Duration

Calculating Earliest Start and Earliest Finish Times

Returning to our barbecue example, the new network diagram shows the earliest start times and earliest finish times for each activity.

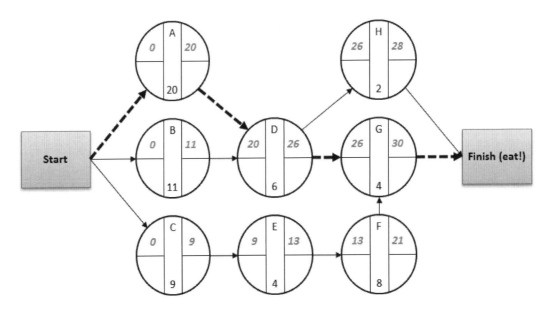

These numbers were derived by working from left to right. Starting at minute zero (0) for the earliest start times of activities A, B, and C and then adding these activities' duration to zero (the ES for these three activities) we come up with the earliest finish times of minute 20, minute 11, and minute 9 for activities A, B, and C, respectively.

The process continues working to the right as we determine each activities' earliest start time. Notice that activity D has two immediate predecessors—activity A and activity B—so in these cases we take the largest earliest finish time of the predecessors and use that number as the earliest start time for the successor, activity D (A's EF = 20 and B's EF = 11, so we make D's ES = 20). When there is only one immediate predecessor we simply make the ES of the successor equal to the EF of the predecessor (C's EF = 9 so E's ES = 9). Again, we see that the overall duration is still 30 minutes, but now we have a bit more detail in the diagram.

Calculating Latest Start and Latest Finish Times

When calculating the latest start times and latest finish times we follow a similar process except we work from right to left. The network diagram below shows the latest start times and latest finish times in the bottom half of the activity nodes.

Starting with activity H we ask ourselves, what is the latest time we can finish this activity without increasing the overall duration of the project? The answer is minute 30, which we input as the latest finish time (LF) for activity H. Working to the left, we subtract the activity's duration from the LF to derive the latest start time (LS), which in the case of activity H would be minute 28.

For activity G we again ask ourselves, what is the latest time we can finish this activity without increasing the overall duration of the project? The answer again is minute 30. Working down, we ask ourselves the same question of activity F, which has only one immediate successor (activity G). The answer is minute 26. The latest finish time of the predecessor (activity F) is equal to the latest start time of the immediate successor (activity G), meaning activity F must be done no later than minute 26 in order to preserve the overall project duration of 30 minutes.

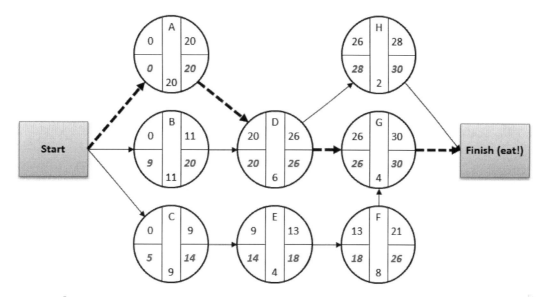

What happens when an activity has two or more immediate successors as is the case with activity D? We must make that activity's latest finish time equal to the smallest latest start time of the successors (G's LS = 26 and H's LS = 28, so we make D's LF = 26). As we continue with these calculations from right to left we end up with the latest start times and latest finish times as depicted in the diagram above.

Calculating Slack Time

It's quite easy to calculate each activity's slack time once we have calculated the latest start times and latest finish times through the entire network. As stated above (in step 3), slack time can be calculated in one of two ways.

- Slack Time = LS – ES, or
- Slack Time = LF - EF

The table below gives us each activity's ES, EF, LS, LF, and slack times.

Activity	Description	Duration	Predecessors	ES	EF	LS	LF	Slack
A	Heat charcoal	20	-	0	20	0	20	0
B	Prepare patties	11	-	0	11	9	20	9
C	Slice tomatoes and onions	9	-	0	9	5	14	5
D	Grill patties	6	A, B	20	26	20	26	0
E	Set out condiments	4	C	9	13	14	18	5
F	Prepare burger buns	8	E	13	21	18	26	5
G	Assemble hamburgers	4	D, F	26	30	26	30	0
H	Ask a blessing	2	D	26	28	28	30	2

Notice that the critical path activities A-D-G have no slack time. In other words, if the duration of any one of these three activities is increased, then the overall duration of the project is also increased. Conversely, we have some flexibility with those activities that are not on the critical, meaning they can be delayed by their slack time without pushing out the overall project duration.

For example, let's suppose you assigned two people to slice tomatoes and onions but only one person shows up. Now instead of taking 9 minutes this activity will take twice as long (18 minutes) and will push out the overall length of the project because that activity only has 5 minutes of slack time (assuming two workers). However, since you know that the activity of preparing patties has 9 minutes of slack time, you reassign that person to help slice tomatoes and onions for 9 minutes. This will delay your patties preparation activity by 9 minutes, but that won't be a problem because that activity had 9 minutes of slack time.

As can be seen in this example, skillful project managers understand that they operate in dynamic environments and know how to use slack time and other knowledge (of resource skills, availability, etc.) to help them adjust plans without adversely affecting overall project schedules.

Project Crashing

__Question__: What does it mean to "crash" a project?

Crashing a project is a methodical process of reducing the project's duration. Slippage to a project's schedule (increased duration) can result in lost revenue (due to a late introduction of a new product), tarnished reputation, or even large contractual penalties (large public works projects). When a project's schedule is at risk of slipping, management may want to intervene by crashing the project.

__Note__ that crashing a project does not mean you can eliminate required activities. You must shorten the project's duration by shortening the duration of critical path activities. This can be done by working overtime, subcontracting, buying or renting extra equipment, and so forth. Crashing involves increasing the project's cost, so care should be taken to crash the project in the most cost-effective manner possible.

__Question__: What are the steps to crashing a project?

1. Identify the critical path.
2. Identify the activity on the critical path that has the lowest crashing cost per period (per day, per week, etc., whichever time bucket is being used).
3. Crash the lowest-cost activity until (a) the crashing objective is met, (b) that activity cannot be crashed further, or (c) a new critical path emerges.
4. If further crashing is required (crashing objective not yet met), then continue by crashing the next critical-path activity that has the lowest crashing cost per period. __Note__ that if two critical paths emerge, see if there is an activity that (a) is common to both critical paths and (b) would be the most cost effective to crash (cheaper than crashing two separate items, one on each critical path).
5. Crashing ends when the objective has been met or the critical path cannot be crashed any further.

Crashing Example

For this example we'll start by taking our previous network diagram, except in this case it won't be for a barbecue. Instead, let's just suppose these are generic activities and the durations are now in weeks and not in minutes as in the barbecue example. Everything else (critical path, slack time, etc.) will be the same.

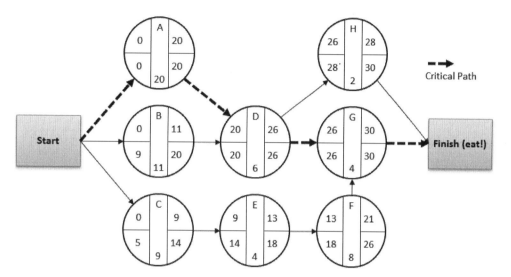

Before walking through this example we will need more information. The table below provides the required information—both given and computed.

		Given Information				Computed Information			
Activity	Pred.	Normal Duration (weeks)	Crashed Duration (weeks)	Normal Cost	Crashed Cost	Normal Duration *minus* Crashed Duration	Crashed Cost *minus* Normal Cost	Crash Cost per Week	Critical Path Activity?
A	-	20	15	$2,000	$3,000	5	$ 1,000	$ 200	Yes
B	-	11	8	$1,200	$1,350	3	$ 150	$ 50	No
C	-	9	9	$1,500	$1,500	0	$ -	n/a	No
D	A, B	6	4	$1,800	$2,100	2	$ 300	$ 150	Yes
E	C	4	3	$ 500	$ 900	1	$ 400	$ 400	No
F	E	8	6	$ 500	$ 600	2	$ 100	$ 50	No
G	D, F	4	2	$ 800	$ 950	2	$ 150	$ 75	Yes
H	D	2	1	$ 500	$1,200	1	$ 700	$ 700	No

Finally, our new objective is to make sure the project takes no longer than 25 weeks (down from the original project duration of 30 weeks). This means we must shorten the project by 5 weeks via crashing.

With all this information we are now ready to walk through the steps of the crashing process.

1. Identify the critical path.

    ➤ <u>Action Taken</u>: Identify A-D-G as the critical path.

2. Identify the activity on the critical path that has the lowest crashing cost per period (per day, per week, etc., whichever time bucket is being used).

> ➤ Action Taken: Identify activity G as the critical path activity with the lowest crash cost per week (A = $200, D = $150, and G = $75). The example below shows how we got this number for activity A and the same process was followed for all the activities in the project.

= (Crashed Cost – Normal Cost)/(Normal Duration – Crashed Duration)
= ($3,000 – $2,000)/(20 – 15)
= $1,000/5
= $200 crash cost per week

3. Crash the lowest-cost activity until (a) the crashing objective is met, (b) that activity cannot be crashed further, or (c) a new critical path emerges.

> ➤ Action Taken: Crash activity G by 2 weeks (from 4 weeks down to 2 weeks) at which point it cannot be crashed further. We must still shorten the project by another 3 weeks, so we proceed to the next step.
> ➤ Cost of crashing activity G by 2 weeks = 2 x $75 = $150.

4. If further crashing is required (crashing objective not yet met), then continue by crashing the next critical-path activity that has the lowest crashing cost per period.

> ➤ Action Taken: No action is appropriate with this step because we now have two critical paths, A-D-G and A-D-H (each being 28 days long), and we therefore must proceed to the next step.

5. If two critical paths emerge, see if there is an activity that (a) is common to both critical paths and (b) would be the most cost effective to crash (cheaper than crashing two separate items, one on each critical path).

> ➤ Action Taken: Crash activity D by 2 weeks (from 4 weeks down to 2 weeks) because it has a lower crash cost per week than activity A (A = $200, D = $150). At this point activity D cannot be crashed further. Now the project has been crashed a total of 4 weeks, still 1 week short of the objective.
> ➤ Cost of crashing activity D by 2 weeks = 2 x $150 = $300.
> ➤ Action Taken: Crash activity A by 1 week. This activity is common to both critical paths so crashing it by 1 week meets the objective of crashing the project by a total of 5 weeks.
> ➤ Cost of crashing activity A by 1 week = $200.

6. Crashing ends when the objective has been met or the critical path cannot be crashed any further.

> ➤ Action Complete: The crashing objective has been met (from 30 weeks project duration down to 25 weeks—shortening the project by 5 weeks).
> ➤ Total cost of crashing the project by 5 weeks = $650.

Upon completion of this crashing exercise, our network diagram appears as follows (with changes to the durations and affected start and finish times).

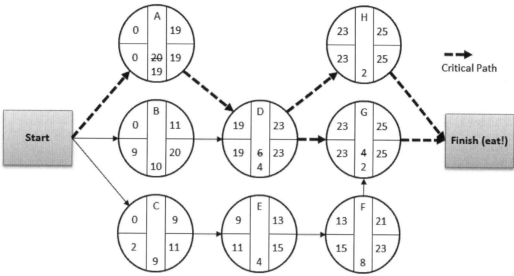

Project Management Software

Now that you understand how network diagrams are constructed, read, and used, you'll be interested to know that there are sophisticated software applications that do this work.

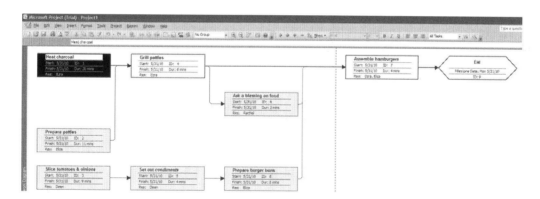

The network diagram above is like our original barbecue "project" network diagram, but the one above was drawn within Microsoft Project (just one of many project management software applications). You will notice that the critical path nodes (activities) are highlighted in red and that each one has configurable fields that can display important information like start and finish times, duration, and resources, among others.

Perhaps the most popular view of a project's schedule is a Gantt chart as shown below (again, a screen shot from Microsoft Project). Gantt charts provide an easy-to-read list of activities or tasks (on left-hand side of the graphic). Gantt charts are great for displaying a concise list of activities and for tracking a project's progress. However, as projects become large and complex, the Gantt chart's view of activity interdependencies is not nearly as intuitive or easy-to-read as that found in a network diagram.

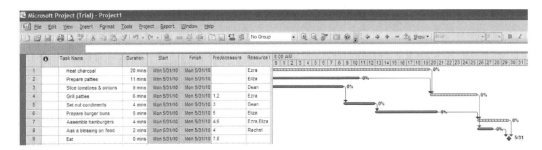

More than Network Diagrams and Gantt Charts

As can be expected, project management software applications offer many features that go beyond project scheduling. Such features include project costing, resource tracking, progress reporting, calendaring, and what-if analysis, to name a few. Hopefully this section has given you a flavor for some of the tools that are available to help project managers.

Chapter Summary

Below are some of the main points you should have garnered from the study of this chapter.

- **Projects are one-time endeavors** as opposed to ongoing operations and are typically staffed and managed with a temporary organization.
- **Projects consist of four phases**: (I) Initiation, (II) Planning, (III) Execution, and (IV) Close Out. The Creation gives us an excellent example of the phases of a project.
- **Project managers need to be good investigators, organizers, communicators, motivators, and negotiators**, but do not have to be experts in all the functional areas involved in the project. In addition to these "soft" skills, project managers should also develop the baseline technical skills of knowing how to manually draw network diagrams, determine earliest and latest start times, compute slack times, and crash projects—even if they use project management software to help with these things.

PLANNING
AND
CONTROLLING
OPERATIONS

Chapter 7

FORECASTING

And truth is knowledge of things as they are, and as they were, and as they are to come.

Doctrine and Covenants 93:24

Our omniscient Father, who knows the beginning from the end, knows all truth, whether past, present or future. Indeed, "We do not worship a God who simply forecasts a generally greater frequency of earthquakes in the last days before the second coming of His Son; He knows precisely when and where all these will occur."[60]

In The Church of Jesus Christ of Latter-day Saints we have a rich tradition of forecasting, we just know it by the name of *prophecy*. We have ancient and modern scriptures that are full of prophecies in addition to countless non-canonized prophetic statements from Joseph Smith and other latter-day Church presidents and apostles—all of whom we sustain as prophets, seers, and revelators. Clearly, the Lord, through His servants, is in the business of forecasting![61]

Chapter Objectives

The world teaches that good forecasting is as much of an art as it is science; requires judgment and experience as much as data and formulas. And if we are to believe in spiritual gifts and in the omniscience of God, then we would also include inspiration as an additional ingredient that leads to successful forecasting—after we have employed our best judgment and applied appropriate tools in our analysis.[62] In this chapter you will learn about the main concepts, tools, and techniques that will help you effectively forecast. Specifically, after studying this chapter you should be able to

1. Understand the critical role of forecasting in making business decisions.
2. Identify the potentially appropriate forecasting methods which can be used for a given set of data or circumstances.

---

[60] Neal A. Maxwell, *All These Things Shall Give Thee Experience* (Salt Lake City: Deseret Book Co., 1979), 7.

[61] See Truman G. Madsen, *Joseph Smith the Prophet* (Salt Lake City: Bookcraft, 1989), 37, where he cites a study that concludes the Doctrine and Covenants contains nearly eleven hundred statements about the future.

[62] See 2 Nephi 23:25 and Doctrine and Covenants 9:7-9.

3. Develop quantitative forecasts using time series and causal models, including moving average, weighted moving average, exponential smoothing, seasonal index, and linear regression.
4. Measure forecast accuracy and interpret the results.

Overview of Forecasting

Question: What is a forecast and how are forecasts used?

Simply put, a forecast is a prediction. More specifically, a forecast is an estimate of the timing and magnitude of future events. Forecasts are used to guide decisions about the future use of resources (people, money, materials, etc.). For example, when Captain Moroni wanted to know how to deploy his resources to repel a Lamanite invasion, he used forecasting. He gathered whatever information he could from his own research (spies) and he also turned to the Prophet Alma to prophecy what the Lamanites would do.

> Behold, now it came to pass that [the Lamanites] durst not come against the Nephites in the borders of Jershon; therefore they departed out of the land of Antionum into the wilderness, and took their journey round about in the wilderness, away by the head of the river Sidon, that they might come into the land of Manti and take possession of the land; *for they did not suppose that the armies of Moroni would know whither they had gone.*
> But it came to pass, as soon as they had departed into the wilderness Moroni sent spies into the wilderness to watch their camp; and Moroni, also, knowing of the prophecies of Alma, sent certain men unto him, desiring him that he should inquire of the Lord *whither the armies of the Nephites should go* to defend themselves against the Lamanites.
> And it came to pass that the word of the Lord came unto Alma, and Alma informed the messengers of Moroni, that the armies of the Lamanites were marching round about in the wilderness, that they might come over into the land of Manti, that they might commence an attack upon the weaker part of the people. And those messengers went and delivered the message unto Moroni.
> Now Moroni, leaving a part of his army in the land of Jershon, lest by any means a part of the Lamanites should come into that land and take possession of the city, took the remaining part of his army and marched over into the land of Manti. [63]

As we can see in this example, Moroni used the forecasted information (prophecy of Alma) to determine where to deploy his forces (resources) to best deal with a future event (attack by the Lamanites). Given the smaller number of Nephites as compared to Lamanites, the accuracy of the forecast was of supreme importance as it guided Moroni to make the best use of his limited resources.

Forecasts are also vitally important in a business context—where resources are usually scarce and should be used as effectively as possible. Forecasts drive important decisions regarding the acquisition and use of resources such as capital, land and equipment, materials, and personnel. With our forecasts—as with

---

[63] Alma 43:22-25 (emphasis added).

prophecy—we have an obligation (even a burden) to make sure we do so as accurately as possible and then do all we can to make them come to pass.

Question: How does forecasting relate to other production and operations planning processes?

As depicted in the graphic below, forecasting is very much a starting point for several planning processes that are part of an integrated production and operations planning and control system. (The next several chapters will cover the other processes besides forecasting.)

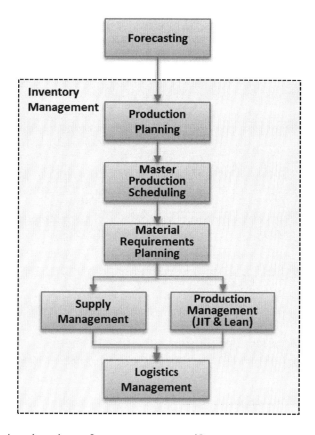

Question: At what level are forecasts created?

Forecasts are created at multiple levels within an organization to drive business decisions over different time horizons. The table below summarizes the personnel levels at which business forecasts are created, as well as the time horizons, units of measure, and decision focus of each.

It should be noted that the longer the forecasting horizon, the more difficult it is to be accurate. Hence, the longer the forecasting horizon, the more generic the unit of measure. For example, a car manufacturer may forecast how many of each vehicle they will sell next month—down to the trim level and color—whereas their mid-range forecast may be expressed at the product family level (total pickup trucks) and finally, the long-range forecast may be in total units (combination of all vehicles) or even in terms of revenue dollars. And as you can see from this example, it is also more difficult to forecast at the detailed product level than it is at a product family level.

Level	Horizon	UOM	Decision Focus
Senior Management	Long Range (3 years or longer into the future)	Dollars	• New products/markets • Facility location/expansion • Capital expenditures
Middle Management	Medium Range (3 months to 3 years)	Product families	• Sales and operations plans • Budgeting
First-Level Management (and their teams)	Short Range (today to 1 year)	Individual products	• Purchasing • Job scheduling • Workforce levels

Question: How are forecasts constructed?

Whether forecasting the moves of a battlefield opponent or the customer demand for a product, the basic process would be the same: (1) gather information or data that relates to the future event, (2) analyze the data, (3) combine the analysis and judgment (or inspiration) to make the prediction, and (4) deploy resources to address the future need or opportunity. There is no such thing as a one-size-fits-all forecasting method, so quite often users will create their own methods from a combination of method building blocks.

Forecasts are most often constructed with a combination of quantitative and qualitative techniques. When looking at the example of Captain Moroni and Alma we can see how these two basic approaches are combined to help Moroni determine how to best deploy his resources. On the one hand, we see Moroni's spies gathering information regarding the Lamanite movements (which direction, how many, etc.), representing the quantitative side of forecasting—driven by data. On the other hand, Moroni seeks the advice of the Lord through the Prophet Alma, representing the qualitative side of forecasting—dependent on judgment or intuition (or inspiration, as with the case of Moroni and Alma). The respective proportions of quantitative and qualitative input are largely dependent on the availability of data.

- When demand patterns are stable and there is an abundance of historical data, then forecasts will rely heavily on quantitative models.
- When historical data is scarce—as is often the case when launching a new product or a new technology—then forecasts rely more heavily on qualitative inputs (opinion and judgment).

Question: What are the main quantitative forecasting methods?

Quantitative forecasting methods come in two varieties: (1) time series models and (2) associative models. Before explaining the time-series models we must first understand what a time series is.

Time Series

A time series is a set of observations (data) arranged in chronological order. Over time, such data will typically display one or more of the following patterns.

- <u>Randomness</u>: the unpredictable movement of data from one time period to the next.

- <u>Trends</u>: long-term directional moves (either up or down) in the data.
- <u>Seasonality</u>: similar repeating patterns within corresponding periods, like December retail sales, summer gasoline sales, month-end auto sales, weekend theater sales, or even mealtimes at fast food restaurants. The "seasons" can be classified as certain hours in the day, days of the week or month, weeks within a quarter, months or quarters within a year, etc.
- <u>Cycles</u>: long-term (multi-year) swings in the data, often associated with the business cycle.

Time Series Models

With this understanding of time series, we are now prepared to examine the most common time series forecasting models.

- <u>Naïve</u>: the simplest model where the forecast is merely equal to the most recent period's actual demand.
- <u>Moving average</u>: the forecast is the average of *n* most recent periods.
- <u>Weighted moving average</u>: the same as moving average except weights are applied to the periods being averaged.
- <u>Exponential smoothing</u>: a special weighted moving average model used when little historical data exists.
- <u>Trend projection</u>: a special kind of regression analysis (a linear regression) that fits a trend line to a time series of data to project future values.
- <u>Multiplicative seasonal</u>: seasonal factors are multiplied by an estimate of average demand.

Associative Models (aka Causal Models)

Associative models use mathematical relationships between variables to predict the future. To explain how associative models work, let's suppose we own a small booth that sells bottled water. When the outside temperature goes up we sell more bottles of water. When temperature goes down we sell fewer bottles.

In the parlance of associative models, we would say that the temperature is the *independent variable* (the "x" value) and that the number of bottles sold is the *dependent variable* (the "y" value). In other words, the number of bottles we sell depends on the outside temperature. A rise in temperature will cause a rise in sales. Hence, we can say that these two variables are *positively* correlated, that is, the number of bottles sold goes in the same direction as the outside temperature.

If we took this example a bit further and said that we also sold hot chocolate, we would likely find that sales of hot chocolate and the outside temperature were *negatively* correlated. That is, when the temperature goes down, sales go up; temperature goes up, sales go down. The sales of hot chocolate and the outside temperature move in *opposite* directions indicating a *negative* correlation.

Below is a list of important terms related to associative models.

- <u>Regression analysis</u>: a statistical procedure for estimating mathematically the average relationship between dependent and independent variables.

- <u>Simple regression</u>: uses one independent variable (as in the bottled water example above).
- <u>Multiple regression</u>: uses two or more independent variables (temperature and price, for example, to determine the sales of bottled water).
- <u>Correlation</u>: is a measure of the relationship between the variables.

In this text we will cover simple regression and linear regression where only one dependent variable and one independent variable are used. We will also learn how to measure the strength in the relationship between these variables to help us know how good our associative-model forecasts are.

Question: What are the main qualitative forecasting methods?

Qualitative forecasting methods rely on opinion and judgment and are used extensively when historical data is limited. The most common methods include:

- <u>Sales force composite</u>: estimates from field salespeople are "rolled up" or aggregated.
- <u>Field sales and product line management</u>: aggregated forecasts from field salespeople are reconciled with projections from product line managers.
- <u>Executive opinion</u>: marketing, production, and finance managers jointly prepare the forecast.
- <u>Delphi</u>: a costly but effective method where experts individually develop forecasts, share their forecasts, and then revise their forecasts until consensus is reached.
- <u>Market surveys</u>: questionnaires or interviews given to potential customers to learn about consumer behavior.

The graphic below provides an overview of all the forecasting methods and how they are categorized (qualitative versus quantitative; time series versus associative).

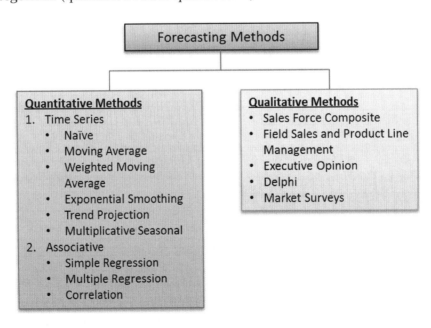

Question: How does the product lifecycle play into the selection of a forecasting method?

Products sell at different levels throughout their lives. Most products go through four lifecycle stages: (1) introduction, (2) growth, (3) maturity, and (4) decline. The newer the product, the less historical data available, the more dependent the product will be on qualitative forecasting methods. As a product matures, growth slows down and historical data is more plentiful, making it easier to effectively employ quantitative forecasting methods.

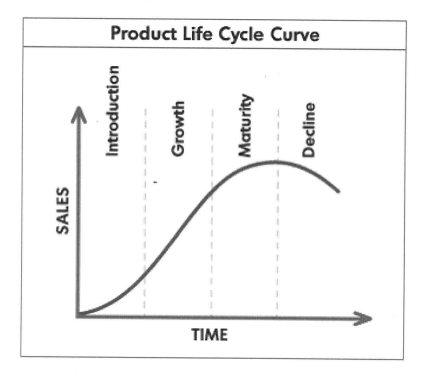

Just because a product is new does not mean that quantitative methods cannot be used. Most new products are not completely new. They may be (1) an updated version of the company's existing product (an example is an iPad 2 being a "new" product, but really just an updated version of the iPad 1), or (2) a product that is new to a company but similar to a competitor's offering (like the Samsung Galaxy Tab is new to Samsung, but not a new product concept given the existing presence of the iPad 1). In many cases of new product introductions, data from the launch of similar products (previous versions or competitor products) can be used to help in the development of forecasts.

Time Series Forecasting Examples

For the time series examples, let's suppose we are dealing with RexCream, an IBC company that sells ice cream novelties during the spring semester. Their 8-week selling season begins in late May and extends into the middle of July. Let's further suppose that we are five weeks into the selling season, meaning we have five weeks of historical data (sales) that we can use to forecast the next week's demand (for week 6). The graphic below contains both an Excel data table and a simple line graph which plots the actual demand data (and shows an upward trend).

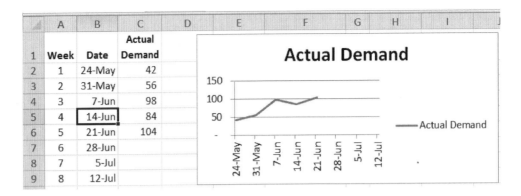

Naïve Method

If we were to use the **Naïve method** to predict sales in week 6, the forecast would be 104. In other words, we would simply use the actual demand from the previous period (104 in week 5) as the forecast for the next period.

Moving Average

As shown in the Excel table below, to compute the 3-week **Moving Average** forecast for week 6, we simply take an average of the previous three weeks' actual demand (cells C4, C5, and C6, as highlighted in yellow and shown in the Excel formula bar). This gives us a forecast of 95.3 units in week 6.

	D7				f_x	=AVERAGE(C4:C6)

	A	B	C	D	E
1	Week	Date	Actual Demand	3-Week MA	
2	1	24-May	42		
3	2	31-May	56		
4	3	7-Jun	98		
5	4	14-Jun	84		
6	5	21-Jun	104		
7	6	28-Jun		95.3	

Weighted Moving Average

Next is the **Weighted Moving Average**, which is very similar to the weighted average forecast. For a 3-week weighted moving average we take the previous three weeks of actual demand data and multiply these numbers by "weights" to arrive at the weighted moving average forecast. Typically, the weights will add up to one (1) with larger weights being assigned to the more recent periods—the thinking being that the more recent data will better reflect any trend in the data.

The Excel table below shows how a 3-week weighted moving average forecast would be computed for week 6. (Note how the cell colors are highlighted to show the matching of factors between the previous three weeks' actual demand and the weights.) In this example we get a week 6 forecast of 97.4 units. Notice that this number is slightly higher than the 95.3 we calculated with the simple (non-weighted) 3-week moving average. This shows how weighting the factors can help the forecast more closely reflect any trend in the data.

	A	B	C	D	E	F	G	H
			Actual	3-Week	3-Week			
1	Week	Date	Demand	MA	WMA		Weights	
2	1	24-May	42				3 Weeks Ago	0.1
3	2	31-May	56				2 Weeks Ago	0.3
4	3	7-Jun	98				Last Week	0.6
5	4	14-Jun	84				Sum of Weights	1.0
6	5	21-Jun	104					
7	6	28-Jun		95.3	97.4			
8	7	5-Jul						
9	8	12-Jul						

Cell E7: =(C6*$H$4)+(C5*$H$3)+(C4*$H$2)

Exponential Smoothing

The next time series method we'll examine is **Exponential Smoothing**, a variation of a weighted moving average. Below is the formula for this method.

$$F_t = F_{t-1} + \alpha(A_{t-1} - F_{t-1})$$

Where

F_t = the forecast in the next period (week 6 in our RexCream example)
F_{t-1} = the forecast from the previous period (week 5 in our example)
α = Alpha, the smoothing constant, a number between 0 and 1
A_{t-1} = the actual demand from the previous period (week 5 in our example)

Cell F7: =F6+$H$2*(C6-F6)

	A	B	C	D	E	F	G	H
			Actual	3-Week	3-Week	Exponential		
1	Week	Date	Demand	MA	WMA	Smoothing		Alpha
2	1	24-May	42			50		0.8
3	2	31-May	56			44		
4	3	7-Jun	98			54		
5	4	14-Jun	84			89		
6	5	21-Jun	104			85		
7	6	28-Jun		95.3	97.4	100		

Here is some additional information you need to know about exponential smoothing.

- When Alpha is closer to 1 than 0 the previous period's demand will be weighted more heavily than the previous period's forecast, thus enabling the new forecast to more closely follow any trends in the data.
- Exponential smoothing requires an arbitrary forecast in the initial period (week 1) and then builds a forecast period by period thereafter.
- Exponential smoothing is a useful method when there is little historical demand data available.

Using exponential smoothing with an initial forecast of 50 units in week 1 and an alpha of 0.8 gives us a forecast of 100 in week 6. Again, we had to build this forecast period by period, from week 2 through week 5, before we could compute the forecast for week 6.

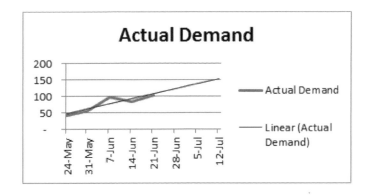

Trend Projection

The **Trend Projection** method of forecasting is based on the *least squares* mathematical technique of fitting the *line of best fit*[64] to the actual demand data. The chart above contains two lines, one representing our original demand data and the other a line of best fit, or a trend line, for that demand data.

When using Excel's "trend" function we tap into this trend line to predict what demand will be in some future period. For week 6, as can be seen below, the trend function returns a value of 122.4.

	G7				f_x	=TREND(C2:C6,B2:B6,B7)	
	A	B	C	D	E	F	G
1	Week	Date	Actual Demand	3-Week MA	3-Week WMA	Exponential Smoothing	Trend
2	1	24-May	42			50	
3	2	31-May	56			44	
4	3	7-Jun	98			54	
5	4	14-Jun	84			89	
6	5	21-Jun	104			85	
7	6	28-Jun		95.3	97.4	100	122.4

The beauty of the trend method is that it allows us to forecast well beyond the next period. For example, the trend function predicts that our sales in the week of July 12—three periods into the future—would be 152.8.[65]

Measuring Forecast Accuracy: MAD and MAPE

In forecasting it's critical to understand the underlying patterns in the data in order to pick or create a forecasting method that is appropriate for that data. And not surprisingly, there are ways to measure forecast accuracy in order to help us determine which method is best for a given set of actual demand data. The two most

---

[64] In this course you will not be required to compute the line of best fit, however, it's important that you understand this concept as it underlies the calculation of the "trend" function within Excel.
[65] You should be careful when using a trend function to predict far into the future as most trends tend to "flatten" as time goes on.

basic methods which we will examine are MAD (Mean Absolute Deviation) and MAPE (Mean Absolute Percentage Error).

H6				f_x	=ABS($C6-D6)									
	A	B	C	D	E	F	G	H	I	J	K	L	M	N	O
1				Forecasting Method				Absolute Deviation				Percentage Error			
2	Wk	Date	Actual Dmd	3-Wk MA	3-Wk WMA	ES	Trend	3-Wk MA	3-Wk WMA	ES	Trend	3-Wk MA	3-Wk WMA	ES	Trend
3	1	24-May	42			50									
4	2	31-May	56			44									
5	3	7-Jun	98			54									
6	4	14-Jun	84	65.3	79.8	89	121.3	18.7							
7	5	21-Jun	104	79.3	85.4	85	112.0	24.7							
8	6	28-Jun	116	95.3	97.4	100	122.4	20.7							
9	7	5-Jul	110	101.3	109.2	113	133.3	8.7							
10	8	12-Jul	126	110.0	111.2	111	134.3	16.0							
11								17.7							
12															
13								Mean Absolute Deviation				Mean Absolute Percentage Error			

In the table above we evaluate three different forecasting methods. These forecasts were generated under the assumption that each was calculated from the data that was available at that time. (For example, the week 4 moving average forecast was based on actual sales from weeks 1 through 3; week 5 from weeks 2 through 4, and so forth).

The foundation for MAD and MAPE calculations is the absolute deviation of actual demand (column C) and the forecast (columns D through G). In cell H6 we have calculated the absolute deviation (18.7 units) between week 4 actual demand (84 units) and the 3-week moving average forecast (65.3 units).

L6				f_x	=H6/$C6									
	A	B	C	D	E	F	G	H	I	J	K	L	M	N	O
1				Forecasting Method				Absolute Deviation				Percentage Error			
2	Wk	Date	Actual Dmd	3-Wk MA	3-Wk WMA	ES	Trend	3-Wk MA	3-Wk WMA	ES	Trend	3-Wk MA	3-Wk WMA	ES	Trend
3	1	24-May	42			50									
4	2	31-May	56			44									
5	3	7-Jun	98			54									
6	4	14-Jun	84	65.3	79.8	89	121.3	18.7	4.2	5.1	37.3	22%	5%	6%	44%
7	5	21-Jun	104	79.3	85.4	85	112.0	24.7	18.6	19.0	8.0	24%	18%	18%	8%
8	6	28-Jun	116	95.3	97.4	100	122.4	20.7	18.6	15.8	6.4	18%	16%	14%	6%
9	7	5-Jul	110	101.3	109.2	113	133.3	8.7	0.8	2.8	23.3	8%	1%	3%	21%
10	8	12-Jul	126	110.0	111.2	111	134.3	16.0	14.8	15.4	8.3	13%	12%	12%	7%
11								17.7	11.4	11.6	16.7	17%	10%	11%	17%
12															
13								Mean Absolute Deviation				Mean Absolute Percentage Error			

- To compute the mean absolute deviation (MAD) we must (1) compute the individual absolute deviation for each forecasting period (cells H6 through H10) and (2) compute the mean of those individual absolute deviations (cell H11). In the example above the MAD for the 3-week moving average forecast is 17.7.
- To compute the mean absolute percentage error (MAPE) we must (1) compute the individual absolute percentage error for each forecasting

period[66] (cells L6 through L10) and (2) compute the mean of those individual absolute percentage errors (cell L11). In the example above the MAPE for the 3-week moving average forecast is 17%.

After making these MAD and MAPE calculations for each of the forecasting methods we end up with the following answers in the table above (row 11). From these calculations (on this limited data set) we can conclude that the 3-week weighted moving average yields the most accurate forecast because it has the lowest MAD (11.4) and the lowest MAPE (10%) of all forecasting methods.

Measuring Forecast Accuracy: Tracking Signal and Bias

As discussed above, MAD and MAPE are useful methods for understanding the average magnitude of forecast errors, however, they do not indicate whether or not there is a bias in the forecast. This is where tracking signal comes into play. It measures the forecast bias, that is, the tendency of the forecast to be above or below the actual demand. Tracking signal is computed by taking the running sum of forecast errors (RSFE) and dividing by the MAD for the same period.

$$Tracking\ Signal = \frac{\sum(Actual\ demand\ in\ period\ i - Forecast\ in\ period\ i)}{MAD\ in\ period\ i}$$

You should note that we **do not** take the sum of the **absolute** forecast errors, rather, we take the sum of the **actual** forecast errors (where some will be positive and others will be negative).

- Tracking signals greater than zero (positive) indicate a bias where actual demand is greater than forecast.
- Tracking signals less than zero (negative) indicate a bias where actual demand is less than forecast.
- Ideally, positive and negative errors should cancel each other out such that the tracking signal remains close to zero, indicating very little forecast bias.

When working with forecasts it's important to recognize these two principles: (1) "the forecast is always wrong" and, its corollary, (2) we must constantly measure and strive to minimize forecast error.

Multiplicative Seasonal

The data set above for RexCream displayed characteristics of randomness and trend. If we were to convert this 1-semester IBC business into a going concern then we would no doubt find that demand for this business also displays seasonality.

Let's suppose that RexCream opened up a new location within a gas station convenience store in Brigham City, Utah. Below we have three years of sales history for RexCream at this location. The data clearly shows a seasonal pattern where

---

[66] The absolute percentage error for one period is computed by dividing the absolute error for that period by the actual demand for the same period.

demand is much higher during the summer months and much lower in the winter months.

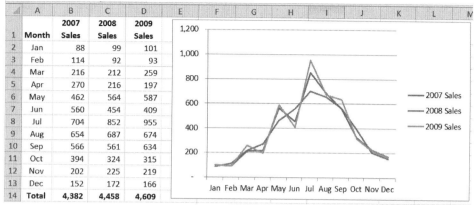

	A	B	C	D
	Month	2007 Sales	2008 Sales	2009 Sales
1				
2	Jan	88	99	101
3	Feb	114	92	93
4	Mar	216	212	259
5	Apr	270	216	197
6	May	462	564	587
7	Jun	560	454	409
8	Jul	704	852	955
9	Aug	654	687	674
10	Sep	566	561	634
11	Oct	394	324	315
12	Nov	202	225	219
13	Dec	152	172	166
14	Total	4,382	4,458	4,609

Now let's further suppose that for 2010 (the next year) the owner is quite optimistic that annual sales will increase to 5,000 total units, and that she wants you to produce a month-by-month forecast of sales. To produce such a forecast we would employ the **Multiplicative Seasonal** method. This is done by taking the following steps. (Refer to the table below to see how these steps are implemented with the data above.)

1. Compute the 3-year average sales by month (example, cell E2). For January the average is 96 units (an average of 88, 99, and 101). *Please note that if we had 4 years of historical data available, we would use a 4-year average by month. If we had 5 years history, then a 5-year average, and so forth*.

2. Compute the 3-year overall average sales for all months combined (example, cell F2). The overall monthly average sales over the 3-year period is 373.6.

3. Compute the seasonal index for each month (example, cell G2). This is done by dividing the average sales by month by the overall monthly average sales. For January the seasonal index is 0.26 (96÷373.6 or cell E2 divided by cell F2). This means that average January sales are about 26% of what overall average monthly sales should be.

	G2			f_x	=E2/F2			
	A	B	C	D	E	F	G	H
1	Month	2007 Sales	2008 Sales	2009 Sales	Monthly Average	Overall Average	Seasonal Index	2010 Forecast
2	Jan	88	99	101	96.0	373.6	0.26	107
3	Feb	114	92	93	99.7	373.6	0.27	111
4	Mar	216	212	259	229.0	373.6	0.61	255
5	Apr	270	216	197	227.7	373.6	0.61	254
6	May	462	564	587	537.7	373.6	1.44	600
7	Jun	560	454	409	474.3	373.6	1.27	529
8	Jul	704	852	955	837.0	373.6	2.24	934
9	Aug	654	687	674	671.7	373.6	1.80	749
10	Sep	566	561	634	587.0	373.6	1.57	655
11	Oct	394	324	315	344.3	373.6	0.92	384
12	Nov	202	225	219	215.3	373.6	0.58	240
13	Dec	152	172	166	163.3	373.6	0.44	182
14	Total	4,382	4,458	4,609				5,000

4. Compute the monthly forecasts for 2010 (example, cell H2 with the formula found in the formula bar at the top of the table). To compute the monthly forecasts, we multiply each month's seasonal index by next year's forecast (5,000 units for 2010) divided by the number of periods in the year (12 months in the year).

H2				f_x =G2*($H$14/12)			
	A	B	C	D	E	F	G	H
	Month	2007 Sales	2008 Sales	2009 Sales	Monthly Average	Overall Average	Seasonal Index	2010 Forecast
2	Jan	88	99	101	96.0	373.6	0.26	107
3	Feb	114	92	93	99.7	373.6	0.27	111
4	Mar	216	212	259	229.0	373.6	0.61	255
5	Apr	270	216	197	227.7	373.6	0.61	254
6	May	462	564	587	537.7	373.6	1.44	600
7	Jun	560	454	409	474.3	373.6	1.27	529
8	Jul	704	852	955	837.0	373.6	2.24	934
9	Aug	654	687	674	671.7	373.6	1.80	749
10	Sep	566	561	634	587.0	373.6	1.57	655
11	Oct	394	324	315	344.3	373.6	0.92	384
12	Nov	202	225	219	215.3	373.6	0.58	240
13	Dec	152	172	166	163.3	373.6	0.44	182
14	Total	4,382	4,458	4,609				5,000

You will notice that the sum of the forecasts in column H (rows 2 through 13) is 5,000. Using the multiplicative seasonal forecasting method allows us to distribute the annual forecast across each month based on the historical proportional sales (seasonal index) of each month.

Associative Forecasting Example

Simple Regression

Let's continue with our RexCream example and see how we can use average daily high temperatures in a **Regression Analysis** to help us predict demand for sales of ice cream novelties.

F2				f_x =CORREL(B2:B13,C2:C13)	
	A	B	C	D	E	F
1	Month	Average Temp	Average Sales		Strength of Correlation	
2	Jan	36	96.0		Coefficient of correlation (r)	0.94
3	Feb	43	99.7		Coefficient of determination (r^2)	0.88
4	Mar	53	229.0			
5	Apr	63	227.7			
6	May	72	537.7			
7	Jun	83	474.3			
8	Jul	91	837.0			
9	Aug	89	671.7			
10	Sep	79	587.0			
11	Oct	66	344.3			
12	Nov	48	215.3			
13	Dec	37	163.3			
14	Prediction	62	358			

To do this we would again use the trend function within Excel, except this time we will use average temperatures and not time periods (weeks) as the independent variables (known x's) with our trend function. We place the trend function in cell C14 and use the average sales data range (C2 through C13) as the known y's, use the average temperature data range (cells B2 through B13) as the known x's, and finally, use the predicted temperature (cell B14) as the new x value. Hence, we can predict that our monthly sales will be 358 units if the weather forecast calls for an average monthly temperature of 62 degrees.

Correlation

How good would this forecast be? According to the two measures of correlation—*r* and *r²*—the data appear to be highly correlated. The formula bar in the graphic above shows the formula for computing r (in cell F2)[67], the coefficient of correlation. Since this number is very close to 1 (0.94), we can say that the average temperature is strongly positively correlated to average monthly sales and hence, a very good predictor of unit sales. (Also note that a strong negative correlation with an r close to -1—as would be the case with hot chocolate sales and outside temperature—would likewise be a good predictor of sales.)

The *r²* value of 0.88 also shows that the correlation is quite strong, although it does not tell whether it is a positive or negative correlation. This means that 88% of the change to sales can be explained by or attributed to the change in temperature.

Chapter Summary

Below are some of the main points you should have garnered from the study of this chapter.

- **Forecasts are vital to effective planning within an organization**. Many company planning processes depend on forecasts to help them line up human resources, materials, land and equipment, marketing plans, and so forth.
- **Creating effective forecasts is as much of an art as it is science**. Forecasts are often created from home-grown methods which can be combinations of basic quantitative and qualitative techniques. When historical data is plentiful and demand is steady, then forecasts tend to be more quantitative. With a lack of data, forecasts tend to be more qualitative.
- Selecting or creating an appropriate forecasting method requires a clear understanding of the patterns exhibited in the historical data. Time series data (data arranged in chronological order) displays patterns such as randomness, trends, seasonality, or cycles. Understanding where a product is in its lifecycle is also essential to effective forecasting.
- It is said that "**the forecast is always wrong**," therefore **there is a great need to measure forecast accuracy** and strive to reduce forecast error.

---

[67] Note that when computing correlation we do not include the values in row 14 within our data ranges because they are predicted values and not historical values. The appropriate data range for correlation is surrounded by a heavy dotted line.

Two common measures of forecast accuracy are MAD (mean absolute deviation) and MAPE (mean absolute percentage error).

Chapter 8

INVENTORY MANAGEMENT

> *Behold, there come seven years of great plenty throughout all the land of Egypt...*
>
> *Now therefore let Pharaoh look out a man discreet and wise, and set him over the land of Egypt.*
>
> *Let Pharaoh do this, and let him appoint officers over the land, and take up the fifth part of the land of Egypt in the seven plenteous years.*
>
> *And let them gather all the food of those good years that come, and lay up corn under the hand of Pharaoh, and let them keep food in the cities.*
>
> *And that food shall be for store to the land against the seven years of famine, which shall be in the land of Egypt; that the land perish not through the famine.*
>
> *Genesis 41:29, 33-36*

We can learn much about managing inventory from the story of Joseph in Egypt—especially from his handling of the food supply in response to Pharaoh's dream. First, we see how decisions regarding inventory (purchase and storage of grain) were largely driven by a "forecast" (Pharaoh's dream). Second, Joseph and the appointed officers were able to make large "forward buys" of food at a significant "quantity discount" given the bounteous harvest (over supply) during the seven fat years. Third, the food was properly stored to extend its "shelf life" such that it would be edible or useful for the entire time it would be needed (seven lean years).

Chapter Objectives

Quite often in business, when we think of inventory, we have a knee-jerk reaction that says we must "reduce inventory" to save on costs. Such thinking often comes when we don't fully understand the many legitimate and useful purposes of inventory. In the story of Joseph, having adequate stocks of "hedge inventory" saved countless individuals and several nations, including the House of Israel. Therefore, the simple and trite platitudinous goal of "reducing inventory" should be supplanted by the more judicious goal of having *the right amount* of inventory given the situation. To help you achieve this and other inventory-related goals, this chapter will give you the ability to

1. Describe the basic categories and functions of inventory.
2. Perform an ABC analysis or classification and use that information to calculate the frequency of inventory cycle counts for each classification.

3. Describe continuous review, periodic review, and single-period inventory systems.
4. Calculate order quantity, reorder point, and safety stock for each inventory system.
5. Use a quantity discount model and compute total annual inventory cost.

Overview of Inventory Management

Inventory management is the branch of business management concerned with the planning and controlling of inventories. Perhaps the **most basic challenge of inventory management** is to balance between inventory investment and customer service levels. To better understand inventory management it will be useful to first learn some basic terms and concepts related to inventory.

Question: What is inventory?

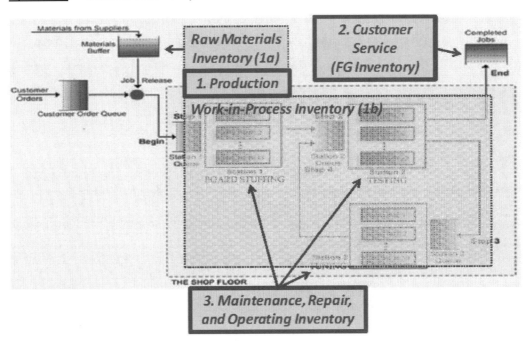

Inventory is stock of items that are used to support:

1. <u>Production</u>. These stocks include **raw materials** and **work-in-process**. Such items are also known as **direct materials**, meaning that stocks of these items will eventually be transformed or assembled into finished goods.
2. <u>Customer service</u>. These stocks include both **finished goods** (items that are sold to customers) and **spare parts** (which are used to service previously sold items).
3. <u>Maintenance, repair, and other activities</u>. These items are sometimes called **MRO** or **indirect materials**. These items do not go on the product, rather they are used to keep equipment and other operations running.

The graphic above superimposes these three basic categories of inventory onto the high-level schematic of a factory simulation. In addition to the three basic inventory categories outlined above, inventory can be categorized further as follows:

- **Cycle inventory**, which includes safety stock, represents the inventory that is required from one supply replenishment to the next.
- **Safety stock** is a quantity of stock planned to be in inventory to protect against fluctuations in demand or supply.
- **Pipeline inventory** is the stock that is in transit between locations.
- **Anticipation inventory** are stocks above and beyond basic pipeline inventory and are used to cover projected trends of increasing demands due to planned sales promotions, seasonal fluctuations, plant shutdowns and vacations.
- **Hedge inventory** is a form of inventory buildup to buffer against an event that may or may not happen. Planning for such inventory involves speculation related to potential labor strikes, price increases, political unrest, and so forth.

ABC Classification and Cycle Counting

Question: What is an ABC classification?

Loosely based on Pareto's law (the 80-20 rule), an ABC classification is a grouping of items in decreasing order of annual dollar volume or some other user-defined criteria. This array is then split into classes called A, B, and C. The A group typically represents 10% to 20% of the item numbers and 50% to 70% of the dollar volume. The next grouping, B, usually represents about 20% of the items and about 20% of the dollar volume. The C class contains 60% to 70% of the items and represents about 10% to 30% of the dollar volume. The ABC principle can be applied to inventories, suppliers, sales, and so forth.

ABC Classification Example

Performing an ABC classification is not difficult from a quantitative standpoint, but it often is difficult to acquire the required data. It also requires attention to detail in following the steps below. We will first start with this data.

1. Compute the Annual Dollar Volume (column D in the spreadsheet graphic below) for each item by multiplying the Annual Unit Volume (column B) by the Unit Cost (column C) for each item.
2. Sort the spreadsheet by column D (Annual Dollar Volume) in descending order (largest to smallest) as shown in the table below. **This is a very important step and it is the step most frequently skipped by students who fail to properly perform an ABC classification**.
3. Compute the % (percent) of Annual Dollar Volume (column E) by dividing the Annual Dollar Volume for each item by the sum of the Annual Dollar Volume for all items. The formula for this calculation in cell E2 can be found in the formula bar in the graphic below.

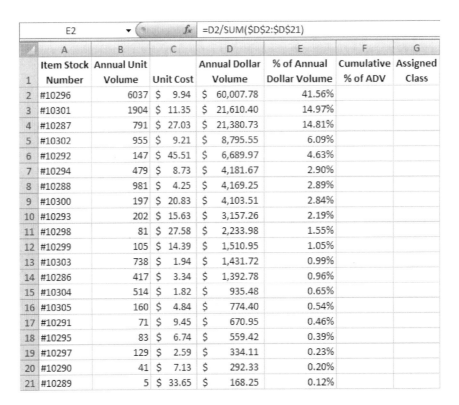

4. Calculate the Cumulative Percentage (%) of Annual Dollar Volume (ADV) for each item in column F. The formula for this calculation in cell F2 can be found in the formula bar in the graphic below.

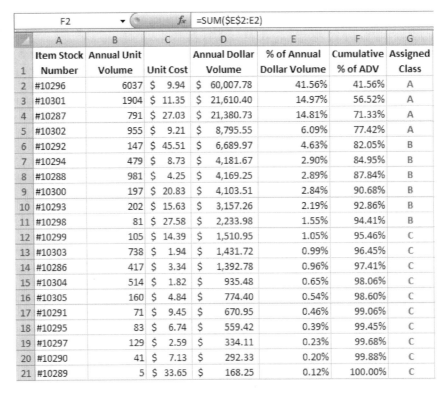

5. Assign the appropriate inventory class to each item in the analysis. (For our purposes, this can be done manually.) As stated above in the explanation of

ABC classifications, the criteria for what constitutes each inventory group is user defined, meaning there is more than one way to perform an ABC classification. For our purposes in this example we will define A items as those items which constitute up to 80% of the total or cumulative annual dollar volume; B items from 80.01% up to 95%; and C items from 95.01% up to 100%. Performing this step gives us

- 4 A items (20% of the items making up 77.42% of the total value)
- 6 B items (30% of the items making up roughly 15% of the total value)
- 10 C items (50% of the items making up roughly 5% of the total value)

Question: What is the value of performing an ABC classification?

The ABC principle states that effort and money can be saved through applying looser controls to the low-dollar-volume class (C) items than will be applied to high-dollar-volume class (A) items (as will be seen in the definition of cycle counting).

Question: What is cycle counting?

Cycle counting is an inventory accuracy audit technique where inventory is counted on a cyclic schedule rather than once a year. A cycle count is usually taken on a regular, defined basis (high frequency for A items, medium frequency for B items, and low frequency for C items). By discriminating in our item-class based cycle counts, we are able to give more attention to the important items and spend less time and resources (money) on keeping track of the lower-value (C) items. Most effective cycle counting systems require the counting of a certain number of items every workday with each item counted at a prescribed frequency.

The **key purpose of cycle counting** is to identify and fix discrepancies between the system's inventory record and what is physically on hand. This way, companies reduce the risk of overcommitting or under committing to customers, as accurate data is required to make and keep delivery commitments.

Cycle Counting Example

Let's start this example by assuming we have one hundred times the number of items used in the ABC classification example above. We'll preserve the same proportions of each item class giving us 400 A items, 600 B items, and 1,000 C items. Let's further suppose that we want to count each class of items as follows:

- 400 A items, each counted once a month (assume 20 working days)
- 600 B items, each counted once a quarter (assume 60 working days)
- 1000 C items, each once a year (assume 250 working days)

How many items will we count each working day?

$$= \left(\frac{400 \; A \; items}{20 \; days}\right) + \left(\frac{600 \; B \; items}{60 \; days}\right) + \left(\frac{1,000 \; C \; items}{250 \; days}\right)$$

Dividing then adding these numbers gives us 20 + 10 + 4 = **34 items per day** need to be counted in order to count all items by the prescribed frequency. This example reinforces the ABC concept that greater attention is given the higher-value A items than the lower-value C items.

Continuous Review Systems

A continuous review system is an independent demand, **fixed-quantity** ordering system which triggers a restocking order whenever stock reaches a certain point (the reorder point). Such systems typically make use of **economic order quantity** or **quantity discount** models to determine *how much* to buy. They also use **reorder point** models to determine *when* to place those orders.

Economic Order Quantity

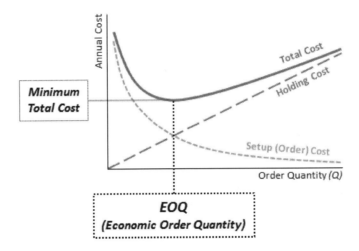

Question: What is the **economic order quantity (EOQ)** and how is it calculated?

The economic order quantity is a type of fixed order quantity model that determines the amount of an item to be purchased at one time. The EOQ formula *perfectly* balances the tradeoff between the cost of acquiring inventory (the ordering costs) and the cost of carrying or holding the inventory. The economic order quantity is that quantity in which the sum of ordering cost and holding cost is minimized (at the intersection of the holding cost and re-order cost lines as seen in the graphic above). In this course we will learn how to work with two basic EOQ formulas.

$$EOQ = \sqrt{\frac{2DS}{H}} \ or \ EOQ = \sqrt{\frac{2DS}{IC}}$$

Where

       D = annual demand
       S = ordering cost (the administrative costs to place an order)
       H = annual holding cost
       I = annual interest rate
       C = the materials cost for one unit

EOQ Example 1

The BYU-Idaho University Store purchases classroom clickers for $360 for each case of 20 units. Annual demand is estimated to be 3,600 units per year. It costs $70 to process and receive an order with a $2.20 holding cost per unit per year.

What is the University Store's Economic Order Quantity (EOQ) for orders placed with its classroom clicker supplier?

In this case, $D = 3{,}600$, $S = \$70$, and $H = \$2.20$. Hence, we input this data into the formula as follows:

$$EOQ = \sqrt{\frac{(2 \times 3{,}600 \times 70)}{2.20}} = 479$$

Here's what this problem looks like when you work it in Excel.

B7		f_x	=SQRT((2*B2*B3)/B4)	
	A	B	C	D
1	Data			
2	D (annual demand)	3,600		
3	S (ordering cost)	$ 70		
4	H (annual holding cost)	$ 2.20		
5				
6	Answers			
7	EOQ	479		

EOQ Example 2

Now let's suppose that the University Store did not have an accurate cost for holding its inventory but it did know that it cost 8% to borrow money to make any purchases and that each clicker cost them $20. Using the alternative EOQ equation would give us the following:

- $D = 3{,}600$
- $S = \$70$
- $I = 8\%$
- $C = \$20$

Hence

$$EOQ = \sqrt{\frac{(2 \times 3{,}600 \times 70)}{(0.08 \times 20)}} = 561$$

Again, turning to Excel, here is what we get:

			f_x	=SQRT((2*B2*B3)/(B4*B5))	
B8					

	A	B	C	D	E
1	Data				
2	D (annual demand)	3,600			
3	S (ordering cost)	$ 70			
4	I (annual interest rate)	8%			
5	C (materials cost)	$ 20			
6					
7	Answer				
8	EOQ	561			

We should be careful to note that in these very simple examples we have been spoon fed the necessary data to perform these calculations. Quite often demand data may be expressed in monthly or weekly terms and costs may be for cases of product and not individual unit costs. Therefore, it is extremely important to make sure the time bucket and unit of measure (UOM) data are consistent within the EOQ equation.

For example, if you are given *monthly* demand data but you only have an *annual* holding cost, you have a *time-bucket mismatch* and must either (1) convert the monthly demand to an annual number by multiplying by 12 or (2) convert the annual holding cost to a monthly holding cost by dividing by 12. Either change will result in the same answer. The important point is to make sure that the time bucket and unit of measure assumptions are consistent in the numerator and denominator of the selected EOQ equation.

Question: Is there a way—without referring to an answer key—to determine if your EOQ calculation is correct?

If you have calculated EOQ properly, the **annual ordering cost should equal annual holding cost**. Let's use the data in Example 1 above to illustrate this fact.

To compute annual ordering cost we multiply the ordering cost (for one order) by the number of orders placed per year. The number of orders placed per year can be found by dividing annual demand by the computed EOQ.

$$Annual\ Ordering\ Cost = Ordering\ Cost \times Number\ of\ Orders\ Placed\ per\ Year$$

$$Annual\ Ordering\ Cost = Ordering\ Cost \times \frac{Annual\ Demand}{EOQ}$$

$$Annual\ Ordering\ Cost\ (for\ Example\ 1) = \$70 \times \frac{3600}{479} = \$526$$

To compute annual holding cost we multiply the annual holding cost (per the designated unit of measure) by the average inventory. **When there is no safety stock**, average inventory is nothing more than the order quantity (Q, or EOQ in this case) divided by 2.

$$Average\ Inventory = \frac{Q}{2}\ or\ \frac{EOQ}{2}$$

In other words, the range of stock goes from zero (when stock is completely consumed) to 479 (when a new replenishment is received). Hence, on average, the level of stock will be one half the order quantity of 479. The graphic below helps to illustrate why average inventory is equal to the order quantity divided by 2.

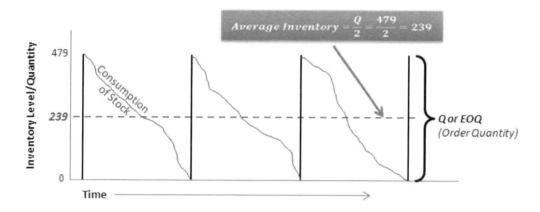

$$Annual\ Holding\ Cost = Annual\ Holding\ Cost\ (per\ UOM) \times Average\ Inventory$$

$$Annual\ Holding\ Cost = Annual\ Holding\ Cost\ (per\ UOM) \times \frac{Q\ (or\ EOQ)}{2}$$

$$Annual\ Holding\ Cost\ (for\ Example\ 1) = \$2.20 \times \frac{479}{2} = \$526$$

B8		f_x =B3*(B2/B7)
A	B	C
1 Data		
2 D (annual demand)	3,600	
3 S (ordering cost)	$ 70	
4 H (annual holding cost)	$ 2.20	
5		
6 Answers		
7 EOQ	479	
8 Annual cost	$ 526	
9 Annual holding cost	$ 526	

B9		f_x =B4*(B7/2)
A	B	C
1 Data		
2 D (annual demand)	3,600	
3 S (ordering cost)	$ 70	
4 H (annual holding cost)	$ 2.20	
5		
6 Answers		
7 EOQ	479	
8 Annual cost	$ 526	
9 Annual holding cost	$ 526	

As we can see in this example, the annual ordering cost = annual holding cost = $526. Here's how the formulas are written in Excel for annual ordering cost and annual holding cost, respectively.

We should note that **in practice, purchase quantities often vary from the calculated EOQ**. For example, if our supplier sells a given item in cases of 400 units but our EOQ is 479, we would likely set our order quantity to 400. Such a case- or lot-size restriction is just one example among several possible reasons why actual purchase quantities may vary from a calculated number. Purchase quantities can be adjusted to support marketing promotions, off-season purchases, transportation efficiencies, quantity discounts, and so forth.

Quantity Discounts

Question: What is the **quantity discount model** and how is it used?

Many companies will offer quantity discounts to their customers in order to increase sales. In such situations, customers will make use of a quantity discount model to determine the best order quantity. A quantity discount model is a variation of the EOQ model. The main difference is that the quantity discount model must look at the total annual inventory cost—including the cost of purchasing the material—and not just at balancing ordering cost and holding cost. The beginning point of this analysis is a schedule of prices based on ranges of order volume. Below is an example of such a schedule (modified from Example 2 above).

Discount Order Quantity	Materials Cost (or Price)	Discount %
1 - 899	$ 20.00	0%
900 - 1799	$ 19.80	1%
1800 or more	$ 19.60	2%

Total annual inventory cost (ordering, holding, material cost) is calculated as follows:

$$Total\ annual\ inventory\ cost = \left(\frac{D}{Q}\right)S + \left(\frac{Q}{2}\right)H + DP$$

Or, if holding cost (*H*) is not given, then *IC* (interest rate X materials cost) should be used to calculate total annual inventory cost.

$$Total\ annual\ inventory\ cost = \left(\frac{D}{Q}\right)S + \left(\frac{Q}{2}\right)IC + DP$$

Where

D = Annual demand in units
Q = Order quantity
S = Ordering or setup cost
I = Annual interest rate
C = Materials Cost (or price per unit)
H = Holding cost per unit per year

When quantity discounts are offered, we must follow a multi-step process to determine the order quantity.

1. Calculate the EOQ for each pricing option when a percentage discount for each option and an interest rate are given. **Note**: if Holding Cost (*H*) is given, then the EOQ will be the same for each option because, in this case, Interest Rate (*I*) and Materials Cost (*C*) are not incorporated into the EOQ formula.
2. Calculate the Adjusted Order Quantity for each quantity discount range. If the calculated EOQ is below the quantity discount threshold, then adjust the order quantity (Q) upward to that threshold amount. This can be done

with a simple IF statement in your spreadsheet. (You may want to insert a new "Minimum Order Quantity" column and an "Adjusted Order Quantity" column to make this step easier.)

3. Using the Adjusted Order Quantity as your baseline, calculate the Average Inventory, the Annual Holding Cost, the Annual Ordering Cost, and the Annual Materials Cost. Note that when Holding Cost (H) is given, use it instead of IC (Interest Rate X Materials Cost) in your Annual Holding Cost calculation.

4. Calculate the Total Annual Inventory Cost for each quantity discount option by summing Annual Holding Cost, Annual Ordering Cost, and Annual Material Cost.

5. Select the quantity discount with the lowest Total Annual Inventory cost.

Let's follow these steps with our modified data from EOQ Example 2 and see which quantity discount is best.

1. Since the given data includes Interest Rate and Materials Cost (or price), we calculate the EOQ for each discount option using IC in the denominator of the EOQ formula. This gives us an EOQ of 458, 461, and 463 for the first, second, and third discount options.

2. We calculate the Adjusted Order Quantity by using an If statement as shown in the formula bar in the graphic below (for cell F8). Since the calculated EOQs for the second and third options do not meet the Minimum Order Quantity thresholds, the Adjusted Order Quantity for these options becomes 900 and 1,800, equal to their respective minimums.

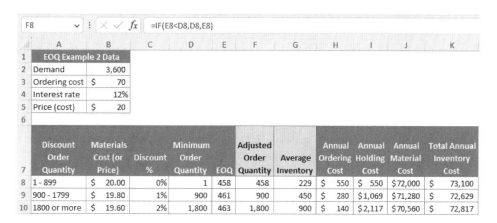

3. Using the formulas discussed on the previous few pages, we calculate the Average Inventory, the Annual Holding Cost, the Annual Ordering Cost, and the Annual Materials Cost. Note that for the first option, where the calculated EOQ of 458 is used, the Annual Holding Cost and Annual Ordering Cost are equal.

4. We calculate the Total Annual Inventory Cost for each option by simply taking the sum of the Annual Holding Cost, Annual Ordering Cost, and Annual Materials cost (the three cells to the left of Total Annual Inventory Cost).

5. We select the second option as the best option because it has the lowest Total Annual Inventory Cost of $72,629.

Reorder Points and Safety Stock

Question: What is the **reorder point (ROP)** and how is it used in a continuous review system?

The reorder point is an inventory level where, if the total stock on hand falls to or below that point, action is taken to replenish the stock. There are several ways reorder point can be calculated, largely determined by the nature of the available data. In this chapter we will cover only one way to compute safety stock (perhaps the most common way). The diagram below not only shows the reorder point, but depicts many other elements of a continuous review (replenishment) system.

- **Demand during the lead time period** is typically the average demand observed from when the stock hits the order point to the time a new replenishment is received.
- **Safety stock**, as noted at the beginning of the chapter, is to guard against fluctuations in demand, such as seen in the second replenishment cycle where lead-time demand exceeds the average and the consumption line dips into the safety stock zone.
- The **equation for reorder point** is demand during lead time plus safety stock.
- The **order quantity** should be matched to the computed EOQ or to the amount computed from utilizing quantity discounts.

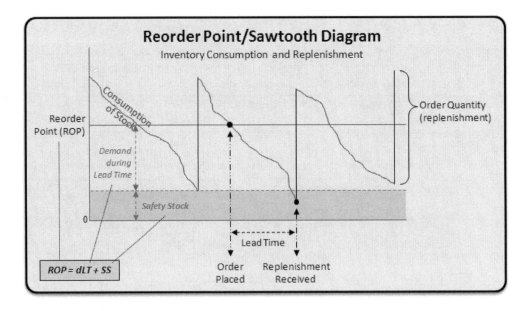

Question: How is reorder point (and its components) calculated?

Computing reorder point is a multi-step process. At a high level the equation is simple: demand during the lead-time period plus safety stock. It is written as follows:

$$ROP = dLT + SS$$

Where

dLT = demand during the lead time period
SS = safety stock

Calculating demand during lead time is simple. For example, if demand is 3 units per day and the lead time is four days, then over the lead-time period demand will be 12 (simply 3 x 4). Calculating safety stock, on the other hand, can be a bit tricky, depending on the available data. For our purposes, where lead time is constant, safety stock can be calculated using one of the two following formulas:

$$(1)\ SS = Z\sigma_{dLT}$$

or

$$(2)\ SS = Z\sigma_d\sqrt{LT}$$

Where

Z = the z-score that corresponds to the desired service level
Tip: Use Excel's NORMSINV function to find the z-score
σ_{dLT} = the standard deviation of demand during the lead time period
σ_d = the standard deviation of demand for a single period
LT = the replenishment lead time

The selection of a safety stock equation depends on the granularity of the given data. More often than not, the second safety stock equation (above) is more closely related to the kind of data that would be available in such cases.

Question: How do you calculate the standard deviation of demand during the lead time period?

The standard deviation of demand during the lead time period is nothing more than the standard deviation for one period times the square root of the lead time.

$$\sigma_{dLT} = \sigma_d\sqrt{LT}$$

ROP Example

A large independent food distributor sells an average of 50 cases of tater tots each day with a standard deviation of daily demand being 7. The replenishment lead time from the tater tots supplier is 9 days. This distributor is very big on customer service and therefore wants to maintain a 98% service level. Given this information, what should be the distributor's reorder point?

d = 50 (average daily demand)
LT = 9
Z = 2.054 (which corresponds to a 98% service level)
σ_d = 7

Populating this data into the (second) equation we get an ROP of 493 (450 + 43).

$$ROP = dLT + SS$$

$$dLT = 50 \times 9 = 450$$

$$SS = 2.054 \times 7 \times \sqrt{9} = 43$$

$$Hence, ROP = 450 + 43 = 493$$

	E3	▼	f_x	=B5*B6*SQRT(B3)	
	A	B	C	D	E
1	**Data**			**Answers**	
2	Average Daily Demand	50		dLT	450
3	Lead Time	9		Safety Stock	43
4	Service Level	98%		ROP	493
5	Z-score	2.05			
6	σ_d	7			

Perhaps the trickiest part of the ROP equation is figuring out safety stock. The Excel graphic above shows how this is done (formula from cell E3 is shown).

The graphic below depicts the reorder point example above (although not to scale). The 98% desired service level is represented by the area under the far right normal distribution which is above the zero (0) line. The 2% of the area below the zero line represents the risk of stocking out. If we had no safety stock at all, then we would have a 50/50 chance of stocking out, as shown by the far left normal distribution.

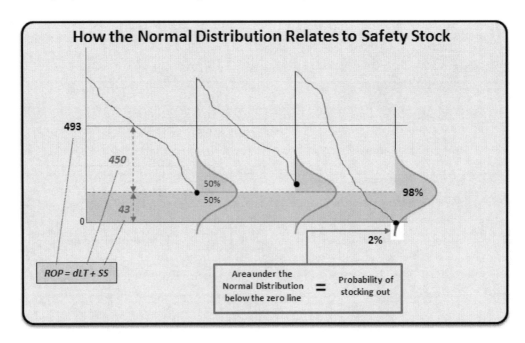

This concludes the discussion and examples related to continuous review systems, namely economic order quantity, quantity discount models, and reorder point.

Periodic Review Systems

A periodic review system is an independent demand, **fixed-period** ordering system which checks inventory levels and places restocking orders at regular intervals. It is also known as an "order up to" system as the order quantity varies depending on how much inventory is required to bring levels "up to" the desired target.

Periodic review systems are well suited to items for which restocking is economical and holding safety stock is inexpensive. Examples of fixed-period systems include vending machines and snack food displays in grocery and convenience stores. Such items are restocked on a regular (or fixed-period) basis.

Relatively speaking, periodic review systems are simple when compared to continuous review systems. In continuous review systems, perpetual inventory records are required, meaning that each addition to or withdraw from inventory must be recorded so that order quantities and order points can be correctly calculated. In a fixed-period system inventory records only have to be updated at the end of the period, just prior to placing the next order.

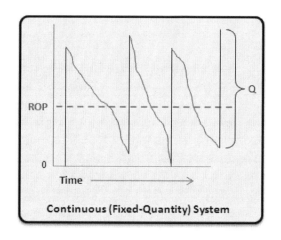

Continuous (Fixed-Quantity) System

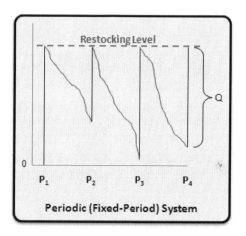

Periodic (Fixed-Period) System

Question: How is the restocking level determined in a periodic system?

The main task with setting up a periodic system is determining the restocking level, R. The equation for calculating R is as follows:

$$R = \mu_{RP+LT} + z\sigma_{RP+LT}$$

Where

RP = the reorder period (the regular time interval between each order)
LT = the order lead time (how long it takes for the order to arrive)
μ_{RP+LT} = average demand during the reorder period plus lead time
σ_{RP+LT} = standard deviation of demand during the reorder period plus lead time
Z = the z-value (which corresponds to the desired service level)

Restocking Level Example

The MC Market sells a variety of snacks, including the "Caramel Cob" popcorn treat. Replenishment orders for this item are placed once a week and there is a 2-day order lead time. The average daily demand is 4 and the standard deviation of demand over the replenishment period plus lead time is 9. The MC Market wants to keep the risk of stocking out at 10%.

What is the MC Market's restocking level (R) for Caramel Cob popcorn treats?

In this case,

$\mu_{RP+LT} = 4 \times (7 + 2) = 36$
$\sigma_{RP+LT} = 9$
$Z = 1.28$ (a 90% service level or 10% chance of stocking out)

Hence,

$$R = \mu_{RP+LT} + z\sigma_{RP+LT}$$

$$R = 36 + 1.28 \times 9$$

$$R = 48$$

Single-Period Inventory Systems

Single-period inventory systems are used in situations where unused items cannot be used elsewhere. Example items include newspapers, magazines, calendars, and Christmas trees. When such items go unused they must be sold at a loss or simply thrown away (at additional cost). In such circumstances companies must weigh the cost of being short against the cost of having excess inventory. The goal of a single-period inventory system is to establish a **target stocking point** that will strike a balance between shortage costs and excess costs.

Question: How is the target stocking point determined in a single-period inventory model?

Determining the **target stocking point** in a single-period inventory model is a 2-step process. We must first determine the **target service level** (a percentage) and then use it as an input into the target service point equation.

Here is the **target service level** equation.

$$SL_T = \frac{C_{Shortage}}{C_{Shortage} + C_{Excess}}$$

Where

$C_{Shortage}$ = shortage cost = revenue *if* demanded – item cost
C_{Excess} = excess cost = item cost + disposal cost – salvage value

Here is the **target stocking point** equation.

$$SP_T = \mu_{Demand} + SL_T \times \sigma_{Demand}$$

Where

μ_{Demand} = average
σ_{Demand} = standard deviation of demand

Target Stocking Point Example

Tie the Knot is an IBC company which sells a variety of neckties to the BYU-Idaho community. As the semester comes to a close they must shut down their business. Of course, they want to maximize profits before shutting down, so they want to make sure they have adequate stock of ties to sell during the last week of business. During the previous six weeks they sold an average of 150 ties per week with a standard deviation of weekly demand being 21. Each tie sells for $7 and costs the company $3. A local merchant has agreed to purchase all excess ties at the end of the week for a price of $2 per tie.

What is Tie the Knot's target stocking point for ties during its last week of business?

We'll start by calculating the target service level.

$$SL_T = \frac{C_{Shortage}}{C_{Shortage} + C_{Excess}}$$

$$SL_T = \frac{(7-3)}{(7-3) + (3-2)}$$

$$SL_T = \frac{4}{5} = 0.80 \; or \; 80\%$$

With the target service level calculated, we're now ready to calculate the target stocking point.

$$SP_T = \mu_{Demand} + SL_T \times \sigma_{Demand}$$

$$SP_T = 150 + 0.80 \times 21$$

$$SP_T = 167$$

Therefore, in order to maximize profit during the last week of sales, Tie the Knot should have 167 ties on hand after it makes its last-time purchase.

Replenishment Models, Independent and Dependent Demand

Continuous review, periodic review, and single-period review inventory models are all examples of **independent demand** replenishment systems. Demand for items is said to be independent when it is largely out of the organization's control. Finished goods items and service parts are examples of independent demand items. The selection of an appropriate replenishment model for such items is largely a function of the nature of product demand (and forecasting method), ordering costs, the quality and availability of inventory data, and the availability of quantity discounts.

Dependent demand items, on the other hand, are items whose demand is directly related to or derived from the bill of material structure for other items or end products. These demands are calculated rather than forecasted, as will be discussed in the MRP and ERP chapter.

Chapter Summary

Below are some of the main points you should have garnered from the study of this chapter.

- **Inventory is stock of items which is used to support production, customer service, and other activities**.
- A basic challenge of inventory management is **balancing the tradeoff between inventory (cost) and customer service (revenue)**. Cycle inventory, safety stock, pipeline inventory, anticipation inventory, and hedge inventory are all used to support customer service.
- **ABC classification enables the efficient tracking of stocks and the reconciling of inventory records with physical inventories**. Inventory record accuracy is critical to making and keeping delivery commitments to customers.
- **There are three types of independent demand item replenishment models** (1—continuous review, 2—periodic review, and 3—single period), each with its own ordering methods. Taking advantage of quantity discounts may require adaptation of the selected replenishment model.

Chapter 9

PRODUCTION PLANNING AND

MASTER PRODUCTION SCHEDULING

Making decisions is probably the most important thing people ever do. Nothing happens until someone makes a decision....

Fortunately the ability and judgment necessary to make decisions can be acquired. Certain methods and practices can bring to us all greater skill in everyday, every-week, every-month opportunities to make decisions....

Collect facts and analyze and use them. Develop and weigh possible solutions to arrive at conclusions. Carry a decision into action with plans and controls. Follow up on the results of the decisions and action.

President Ezra Taft Benson[68]

Whether formal or informal, effective or ineffective, planning and decision-making processes are present within virtually all organizations. As President Benson states, we can acquire greater skill in our decision-making abilities, and this often starts by understanding basic planning processes.

In most organizations, planning occurs on several levels and at different frequencies. This is especially true in organizations that endeavor to push decision making to the lowest levels possible (much like what we find within the Church and family).

Chapter Objectives

In this chapter we will take a look at basic planning processes, which apply in one form or another to manufacturing and service organizations. A common theme or objective of the basic planning processes is to find the best way to make supply (production) equal demand (customer volume and timing requirements). After studying this chapter you should be able to

1. Distinguish among strategic business planning, sales and operations planning, master production scheduling, and material requirements planning processes.

---

[68] Ezra Taft Benson, *God, Family Country: Our Three Great Priorities*, (Salt Lake City: Deseret Book Co., 1997), 145-46.

2. Describe each of the three basic build plan strategies and the conditions under which each would be most appropriate for creating an aggregate production plan.
3. Create aggregate production plans utilizing each of the three basic strategies, including with the use of Excel's Solver function.
4. Describe master production scheduling and the different levels at which it should be expressed (including a 2-level MPS), depending on product structure.
5. Create a master production schedule and compute available-to-promise (ATP).
6. Describe ATP and its importance—especially to production and marketing.

Overview of Manufacturing Planning and Control System

Question: What planning processes are found within manufacturing planning and control system?

A manufacturing planning and control system is composed of many levels of coordinated and connected planning activities, each focusing on different views or aggregations of products, occurring on various cycles, and driven by different levels of personnel. *Each planning level focuses on finding the best way to* **make supply meet demand** *(in other words, make supply = demand, a difficult task).*

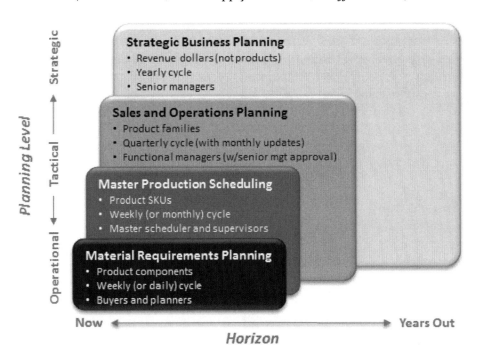

Below is a brief description of each of the planning activities as depicted above, starting with the most strategic and working our way to the operational level.

- **Strategic business planning** is the process of creating a statement of revenue, cost, and profit objectives. Output from this process is translated into and synchronized with functional plans within the sales and operations planning process. Business planning usually speaks in terms of dollars, takes place on an annual basis, extends more than a year into the future, and is under the direction of senior management.

- **Sales and operations planning (S&OP)** is the process of creating tactical plans for functional groups, based on the strategic business plan. Its main outputs are the **sales plan** and the **production plan** (hence, "sales and operations planning"); however, other functions such as engineering, finance, and human resources participate and make their respective plans as well. S&OP speaks in terms of product families, occurs on a monthly or quarterly basis, and is driven by functional managers.
- **Master production scheduling** takes the production plan (an output from sales and operations planning) as its starting point and then disaggregates that family-level plan into SKU or item-specific production schedules, typically by week. The master schedule is the hub of production planning activity, driving materials and capacity requirements while, at the same time, considering the availability of these key resources.
- **Material requirements planning is a process that** incorporates the master production schedule, inventory data, bill of material data, and other rules to make time-phased recommendations on the release of production and materials (purchase) orders.

In our further discussion of planning processes we will begin with sales and operations planning, as this is where functional-based personnel take charge (as opposed to strategic business planning where senior managers lead).

Sales and Operations Planning (S&OP)

A family-level production plan, in monthly (or quarterly) quantities, is one of the key outputs of the sales and operations planning process. Sales and operations planning is a coordinating activity not only among internal organizations, but it also looks at the capabilities of suppliers and logistics service providers. All internal and external constraints must be considered during this process when developing the production plan. Arriving at this plan requires considerable give-and-take among organizations as there are competing objectives that usually cannot all be met.

<u>Question</u>: What are some of the competing objectives when trying to manage the inherent conflicts between supply and demand?

- **Senior managers** want to maximize profits while many **middle managers** want to make investments to improve their respective organizations (investments that may hurt short-term profitability).
- **Sales and marketing personnel** want to maximize product availability for customers—which means producing or acquiring lots of finished goods inventory—while **finance personnel** want to minimize inventory investment.
- **Customers** want to commit to purchases as late as possible and have the flexibility to make last-minute changes to their orders while **supply-side personnel** (production, purchasing, suppliers, human resources) desire

stable, long lead-time demand (lots of visibility) to facilitate efficient operations.

No matter where you find yourself in the business world, you should always be cognizant of these conflicting objectives. Sales and operations planning is the main coordinating vehicle for addressing these supply and demand challenges.

Question: What production plan strategies are used to address the competing requirements of supply and demand?

There are three primary build plan strategies for addressing the mid-range competing requirements of supply and demand.

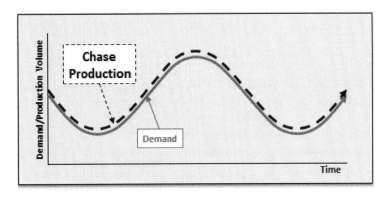

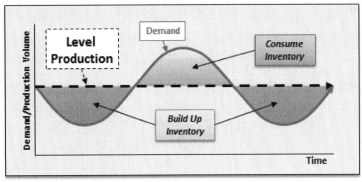

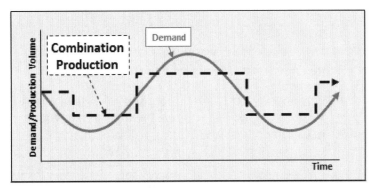

1. Alter production levels to *chase* the demand ("chase" strategy).
2. Maintain *level* production while using inventory to buffer against the ups and downs in demand ("level" strategy).
3. Employ a *combination* of the chase and level strategies ("combination" strategy).

Inventory Shelf Life

Short ◄- - - - - - - - - - - - - -► Long

Capacity: Flexible ▲ / Inflexible ▼

	Short	Long
Flexible	Chase	Chase or Combination (w/Inventory)
Inflexible	Combination (w/Overtime or Subcons)	Level (w/Inventory)

Several key factors drive the decisions regarding production plan strategy. While the use of pure strategies do exist (pure "chase" or pure "level" strategy), in reality, most organizations employ some sort of combination strategy. The graphic above provides a framework for when each strategy should be employed. Consistent with this framework, the table below adds detail and summarizes the main factors or characteristics which favor one strategy versus another.

Plan Strategy	Environmental Factors which Call for Production Plan Strategy
Chase	• Perishable demand • Short product lifecycles • Short shelf life or non-stock-able product or service (unable to prebuild and store inventory, as in a service offering. For example, how do you prebuild and store a haircut or doctor visit?) • Easy to increase capacity • Firm offers complementary seasonal products which utilize similar production processes (Think of Polaris which produces snowmobiles, ATVs, motorcycles, etc. Each product type can "chase" the demand within its given season.) • **Examples**: mid-tier manufacturers (suppliers) who cannot influence demand, service industries like grocery and consumer banking
Level	• Durable, changeable demand (through promotions, discounts, etc.) • Long lead-time demand, long product lifecycles • Stock-able product, long shelf life • Difficult to increase capacity (expensive and specialized equipment) • Stringent quality requirements best met with stable workforce • **Examples**: automobile manufacturing, hotels, airlines, chemical processing (where it is difficult to shut down and restart equipment)
Combination	• Most appropriate where demand is perishable • Can use some overtime or subcontractors to increase capacity • Modular product designs (to address short product lifecycles) • Some ability to stock subassemblies/modules • **Examples**: make-to-order personal computers, fast food restaurants (components precooked—level—then assembled to demand—chase)

Question: What *internal* and *external* tactics are commonly employed to alter or manage the supply and demand sides of the "make supply = demand" objective?

There are many options available to companies as they balance supply and demand, and they fall into two basic categories: (1) focus on altering supply and (2) focus on altering demand. The table below contains a summary of the internal and external tactics which can be employed to alter both supply and demand.

Internal Tactics (focus on supply)	External Tactics (focus on demand)
To increase supply • Hire workers, including temporary workers. • Run overtime. • Subcontract a portion of production. • Build up inventory when capacity exceeds demand (to be consumed when demand exceeds capacity).	**To increase demand** • Lower prices. • Give quantity discounts. • Advertise. • Run promotions. • "Package" or "bundle" product offerings. • Take reservations (appropriate in service operations).
To decrease supply • Fire workers, including temporary workers. • Employ slack time (assign workers to non-production activities). • Change (lower) production rates.	**To decrease (manage excess) demand** • Increase prices. • Take reservations. • Pre-book orders. • Accumulate order backlog. • Decline orders.

Examples for Each Plan Strategy

With the above conceptual grounding for each production plan strategy, we are now prepared to examine examples of how the production plan would be developed for each. For our examples let's suppose that we are trying to develop the production plan for a small manufacturer of high-end toy cars and trucks. Cost and constraint data can be found in the table below. These data will be used to determine which production plan strategy has the lowest total cost.

Cost and Other Information	
Production rate (units/emp/qtr)	500
Max subcontract production/mo	3,000
Regular production cost/unit	$ 20
Subcontract production cost/unit	$ 20
Holding cost/unit/quarter	$ 2
Hiring cost/employee	$ 1,500
Firing cost/employee	$ 4,500

Chase Production Plan

The tables below provide the summary data for the "chase" production plan. With chase production we create a plan that holds no inventory at the end of each quarter. In Q1 we subtract beginning inventory of 2,000 from the forecasted sales of 16,000 to get 14,000 units of regular production. Employees are hired and fired as needed in order to match regular production capacity and output with demand. Based on the production plan in the first table we are able to calculate the costs in the second. For example, Q1 regular production cost = 14,000 units X $20/unit = $280,000. Q2 fire cost = 2 employees fired X $4,500 per fired employee = $9,000. Summing all costs for four quarters gives a total cost of $1,187,000 for this production plan.

"Chase" Production Plan

Supply and Demand		Q1	Q2	Q3	Q4
Forecasted sales		16,000	13,000	14,000	17,000
Regular production		14,000	13,000	14,000	17,000
Subcontract production		-	-	-	-
Ending inventory	2,000	-	-	-	-
Hired employees		4		2	6
Fired employees		-	2	-	-
Total employees	24	28	26	28	34

Calculated Costs	Q1	Q2	Q3	Q4	Year Total
Regular production cost	$ 280,000	$ 260,000	$ 280,000	$ 340,000	$ 1,160,000
Subcontract cost	$ -	$ -	$ -	$ -	$ -
Inventory holding cost	$ -	$ -	$ -	$ -	$ -
Hire cost	$ 6,000	$ -	$ 3,000	$ 9,000	$ 18,000
Fire cost	$ -	$ 9,000	$ -	$ -	$ 9,000
Total Cost by Period	$286,000	$269,000	$283,000	$349,000	$1,187,000

Level Production Plan

Continuing with this same process gives the numbers below for the "level" production plan. Notice that the production plan is level at 14,500 units per quarter. To arrive at this number, we take total forecasted sales, net out (subtract) beginning inventory, then divide by the number of periods: (16k + 13k + 14k + 17k − 2k)/4 = 14,500. When output exceeds demand, inventory is stored (as in Q1, Q2 and Q3). When demand exceeds output, stored inventory is consumed to make up the difference (as in Q1 and Q4).

"Level" Production Plan

Supply and Demand		Q1	Q2	Q3	Q4
Forecasted sales		16,000	13,000	14,000	17,000
Regular production		14,500	14,500	14,500	14,500
Subcontract production		-	-	-	-
Ending inventory	2,000	500	2,000	2,500	-
Hired employees		5	-	-	-
Fired employees		-	-	-	-
Total employees	24	29	29	29	29

Calculated Costs	Q1	Q2	Q3	Q4	Year Total
Regular production cost	$ 290,000	$ 290,000	$ 290,000	$ 290,000	$ 1,160,000
Subcontract cost	$ -	$ -	$ -	$ -	$ -
Holding cost	$ 1,000	$ 4,000	$ 5,000	$ -	$ 10,000
Hire cost	$ 7,500	$ -	$ -	$ -	$ 7,500
Fire cost	$ -	$ -	$ -	$ -	$ -
Total Cost by Period	$298,500	$294,000	$295,000	$290,000	$1,177,500

Combination Production Plan

For the "combination" production plan, we have used a level internal production of 14,000 units per quarter (after hiring 4 employees in Q1), subcontract production in Q2 and Q3, and stored inventory in Q2 and Q3 to help satisfy demand in Q4, where demand exceeds regular production.

"Combination" Production Plan

Supply and Demand		Q1	Q2	Q3	Q4
Forecasted sales		16,000	13,000	14,000	17,000
Regular production		14,000	14,000	14,000	14,000
Subcontract production			1,000	1,000	-
Ending inventory	2,000	-	2,000	3,000	-
Hired employees		4	-	-	-
Fired employees		-	-	-	-
Total employees	24	28	28	28	28

Calculated Costs	Q1	Q2	Q3	Q4	Year Total
Regular production cost	$ 280,000	$ 280,000	$ 280,000	$ 280,000	$ 1,120,000
Subcontract cost	$ -	$ 20,000	$ 20,000	$ -	$ 40,000
Holding cost	$ -	$ 4,000	$ 6,000	$ -	$ 10,000
Hire cost	$ 6,000	$ -	$ -	$ -	$ 6,000
Fire cost	$ -	$ -	$ -	$ -	$ -
Total Cost by Period	**$286,000**	**$304,000**	**$306,000**	**$280,000**	**$1,176,000**

This "combination" plan gives us the lowest cost so far. Is this the lowest cost possible for a combination plan? To answer this question we'll discuss the use of advanced mathematical models to help in the creation of production plans.

Overview of Excel's Solver Function

Companies will often employ complex mathematical models to optimize the tradeoffs among the many tactics which can be employed to make supply meet demand in the production plan. Such models are usually part of Advanced Planning and Scheduling (APS) software. An exploration of such applications is beyond the scope of this book, but we will take a look at Excel's "Solver" function to better understand how APS works.

Solver is a what-if analysis tool that can help you with planning, budgeting, and optimization. It consists of 4 components.[69]

- **Objective**—where you specify your goal within a target cell. For example, you may want Solver to minimize costs or maximize profit. The objective cell must be a formula.
- **Variables**—where you tell Solver which cell values can be changed to meet your objective. For example, you can tell Solver to maximize profit by changing product prices (data values within your variables cells).
- **Constraints**—where you set boundaries of what is acceptable for Solver to do with your variables.

---

[69] Refer to Microsoft Excel Help or Google "solver" to learn more about using this powerful function.

- **Method**—where you select the type of "engine" that will be used to solve your problem. In this class we will use the "Simplex LP" engine.

Combination Production Plan with Excel's Solver Function

To use Solver on our production planning problem, we start with tables that are similar to the ones used in the previous examples. When we open Solver (from Excel's "Data" menu) we get a new window like this one below and are asked to provide a variety of information to help Solver compute an optimal answer.

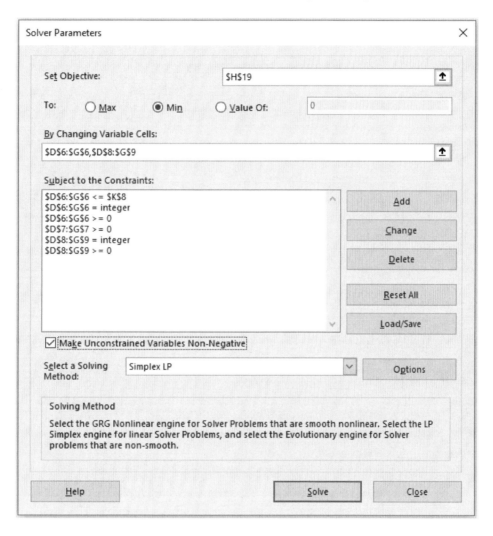

- Our **objective** function is to minimize total plan cost (cell H19).
- The **variables** are subcontract production (cells D6–G6) and hiring and firing of employees (cells D8–G9), which affect regular production.
- The **constraints** can be seen in the graphic above. In this example we have told solver that all the variables must be integers (whole numbers) and that subcontract production must be less than or equal to 3,000 units per month (cells D6–G6 ≤ K8). We also specify that ending inventory must be greater than or equal to zero (cells D7–G7).
- We select the Simplex LP (linear program) as the **method** for this model.

"Combination" Production Plan (using Excel's Solver)

Supply and Demand		Q1	Q2	Q3	Q4
Forecasted sales		16,000	13,000	14,000	17,000
Regular production		12,500	12,500	12,500	12,500
Subcontract production		1,500	500	3,000	3,000
Ending inventory	2,000	-	-	1,500	-
Hired employees		1	-	-	-
Fired employees		-	-	-	-
Total employees	24	25	25	25	25

Calculated Costs	Q1	Q2	Q3	Q4	Year Total
Regular production cost	$ 250,000	$ 250,000	$ 250,000	$ 250,000	$ 1,000,000
Subcontract cost	$ 30,000	$ 10,000	$ 60,000	$ 60,000	$ 160,000
Holding cost	$ -	$ -	$ 3,000	$ -	$ 3,000
Hire cost	$ 1,500	$ -	$ -	$ -	$ 1,500
Fire cost	$ -	$ -	$ -	$ -	$ -
Total Cost by Period	$281,500	$260,000	$313,000	$310,000	$1,164,500

Once all of these parameters are set we click on the "Solve" button and the model will return a value of $1,164,500. As expected, this is the lowest-cost option of the four examples above. Solver was able to quickly consider all the possible tradeoffs to arrive at an optimal plan.

Notice how this plan makes use of both inventory and subcontract production when regular production capacity is insufficient to meet demand. Again, Solver can explore all the options quickly, much faster than a human can do via trial and error—especially when dealing with real-life models which are much more complex than this simple example.

Build Plans Summary

After creating these four plans we can summarize their results (as shown below). We should note that the examples above merely provide a very simplified view of how production plans can be created and evaluated to help organizations make decisions on how to best meet customer demand.

Summary of Production Plan Costs

Costs	Chase	Level	Combination w/o Solver	Combination w/Solver
Hire cost	$ 18,000	$ 7,500	$ 6,000	$ 1,500
Fire cost	$ 9,000	$ -	$ -	$ -
Production cost	$1,160,000	$1,160,000	$ 1,120,000	$ 1,000,000
Subcontract cost	$ -	$ -	$ 40,000	$ 160,000
Holding cost	$ -	$ 10,000	$ 10,000	$ 3,000
Total Cost	$1,187,000	$1,177,500	$ 1,176,000	$ 1,164,500

Question: Are there additional considerations to be made when creating the production plan?

As is the case with many quantitative analyses, care should be taken to look beyond the numbers before making decisions. Following is a sampling of questions (not a comprehensive list) which might be considered when determining which tactics to employ in the production planning process.

- Will subcontract production meet our quality requirements? Will we be at risk of losing important intellectual property (IP) if we subcontract? Will they meet our schedule requirements?
- Will firing employees (to shrink capacity) have an adverse effect on the morale of those who aren't fired? How long will it take newly-hired employees to be able to match the quality of the long-time employees?
- Does our plan call for so much overtime that employees will get tired (and not even care about the overtime pay)? Does our plan have so much idle time that we would be better off to lay off some employees (even if morale might suffer)?
- If we plan to build up inventory (when capacity exceeds demand), do we run the risk of the inventory going bad or becoming obsolete? Have we properly accounted for all the costs related to storing the inventory?
- Are there additional measures that can be taken to manage the quantity and timing of demand (through the "demand management" process) and thereby make it easier for us to make and keep commitments to customers?

Master Production Scheduling (MPS)

The master production schedule (or simply, the master schedule) is the next step in an organization's planning hierarchy. The key input into the master schedule is a finalized production plan that is an outcome of the sales and operations planning process.

The quantities in the master schedule should match those of the production plan, although at a more detailed level of granularity. Within the master scheduling process, the production plan—typically expressed at the product family level in monthly or quarterly buckets—is "disaggregated" into item-specific, "buildable" or "sellable" products, expressed in weekly production quantities. This additional granularity or detail enables the master schedule to become the primary "interface" between the production system and external customers, providing an item-specific statement of supply against which commitments to customers can be made. The master schedule should extend far enough into the future to cover the longest cumulative lead time of the items being produced (usually three months or more).

Question: How are forecasts and customer orders treated within the master schedule?

Along with the production plan, forecasts and customer orders—the two components of demand—are also important inputs into the master schedule. Given customers' general reluctance to commit to purchases long in advance of the need date, companies must rely on forecasts (not merely customer orders) to drive decisions regarding the use of production-related resources (personnel, materials, equipment, etc.). The graphic below provides a conceptual view of a demand profile, where customer orders "consume" the forecast and drive the master schedule in the near term, while unconsumed forecast drives the master schedule further out in the future.

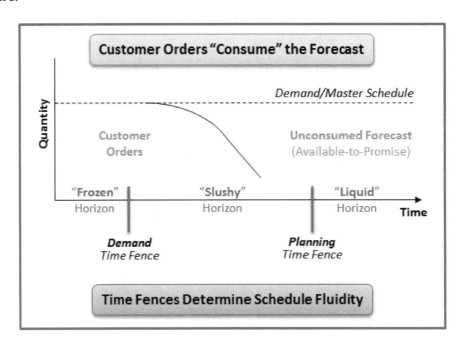

Question: What are time fences and planning horizons, and how do they relate to the master schedule?

Time fences are policy triggers which are used to note where restrictions or changes to operating procedures take place. The **demand time fence** separates the "frozen" planning horizon from the "slushy" planning horizon; the **planning time fence** separates the "slushy" from the "liquid" planning horizon.

- Within the **frozen horizon** the master schedule is considered unchangeable or "frozen" because changing the schedule in this period puts existing

134

customer commitments at risk and wreaks havoc on production execution (productivity). Typically only senior managers can authorize changes in the frozen horizon. In this horizon the forecast is often ignored such that customer orders alone drive master schedule calculations.

- The **slushy horizon** spans from the demand time fence to the planning time fence. Changes to the schedule in this horizon require management approval and extensive analysis by supply management personnel—production planning, production supervisors, purchasing (suppliers)—to make sure such changes can be supported. The master schedule is driven by the combination of customer orders and unconsumed forecast.
- The **liquid horizon** begins at the planning time fence and extends into the future. The planning time fence is set equal to or slightly larger than the cumulative lead time of the product (including its components). In the liquid horizon customer orders may be booked and changes to the master schedule can be made within the constraints of the production plan, without management approval.

Question: What is the Available-to-Promise (ATP) and how is it calculated?

As can be seen in the graphic on the previous page, the available-to-promise represents that portion of the master schedule which is uncommitted to existing customer orders. In other words, this uncommitted supply is "available to promise" to new customers. The ATP provides invaluable information to production and sales personnel as they work to schedule customer order shipments. Calculating ATP can be confusing. The example of MPS-related data in the table below will help us understand how ATP and projected available balance (PAB) are calculated.

MPS/ATP Example

Week	0	1	2	3	4	5	6	7	8	9
Forecast		80	80	80	70	70	70	70	70	70
Customer Orders		83	78	65	61	49	51	34	17	11
Projected Available Balance (PAB)	110	27	99	19	99	29	109	39	119	49
Available-to-Promise (ATP)		27	7	-	40	-	65	-	122	-
Master Production Schedule (MPS)		-	150	-	150	-	150	-	150	-

For this example we will assume there is a 2-week demand fence, meaning we will ignore any forecasts in week 1 and week 2. Only customer orders will be used to calculate both ATP and PAB within this frozen planning horizon. In fact, throughout the horizon, ATP makes its calculations only from (1) beginning on-hand inventory in week 0, (2) MPS replenishments throughout the schedule, and (3) customer orders on the demand side. The PAB, on the other hand, will incorporate the greater of forecast and customer orders, outside the frozen period (week 3 and beyond), not just customer orders. Let's walk through some specific examples.

- ATP in week 1 is calculated by taking the beginning inventory and subtracting customer orders up until the week of the next MPS replenishment (which is in week 2). Hence, ATP in week 1 = 110 – 83 = 27.
- ATP in week 2 is calculated by taking the MPS quantity in week 2 and subtracting all customer orders from week 2 until the next MPS replenishment (which is in week 4). Hence, ATP in week 2 = 150 – (78 + 65)

= 7. *Note that the ATP calculation is not cumulative*. It goes from one MPS period to the next.

- ATP in week 4 = 150 − (61 + 49) = 40.

What should you do if a customer requested 39 units in week 3? Three options come to mind.

- See if the customer would be willing to accept 34 units in week 3 (27 + 7 = 34 from previous period ATPs) and the balance of 5 units in week 4 (to be drawn from the week 4 ATP of 40.
- See if sufficient materials and capacity are available to increase the week 2 master schedule by 5 units in order to ship all 39 units together in week 3.
- If neither of the two previous options will work, then do not take the order.

Below are some examples of how projected available balance is calculated, both inside and outside the demand fence.

- PAB in week 1 (inside the demand fence) is calculated by adding PAB from the previous period to the MPS in week 1 and then subtracting customer orders from week 1. PAB in week 1 = (110 + 0) − 83 = 27.
- PAB in week 2 (again, inside the demand fence, so forecast is ignored) = (27 + 150) − 78 = 99.
- PAB in week 3 (outside the demand fence, so we subtract the greater of forecast and customer orders) = (99 + 0) − 80 = 19. *Note that a projected available balance is shown in each week*, not just in the weeks when there is an MPS replenishment (as is the case with ATP).

Question: What is a two-level master schedule and when is it used?

In an assemble-to-order (ATO) production environment, a two-level master schedule is used for end products or families which contain multi-option features. One level of the master schedule is used for the base product or family and the other level focuses on the features. It may sound complicated, but this approach *greatly* simplifies planning for products which offer many features and options. It also enables organizations to more effectively market products based on component availability.

Feature	Bread	Meat	Cheese
Option 1	White	Roast beef	American
Option 2	Wheat	Turkey	Swiss
Option 3	Oat	Chicken	Provolone
Option 4	Parmesan	Cold cuts	Pepper jack

To help illustrate how a two-level master schedule is used, let's look at a sandwich shop (think of Subway) that uses an assemble-to-order process for its main product offering—sandwiches. For this example one level of the master schedule will be for the sandwich (base product) and the other level will be for all of the features and options.

With this simplified product structure, how many unique sandwiches can be produced? The answer is 64 (4 bread types X 4 meat types X 4 cheese types = 64 combinations). If we were to include all the options for each of the features above, and if we were to include other features with their numerous options (vegetables, condiments, toasted or not, etc.) we would end up with *literally thousands* of potential unique sandwich combinations or products. In such environments, where thousands of unique end products are possible, it becomes virtually impossible to accurately forecast demand for each of these end products.

A two-level master schedule allows each base product and each feature to be forecasted and planned separately. In other words, instead of forecasting and planning for 64 unique sandwich combinations, the sandwich shop merely has to (1) forecast or plan the number of sandwiches to be sold per day and (2) apportion that number across the options within each feature, probably using historical averages for each option.

The table below shows a simple product structure and the percentage breakdown of demand across each option. Notice that in this example the sum of the option percentages for each feature exceeds 100% (sum of bread options, meat options and cheese options are 105%, 103%, and 104%, respectively). This "overplanning" is done intentionally as a "mix hedge" to provide flexibility at the component or option level in case the actual option demand or mix is different than what is forecasted. In other words, it is much easier, more practical, and more cost effective to stock excess supplies of components than it is to stock extra finished goods (finished sandwiches).

Feature	Bread	Meat	Cheese
Option 1	35% - White	33% - Roast beef	24% - American
Option 2	25% - Wheat	30% - Turkey	35% - Swiss
Option 3	15% - Oat	25% - Chicken	20% - Provolone
Option 4	30% - Parmesan	15% - Cold cuts	25% - Pepper jack

Another benefit of this 2-level approach is that it provides valuable information that can be used by marketing. For example, let's say that the sandwich shop made a large, heavily-discounted forward buy on roast beef and they wanted to use it all up before its expiration date. They may want to run a special on all roast beef sandwiches in order to steer demand in that direction. They could also use pricing to steer demand away from components that may be short. A modular bill of material and option-level planning process enables this type of agility. Dell Computer is a master of this.

Question: How does the selection of build strategy affect customer input into the design of the finished product (and lead time)?

If we stick with our food examples, it's easy to see the varying degree of customer input that is facilitated with each build strategy (as shown in the graphic below).

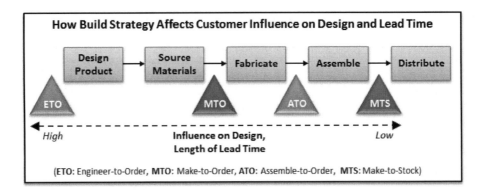

How Build Strategy Affects Customer Influence on Design and Lead Time

Design Product → Source Materials → Fabricate → Assemble → Distribute

ETO   MTO   ATO   MTS

High ←---------- Influence on Design, Length of Lead Time ----------→ Low

(ETO: Engineer-to-Order, MTO: Make-to-Order, ATO: Assemble-to-Order, MTS: Make-to-Stock)

- **Make-to-stock** items allow for virtually no customer input into the design of the item. Think of a package of cookies on a convenience store shelf. You can't change the design of the product. It has been designed in response to marketing research, produced in response to a forecast and stocked on a shelf until purchased. A major benefit of this build strategy is very short lead times as the finished product is available on store shelves.
- **Assemble-to-order** items allow customers to provide input as to how the semi-finished goods or subassemblies are configured. Again, think of Taco Bell where it is fairly easy to request changes that differ from a standard product (for example, extra sour cream), however, those changes are limited to adjusting the mix of existing subassemblies. This build strategy balances the benefits of increased product variety with relatively short lead times.
- **Make-to-order** items allow for extensive input by customers into the design process, limited by acceptable design constraints and available raw materials. In a fine restaurant customers can make requests down to the ingredient level as many or most dishes are prepared from scratch, not merely assembled from existing semi-finished goods.
- **Engineer-to-order** items allow maximum input by customers into the design process. This would be analogous to designing any food item and then having the freedom to procure materials from wherever is necessary.

<u>**Question**</u>:   How does product structure (or the bill of materials) affect the master production schedule?

Consider our ATO example above (sandwiches) where production is planned at the ingredient level, prior to assembly of the final product. The number of ingredients is much smaller than the number of possible finished sandwiches configurations. Hence, it is better to forecast and plan production of sandwiches at the ingredient level, or the narrowest point in the bill of material (as seen in the graphic below).

Likewise, each of the basic build strategies calls for the MPS to be created at different points in the product structure. The "shape" of a product's bill of material (BOM) can vary greatly, with the three basic shapes shown in the graphic below, and each requiring a slightly different approach to master scheduling. For example, the shape for the MTS item (far right side of the graphic) denotes that many raw material inputs will result in a relatively small number of sellable products. (The shape is broader at the base than at the top.) The master schedule for such products (pre-packaged foods, etc.) is expressed at the finished product level. For instance, the schedule would tell how many of a specific sellable item would be produced per week.

The middle "hourglass" can best be explained by Taco Bell. A relatively small number of semi-finished goods—represented by the narrow part of the shape—are mixed and matched to create a much wider variety of finished goods. The master schedule is more generic than the previous example, being expressed in terms of how many base products (tacos, burritos, etc.) will be sold and how much of each semi-finished ingredient will be needed.

Such an approach to master scheduling is much simpler than trying to schedule production for the many, many end items—as represented by the top of the shape. (For a fun exercise, go to Taco Bell and see how many unique end items they can produce and compare that number to the total number of ingredients that they use. You will find that the number of ingredients is much smaller than the number of unique items they can produce.)

Finally, the MTO shape represents those many items that can be made from few common ingredients. For example, a fine restaurant can mix and match a relatively small number of ingredients into a nearly limitless variety of gourmet dishes. Likewise, petroleum can be refined into many, many products (gasoline, motor oil, Vaseline, plastics, etc.). In such build environments, planning is done at the ingredient level.

Chapter Summary

Below are some of the main points you should have garnered from the study of this chapter.

- **Planning processes will differ by industry and by company**, but most organizations will employ, in one form or another, multi-level planning processes similar to those discussed in this chapter. From most strategic to most granular, **the basic planning processes are** (1) strategic business planning, (2) sales and operations planning, (3) master production scheduling, and (4) materials requirements planning.

- **Sales and operations planning** (S&OP) is a monthly or quarterly planning activity focused on aligning supply with demand at a product family level. To achieve this objective or alignment, functional managers must often make tradeoffs among competing objectives.

- **A key output from S&OP is the production plan**, which will employ **one of three build plan strategies**: (1) chase, (2) level, or (3) combination. Organizations often employ sophisticated mathematical models (usually within specialized software packages) to help create optimal production plans.

- The family-level or "aggregate" production plan is "disaggregated" and converted into an SKU-level master production schedule (MPS). The MPS becomes a statement of supply and interface against which commitments to customers can be made.

- A product's bill of material structure and selected build strategy (ETO, MTO, ATO, or MTS) can have a huge bearing on lead time, flexibility, and customer input into the design process.

Chapter 10

MATERIAL REQUIREMENTS PLANNING (MRP) AND INFORMATION SYSTEMS

Now these are the names of the different pieces of their gold, and of their silver, according to their value...

Now the reckoning is thus—a senine of gold, a seon of gold, a shum of gold, and a limnah of gold.

A senum of silver, an amnor of silver, an ezrom of silver, and an onti of silver.

A senum of silver was equal to a senine of gold, and either for a measure of barley, and also for a measure of every kind of grain.

Now the amount of a seon of gold was twice the value of a senine.

And a shum of gold was twice the value of a seon.

And a limnah of gold was the value of them all.

And an amnor of silver was as great as two senums.

And an ezrom of silver was as great as four senums.

And an onti was as great as them all.

Now this is the value of the lesser numbers of their reckoning—

A shiblon is half of a senum; therefore, a shiblon for half a measure of barley.

And a shiblum is a half of a shiblon.

And a leah is the half of a shiblum.

Now this is their number, according to their reckoning.

Now an antion of gold is equal to three shiblons.

Alma 11:4-19

Why would Mormon include so many verses related to Nephite coinage in the Book of Mormon? Are there some important things we learn from them? Here are two (plus an interesting aside).

- **Standardization enables organizational growth and unity**. Prior to "the reign of the judges" the Nephites had "altered their reckoning and their measure according to the minds and the circumstances of the people." One can safely assume that such variation in reckoning and measures among different locales (cities, provinces, regions) caused confusion and hindered trade and the development of a cohesive Nephite society. The standardization of coinage and measures is a great testament to the inspiration and far-sightedness of King Mosiah, who engineered the transition of Nephite society from a monarchy to the rule of the judges, as elected by the voice of the people.

- **Hierarchical structure enables working knowledge of complex relationships.** The hierarchical relationships of Nephite coinage provides a quick reference of relative value, highly intuitive and easily understood by all who dealt with money—especially when viewed in a hierarchical graphic like the one below.

- **Finally, an interesting aside**...Nephite currency was ultimately tied to something of true value—grain or food.

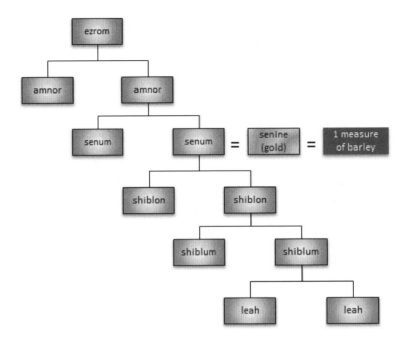

Chapter Objectives

Just as standardized coinage and measures were essential to the growth of Nephite society, standardized data and systems are essential to the successful management and growth of a business. Of course, today's corporations deal with much greater complexities than Nephite coinage, but the principles surrounding standardization and organization of data are the same.

This chapter is a natural successor to the previous chapter's discussion on production planning as it dives deeper into the realm of material requirements planning (MRP) and the supply chain systems which support this and other planning processes. After studying this chapter you should be able to

1. Draw and interpret a bill of material.
2. Describe the inputs to and outputs from MRP.
3. Make MRP calculations under various sets of assumptions.
4. Describe enterprise resource planning (ERP) and distinguish between front-office systems and back-office systems.
5. Name the supply chain macro processes and main system transactions related to each one.

Overview of Material Requirements Planning (MRP)

Material requirements planning is a set of techniques used to calculate requirements for materials. As mentioned in the Inventory Management chapter, MRP is used to calculate demand for *dependent* items—the components or ingredients which are buried in a bill of material.

For example, sandwiches at a delicatessen would be considered **independent** *demand items* whereas the components (ingredients) would be **dependent** *demand items*. The delicatessen might use forecasts to determine how many sandwiches they will sell whereas they would use MRP logic to calculate the demand for the components (meats, cheeses, etc.) based on the forecast for sandwiches.

Question: What are the **inputs** to and **outputs** from MRP? How does MRP work?

The main input into MRP is the **master production schedule**. Via MRP logic, this schedule for the production of end items is "exploded" through the product's **bill of material** (or "BOM," an MRP input) and netted against the **inventory status** for each component (an MRP input) to ultimately derive time-phased requirements for each component within the BOM. These requirements become part of either a *purchasing action plan* or a *production action plan*, depending on whether the component is a "**buy**" item (an item that is purchased from a supplier) or a "**make**" item (an item that is produced or assembled internally).

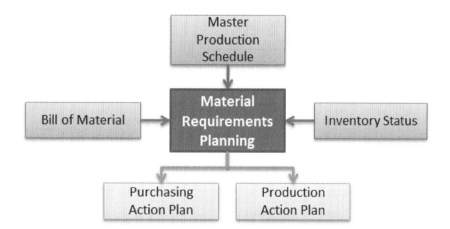

MRP Mechanics

Suppose we are a toy manufacturer and we want to plan the material requirements for one of our toy cars. To do so we will need the following inputs: a master production schedule, a bill of material, and inventory status for the toy car and each of its components. In addition to the above inputs, we also will make use of several MRP worksheets (one for the toy car and one for each component) that will help us organize these inputs so that we can make the required MRP calculations. (Note that MRP is generally done with sophisticated MRP software. However, in this text we will employ Excel-based MRP sheets to show how MRP logic works.)

Below is the graphical bill of material for this toy car. This view of the bill of material clearly shows the parent-child relationships for all levels of the BOM. For example, the toy car final assembly is the "parent" to two "children" components: the body and the wheel assembly. Notice that the wheel assembly is also a parent to two children: the axle and the wheel. The top level assembly in the BOM is said to be "level 0" with each succeeding level being called level 1, level 2, and so forth until the bottom of the hierarchy is reached (level 2 in this case).

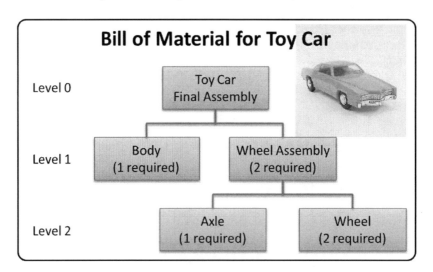

The BOM also shows (in parentheses) how many children are required for each parent. For example, each toy car requires one body and two wheel assemblies. Each wheel assembly requires one axle and two wheels.

The master production schedule and inventory status—both key inputs to the MRP process—can best be shown in an MRP worksheet or table, along with other key data which are required for making MRP calculations. Each item in the BOM of our toy car example will have its own worksheet, but to keep things simple we'll begin just with the MRP worksheet for the top-level assembly, the toy car final assembly.

Toy Car			On Hand	1-Aug	8-Aug	15-Aug	22-Aug	29-Aug	5-Sep	12-Sep	19-Sep	26-Sep
LT (wks)	1	Gross Requirements				1,000		1,600		2,000		2,400
Lot Size	250	Scheduled Receipts		500								
Type	M	Projected On-Hand	200									
		Net Requirements						Given data				
		Planned Order Receipts						(Do not change it!)				
		Planned Order Releases										

In the left-hand side of the table we are given information that governs how MRP will be calculated for this particular item. In descending order we see that this item has a 1-week lead time (LT), a lot size of 250, and that this is an "M" or "make" item (Type of item). Here are the descriptions of the row headings found in the third column of the table.

- Gross Requirements: The total of independent demand (**master production schedule**) and dependent demand (MRP calculated) for a component before the netting of on-hand inventory and scheduled receipts.

- <u>Scheduled Receipts</u>: An open, confirmed, and committed purchase order or production order that has an assigned due date. These differ from planned order receipts, which are merely computer-generated suggestions, and not yet opened, confirmed, and committed to purchasing and production schedules.
- <u>Projected On-Hand</u>: Current **inventory status** (week zero) and inventory balance projected into the future. It is the running sum of on-hand inventory minus requirements plus scheduled receipts and planned orders.
- <u>Net Requirements</u>: the requirements for a part or an assembly derived by taking gross requirements for the period and subtracting the sum of the previous period's projected on-hand balance and the current period's scheduled receipts. (If this number is less than zero, then simply put zero.)
- <u>Planned Order</u>: A computer-generated suggested order, greater than or equal to net requirements, divisible by the designated lot size. Typically, planned orders for "buy" items **"graduate"** to become **actual purchase orders** once a buyer reviews and approves them. Planned orders for "make" items become **actual production orders** once a production planner has reviewed and approved them. In MRP worksheets and systems, these approved purchase orders and production orders show up as scheduled receipts.
  - *Planned Order Receipts:* The planned receipt date and quantity of planned orders. Planned order receipts differ from scheduled receipts in that they have not been "graduated" or released by a buyer or planner (not yet opened, confirmed, and committed).
  - *Planned Order Releases:* The planned release date (to a supplier or to production) of planned orders. Each planned order release quantity and date will correspond to a planned order receipt quantity and date, offset by the lead time. Planned order receipts and releases are like two sides of the same coin (the coin being planned orders).

MRP Process Steps for Top-Level Items

With the above descriptions, we are now ready to review the steps required to fill in all the data in this MRP sheet. Before enumerating the steps, we must first emphasize the following points.

- **Do not change any data in the gross requirements row** as this is given data and must not be changed in order to properly complete this worksheet.
- **Do not change any data in the scheduled receipts row** as this is given data and must not be changed in order to properly complete this worksheet.
- **Do not change the initial "On Hand" quantity** which is given before the first week of the worksheet. (You will compute projected on-hand quantities for all dated weeks in the worksheet.)

The steps for the top-level assembly are as follows:

1. **Compute net requirements** in the first week (gross requirements minus the sum of the previous period's projected on-hand balance and the current

period's scheduled receipts). Note that if this number is zero then net requirements for that week is simply zero.

2. **Determine planned order receipts** in the first week.

- If there are no lot-sizing restrictions, then planned order receipts will equal net requirements.
- If there are lot-sizing restrictions, then planned receipts must be greater than or equal to net requirements **and** divisible by the lot size.

3. **Determine planned order releases** in the first week (equal to planned order receipts, but offset or pulled back by the number of lead time (LT) periods.

4. **Compute projected on-hand balance** in the first week (previous period's projected on-hand plus the current period's scheduled receipts and planned order receipts minus the current period's gross requirements).

5. Repeat steps 1–4 for each week.

Top-Level Assembly Example

Toy Car			On Hand	1-Aug	8-Aug	15-Aug	22-Aug	29-Aug	5-Sep	12-Sep	19-Sep	26-Sep
LT (wks)	1	Gross Requirements				1,000		1,600		2,000		2,400
Lot Size	250	Scheduled Receipts		500								
Type	M	Projected On-Hand	200	700	700	200	200	100	100	100	100	200
		Net Requirements				300		1,400		1,900		2,300
		Planned Order Receipts				500		1,500		2,000		2,500
		Planned Order Releases			500		1,500		2,000		2,500	

Now that we have outlined the process that MRP follows, we are ready to walk through the steps with our toy car top-level assembly.

1. Compute net requirements in the first week (1-Aug).

   ➤ Action Taken: **Input zero** (or leave cell blank). There were no gross requirements in the first week, so net requirements will also be zero.

2. Determine planned order receipts.

   ➤ Action Taken: **Input zero** (or leave cell blank). There were no net requirements in the first week, so planned order receipts will also be zero.

3. Determine planned order releases.

   ➤ Action Taken: **Nothing**. Actually, planned order releases for the first week (1-Aug) will correspond to the planned order receipts from the second week (8-Aug) due to the 1-week lead time for this item. In other words, we must first see if there are any planned order receipts in the second week (8-Aug) before we can input the proper value—zero in this case—into planned order releases for the first week.

4. Compute projected on-hand balance.

   ➢ Action Taken: **Input 700**. Following the detailed description in step 4 above, we get 200 + 500 + 0 – 0 = **700** (previous week's on-hand plus the current period's scheduled receipts plus current period's planned order receipts minus current week's gross requirements).

Now let's step forward a few weeks and do the same calculations for week 3 (15-Aug). This will give us more variety, more opportunity to see how lead time and lot sizing rules come into play.

5. Compute net requirements for week 3 (15-Aug).

   ➢ Action Taken: **Input 300**, derived from 1,000 – 700 – 0 (gross requirements minus previous week's on-hand balance – current week's scheduled receipts).

6. Determine planned order receipts.

   ➢ Action Taken: **Input 500**. Since there is a lot-sizing restriction of 250 units, we must input the minimum value which is greater than or equal to the net requirements of 300 and divisible by 250.[70] That number is 500.

7. Determine planned order releases.

   ➢ Action Taken: **Input 500 in week 2** (8-Aug). With a 1-week lead time, the planned order releases must be input into the field which is one week before the planned order receipts (15-Aug). Think of it this way. With a 1-week lead time, in order for completed production units to be received week 3 (planned order receipts) the units must be released to production in week 2 (planned order releases).

8. Compute projected on-hand balance.

   ➢ Action Taken: **Input 200**, derived from 700 + 0 + 500 – 1,000 (previous week's on-hand balance plus current week's scheduled receipts plus current week's planned order receipts minus current week's gross requirements).

Be careful in this process! You should note that projected on-hand balance is the last item computed in this process, even though planned order receipts and planned order releases appear lower in the worksheet. Make sure you focus on walking through these steps as numbered and not as the titles appear in the worksheet.

---

[70] Lot-sizing restrictions are production (or purchase) order policies which say, in effect, "We're not going to produce any units unless we can produce in increments of 250 (or whatever the number may be).

MRP Process Steps for Components (or "child" items)

The process for filling out an MRP worksheet for the components or "child" items in the bill of material is nearly identical to the steps above. The only difference is that *we must first compute gross requirements* from the direct "parent" item *before* we proceed with step 1. For the top-level assembly, gross requirements typically come from a combination of sales forecast and customer orders. However, for child items, gross requirements are computed as follows:

- Take the planned order releases (quantities by date) for the direct parent item and multiply those quantities by the number of child items required per parent item (from the bill of materials).

Component Example

For our example we will use the wheel assembly. It is both a "parent" and a "child" item—a parent to the axle and wheel and a child to the toy car (top-level assembly).

Toy Car			On Hand	1-Aug	8-Aug	15-Aug	22-Aug	29-Aug	5-Sep	12-Sep	19-Sep	26-Sep
LT (wks)	1	Gross Requirements				1,000		1,600		2,000		2,400
Lot Size	250	Scheduled Receipts		500								
Type	M	Projected On-Hand	200	700	700	200	200	100	100	100	100	200
		Net Requirements				300		1,400		1,900		2,300
		Planned Order Receipts				500		1,500		2,000		2,500
		Planned Order Releases			500		1,500		2,000		2,500	

Wheel Assembly			On Hand	1-Aug	8-Aug	15-Aug	22-Aug	29-Aug	5-Sep	12-Sep	19-Sep	26-Sep
LT (wks)	1	Gross Requirements		-	1,000	-	3,000	-	4,000	-	5,000	-
Lot Size	800	Scheduled Receipts										
Type	M	Projected On-Hand	1,500	1,500	500	500	700	700	700	700	500	500
		Net Requirements					2,500		3,300		4,300	
		Planned Order Receipts					3,200		4,000		4,800	
		Planned Order Releases				3,200		4,000		4,800		

Recall from our bill of material above that there are two wheel assemblies for each toy car. Therefore, to compute gross requirements for the wheel assembly we take the planned order releases for the toy car—the direct parent of the wheel assembly—and we multiply those quantities by two and input the product of these factors into the gross requirements row of the wheel assembly (as seen in the graphic above).

Just to be thorough, we should work this process through one more level in the bill of material. Below we see the complete MRP worksheet table for the wheel assembly and the wheel. The planned order releases for the wheel assembly are multiplied by two and input into the gross requirements row for the wheel. Once done, we can fill out the remainder of the wheel's MRP table.

Take note that our disciplined and precise MRP thought process does not ask, "How many wheels are there per toy car assembly?" Rather, it asks, "How many wheel assemblies are there per toy car?" and then, "How many wheels per wheel assembly?" MRP calculations follow this disciplined, step-by-step, level-by–level methodical process.

Wheel Assembly			On Hand	1-Aug	8-Aug	15-Aug	22-Aug	29-Aug	5-Sep	12-Sep	19-Sep	26-Sep
LT (wks)	1	Gross Requirements		-	1,000	-	3,000	-	4,000	-	5,000	-
Lot Size	800	Scheduled Receipts										
Type	M	Projected On-Hand	1,500	1,500	500	500	700	700	700	700	500	500
		Net Requirements					2,500		3,300		4,300	
		Planned Order Receipts					3,200		4,000		4,800	
		Planned Order Releases				3,200		4,000		4,800		

Wheel			On Hand	1-Aug	8-Aug	15-Aug	22-Aug	29-Aug	5-Sep	12-Sep	19-Sep	26-Sep
LT (wks)	2	Gross Requirements		-	-	6,400	-	8,000	-	9,600	-	-
Lot Size	500	Scheduled Receipts		3,000								
Type	M	Projected On-Hand	1,000	4,000	4,000	100	100	100	100	-	-	-
		Net Requirements				2,400		7,900		9,500		
		Planned Order Receipts				2,500		8,000		9,500		
		Planned Order Releases		2,500		8,000		9,500				

Output from MRP will drive purchasing and production decisions. At times, the master production schedule may need to be adjusted when purchasing and production cannot support the material and capacity requirements from MRP. In such cases, MRP becomes an iterative process, adjusting the MPS until it can be fully supported.

Bill of Material Considerations

BOM Accuracy

The toy car examples above are quite simple as we are dealing with a simple 3-level bill of material. Contrast that with the bill of material for Boeing 787 Dreamliner where there are thousands upon thousands of components and many, many levels. When all the BOM structures are properly set up and when inventory data is accurate, MRP can be an extremely powerful tool to help organizations manage their complex material planning challenges. Needless to say, MRP is very data intensive and MRP systems have exceedingly high standards for data accuracy (well over 99% accuracy) in order to be effective.

Single Bill of Material Database is Critical

The bill of material is central to a company. Materials are ordered based on the BOM. Product cost is calculated based on the BOM. Production and supplier schedules are connected to the BOM. Product features, important to marketing and engineering, are tied to the BOM. In large corporations, where the uses of the BOM may vary across departments, there is a strong temptation to create department-specific BOMs to meet those diverse needs. However, wise companies put forth the effort to make sure there is a single bill of material database for the entire company and that the bills of material contained therein meet the diverse needs of all internal users.

Yes, this is an abstract discussion for most of you. Think of it this way. How much confusion in the Christian world is there because of the multiple versions of the Bible and even more interpretations of the same? Multiple bill of material databases are kind of like having multiple Bibles within an organization. A single bill of material database provides "one version of the truth" which greatly aids in keeping unity within an organization.

Bill of Material Change Control and Managing a BOM Cutover

Strict cross-functional controls must be put in place to keep all concerned parties "on the same page" with respect to BOMs. Bills of material are living documents that change over a product's lifecycle. Most manufacturers have some sort of "change control board" (CCB) process for reviewing, approving and preparing for all changes to the bill of material. A detailed discussion of CCB management is beyond the scope of this book, but perhaps the following scenario will provide some sufficient food for thought.

How should an organization handle the transition to a new component in one of its products? Suppose a computer manufacturer wants to switch to a new disk drive supplier, one with better quality and performance. Let's suppose that they also have a two months' supply of the current disk drives. Let's further suppose that their savvy customers know this change is coming. When should they make the transition to the new disk drives? Marketing, engineering, and quality assurance might want to cut over immediately to keep customers happy and minimize quality risks. On the other hand, finance and purchasing might want to use existing inventory to minimize scrap costs. Who wins? This is where a change control board comes in. A change control board—a committee composed of all internal stakeholders, with potentially conflicting interests—meets and determines how such decisions are handled.

Information (Supply Chain) Systems

The discussions on MRP and BOMs above are fairly technical and comprise merely one area within a larger environment of supply chain management systems. When we look at all the systems required to run an organization, especially a large multi-national manufacturing organization, we may feel a bit overwhelmed at the scope of data, information, and transactions contained therein. We may ask, "Isn't there an easier way to keep track of all these business transactions? Is all the effort to set up and organize such systems really worth it?" The simple answer is, "Yes."

At the end of the June 21, 2003 Worldwide Leadership Training Meeting, President Gordon B. Hinckley posed a similar question to Church leaders (stake presidents and bishops, in particular) who had been given counsel on how to best manage their many, many responsibilities.

> As I have been listening with you, a question has arisen in my mind as I believe it has in each of yours. That question is, "How can I find the time to do it all?" Let me say that there is never enough time to do it all. There is so much more than any of us can singlehandedly give attention to.

I think I know something of this. I have been where many of you are today. There is only one way you can get it done. That is to follow the direction which the Lord gave Joseph Smith. To him He said, "Organize yourselves; prepare every needful thing" (D&C 88:119).

This counsel highlights the connection between getting organized and being productive, getting as much done as possible. Information technology is crucial to organizing the work of a vibrant business.

Enterprise Resource Planning

Question: What is enterprise resource planning (ERP)?

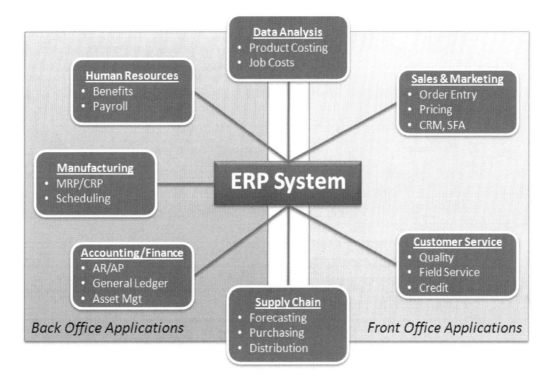

ERP is "a framework of system modules for organizing, defining, and standardizing the business processes necessary to effectively plan and control an organization so the organization can use its internal knowledge to seek external advantage."[71]

An **ERP system** is an integrated information system or set of applications that serves all departments within an enterprise. ERP evolved out of the manufacturing industry and MRP systems, and implies the use of packaged software—usable by many customers—versus custom software written for one customer. ERP systems typically include software for manufacturing, order entry, accounts receivable and payable, general ledger, purchasing, warehousing, transportation and human resources. Major ERP vendors include SAP, Oracle (PeopleSoft and J.D. Edwards), SSA Global (Baan) and Microsoft.

---

[71] APICS Online Dictionary, 12th edition, www.apics.org.

Question: What are front office applications and back office applications?

ERP applications are often classified as "front office" and "back office" applications. Front office applications are those software modules that face customers directly. They provide functionality and data necessary to take orders, configure products, and provide effective service and support to customers. Modules include customer relationship management (CRM), sales force automation (SFA), customer support and field service.

Back office applications do not interact directly with customers. They provide functionality for internal operations such as inventory control, production and all of the supply chain activities associated with procuring goods, services and raw materials.

You should note that in service operations, the "front room" is where the customer comes into contact with the service operation. The "back room" refers to the part of the service operation that is completed without direct customer contact.

Supply Chain Macro Processes and System Transactions

Question: What are the macro supply chain processes which are supported by supply chain systems?

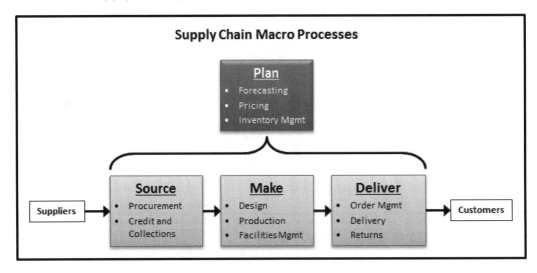

Supply chain systems are designed to support the sourcing, making, and delivering of goods and services, as well as all related planning activities. These basic macro processes are part of virtually all organizations' supply chains, whether they be service firms or manufacturers.

Question: What are a firm's basic systems transactions related to sourcing, making, and delivering of goods and services?

The diagram below shows both the physical (material) flows and information flows that are associated with the system transactions which support sourcing, making, and delivering of goods and services.

The basic supply chain transactions depicted on the next page are:

- <u>Purchase orders</u>, which support **sourcing** from suppliers.
- <u>Production orders</u>, which support **making** of goods and services.
- <u>Transfer orders</u>, which support **delivering** to inter-plant customers.
- <u>Sales orders</u>, which support **delivering** to customers.

If you think about it, systems transactions occur every time you make a purchase from a retailer, although most retailer-to-customer transactions are less formal. There are some small differences, however. When consumers make retail purchases, they do not first create a formal purchase order in some sort of system. However, the retailer will log a sales (order) transaction which is recorded in its computerized inventory system. You should also note that purchase orders and sales orders are two systems transactions—one on the customer's system and one on the supplier's system—that relate to the same movement of material.

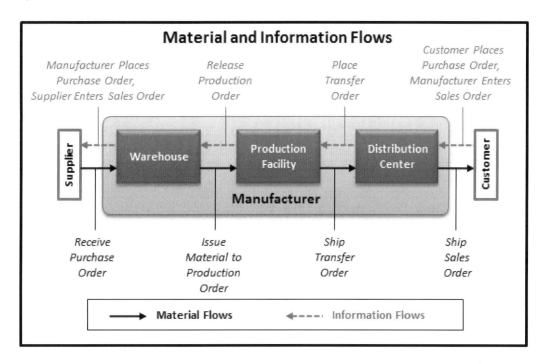

Master Data – Foundation for System Transactions

<u>Question</u>: What is master data and how does it relate to system transactions?

Master data refers to that permanent information which is found in a master file or main reference file. Each ERP module requires a significant amount of setup in order to support the myriad transactions that correspond to business processes. (The list above of basic supply chain system transactions only begins to scratch the surface of the many transactions that are captured in an ERP system.) This setup is performed within master files, which files are maintained on a periodic basis. Examples of master files include

- **Item Master**—a file which contains descriptive data (size, unit of measure, etc.) and control values (lead time, lot size, etc.) for an item.
- **Location Master**—a file which contains all possible inventory locations.

- **Bill of Material**—a product structure record which defines the relationship of one component to its immediate parent item and governs how material requirements are computed.
- **Routing Sheet**—contains a listing of all the operations to be performed within a given process.
- **Approved Vendor List** (AVL)—a list of suppliers which have been approved through the firm's formal vendor selection process.
- **Vendor Master**—contains the name, address, terms, quality rating, and shipping method for each vendor.
- **Customer File**—contains contact information, discount schedule, credit rating, billing and ship-to addresses, and other related information.
- **Employee Master**—contains pertinent information on each employee such as hire date, birth date, title, wage, and job class.

Think of it this way, master files are like the streets in a city and transactions are like the driving routes individual cars take. Master files govern how transactions will take place just as streets govern where the cars can go.

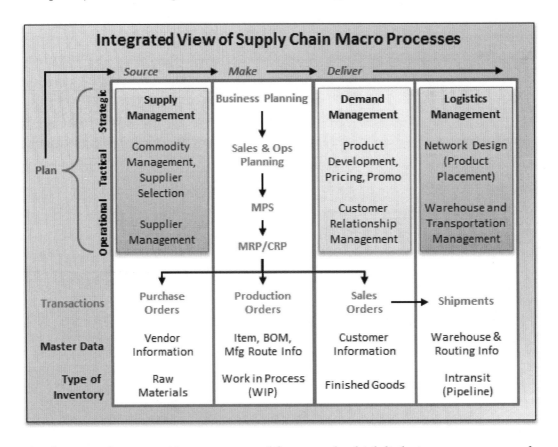

The diagram above provides a conceptual framework which links inventory type and master data titles with corresponding supply chain system transactions. Additionally, it attempts to connect some of the planning concepts in this chapter (MRP) with some of those discussed in other chapters (business planning, sales and operations planning, master production scheduling, supply management, demand management, and logistics management).

When companies make the effort to organize business processes and supporting supply chain systems (which collect, process, and disseminate information), employees can be more productive in their planning, decision making, and operational control processes. Lack of such a foundation can bring an organization to its knees, while business process and information technology excellence can facilitate rapid and sustained growth.[72]

Chapter Summary

Below are some of the main points you should have garnered from the study of this chapter.

- **Output from the MPS drives MRP**, which calculates requirements for dependent demand items. MRP output drives purchasing and production decisions.
- **MRP is highly dependent on data accuracy, particularly in the bill of material**.
- **Standardized data and systems are essential to the successful management and growth of a business**. Adequate effort invested in system and master data setup and maintenance will result in opportunities to automate business processes and system transactions, helping to improve productivity.

---

[72] Wal-Mart, Dell, Cisco Systems, and Oracle all provide great examples of how companies have effectively used information technology to support both organic growth and growth through acquisition.

Chapter 11

JIT AND LEAN PRODUCTION

*You and I can put Christ at the center of our lives and become one with Him as He is one with the Father (see John 17:20-23). We could **begin by stripping everything out of our lives and then putting it back together in priority order** with the Savior at the center....In this way the essential will not be crowded out of our lives by the merely good, and things of lesser value will take a lower priority or fall away altogether.*

Elder D. Todd Christofferson[73]

A life of lasting value is based on eliminating non-essential activities and putting into our lives—in priority order—those things which will help us become one with the Savior. In similar fashion, JIT and lean production have a central focus on eliminating non-value-added activities (waste) and only doing those things which the customer will value.

Chapter Objectives

Successful organizations relentlessly seek for ways to eliminate waste and focus on activities that are of the greatest value to their customers—**where value is defined as a service or change in a product's configuration such that a customer would be willing to pay for that service or change**. This is the essence of the JIT and lean philosophies and will form the foundation of our discussion in this chapter. After studying this chapter you should be able to

1. Explain the history and philosophy of JIT and lean production.
2. Identify the "seven wastes" as outlined by Taiichi Ohno.
3. Describe the JIT philosophy on production layout and how it differs from process and product layouts.
4. Describe "pull" production and how a kanban system helps synchronize production to meet customer needs.
5. Contrast JIT with MRP, how they differ and how they can work together.
6. Describe value stream mapping and calculate process cycle efficiency (PCE).
7. Calculate optimal product quantity and describe how reduction in setup costs lead to efficient small-batch production.

---

[73] D. Todd Christofferson, "Always Remember Him," BYU-Idaho Devotional, January 2009 (emphasis added).

8. Calculate the size of kanban containers and number of kanban cards required in a given production environment.

History and Philosophy of JIT and Lean Production

Some believe that the concept of "lean" production is merely the latest buzzword to represent the Just-in-Time philosophy of production and operations. While pieces of this philosophy have been around for many, many years—like interchangeable parts (Ely Whitney, 1799) and the assembly line (Henry Ford, 1910), JIT really came into its own in the automobile industry in Japan after World War II. Clearly, the poster child for JIT and lean production is Toyota Motor Company with its world famous Toyota Production System (TPS, formerly known as "Just-in-Time Production").

Question: How do JIT, lean, and TPS differ? Or are they all the same?

If there is any distinction between JIT, lean, and TPS, it would be in each one's primary focus.

- JIT emphasizes the identification and elimination of waste.
- Lean builds upon JIT and emphasizes only performing activities that add value for the customer.
- TPS is Toyota's particular brand of JIT and emphasizes continuous improvement through employee learning and empowerment.

No matter what you call it, JIT "encompasses the successful execution of all manufacturing activities required to produce a final product, from design engineering to delivery, and includes all stages of conversion from raw material onward. The primary elements of Just-in-Time are to have only the required inventory when needed; to improve quality to zero defects; to reduce lead times by reducing setup times, queue lengths, and lot sizes; to incrementally revise the operations themselves; and to accomplish these activities at minimum cost."[74]

Question: Who was Taiichi Ohno and what are his seven wastes?

Taiichi Ohno was a Toyota engineer, considered to be the father of TPS, who identified seven major sources of waste.

1. **Overproduction**—Producing more than is ordered or producing early (before it is ordered) is usually caused by inflexible or unreliable processes.
2. **Queues**—Inventory waiting to be processed is caused by imbalanced, poorly designed, or unreliable processes, or poor production layout.
3. **Unnecessary transportation**—This increases the risk of damaged goods and is often caused by poor layout.
4. **Overprocessing**—This occurs when complex processes are used when simple ones are adequate to satisfy customers.
5. **Unnecessary inventory**—Excess inventory at all levels—raw materials, WIP, and FG—is often used to mask a multitude of problems and waste.

[74] American Production and Inventory Control Society, Online Dictionary, 12th edition, www.apics.org.

6. **Unnecessary motion**—Caused by poor product and process designs.
7. **Defects**—The ultimate waste because they consume labor, materials, and equipment that could have been used to make good products.

Question: What are the main JIT mechanisms which help in the identification and elimination of waste?

There are a number of JIT practices or mechanisms which were initially put in place by Toyota and other Japanese manufacturers. Some terms for these practices are listed below.

- **Andon**—A visual signaling system (an electronic number board) which provides visibility of the production floor status: **green** = running, **red** = stop, and **yellow** = needs attention. When team members (workers) encounter a problem on the floor they pull an **andon cord** which sends a visual signal (yellow light on the number board corresponding to their workstation) to inform team leaders of the problem. If the problem cannot be solved within a specified time, the yellow light is replaced with a red light and the production line stops until the problem is resolved.
- **Genba**—Refers to the place where value is created, like the factory floor. Doing a "*genba walk*" means going to "where the rubber meets the road" or where the process takes place and is often the best way to solve problems and find opportunities to eliminate waste and make other improvements.
- **Heijunka**—An approach to level production to match the planned rate of end product sales.
- **Jidoka**—The practice of stopping the production line when a defect occurs, thus bringing instant attention to the problem so it can be resolved as soon as possible.
- **Kaizen**—A continuous-improvement mindset, necessary for all levels of personnel, to eliminate waste in production methods.
- **Kanban**—A move card or container which authorizes production for a workstation within a "pull" production system. (Production is "pulled" through the system by end customer demand, thus eliminating overproduction.)
- **Poka-yoke**—Mistake-proofing techniques, in product or process design, which prevent errors. A simple example of the concept would be USB plug which can only be inserted one way. Components designed this same way eliminate errors in the assembly or production process.

Question: What are the 5 Ss and how do they improve the workplace?

The 5 Ss come from a series of Japanese words and embody the elements of an organized and effective operation. Roughly translated, here are the terms in English.

- **Sort**—Within the workplace, determine (sort) what is needed and what is not. Remove what is not needed. "*When in doubt, throw it out!*"
- **Straighten**—Put needed items in convenient places so they are readily available for work. "*A place for everything, and everything in its place.*"
- **Shine**—Clean the area and keep it clear of dirt, contamination, and clutter.

- **Standardize**—Remove variation from the process (tools, methods, and training) so that deviations are apparent and can be addressed quickly.
- **Sustain**—Train and develop attitudes to establish and maintain orderliness as part of the organization culture.

With the above foundation on JIT and lean history and philosophy, we are now ready to discuss four specific areas: (1) JIT and production layout, (2) JIT and inventory, (3) value stream mapping, and (4) JIT-related calculations.

JIT and Facility Layout

Facility layout has a huge bearing on the organization's level of waste. Poorly designed layouts can contribute to long wait times and excessive inventory, transportation, and motion. Not surprisingly, JIT layouts focus on flexibility and the reduction of inventory, movement, and labor; on producing what is needed to meet customer demand as quickly as possible.

Requirements Cellular Layouts

In many ways, a cellular layout is a hybrid layout, combining the flexibility of a functional layout with the efficiency of a product layout. (You may want to review the descriptions of these layouts in chapter two in order to better understand the benefits of a cellular layout.)

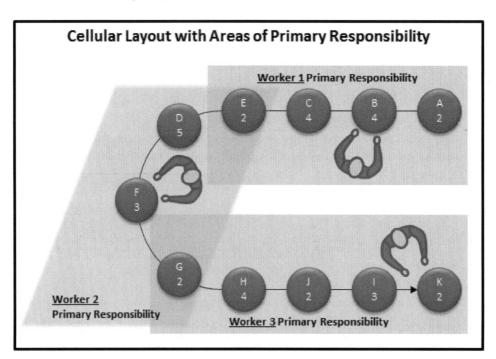

The following requirements must be met in order to properly set up a cellular layout.

- Identify product families where manufacturing process steps similar for all products within the family.
- Set aside (dedicate) specific equipment and personnel to the manufacture of these products.

- Cross train personnel within the cell so that each can perform all the tasks. This helps balance the work cell and gives more variety to the job of the workers.

Suppose we continued with the Lenny's Lawnmower line balancing example in Chapter 2, except now Lenny wants to broaden his product offering to include a variety of lawnmowers. In order to strike an optimal balance between efficiency (lower cost) and flexibility (more lawnmowers), Lenny should give serious consideration to replacing his production line set up with manufacturing cells to produce his products (as depicted in the graphic above). Not all lawn mowers would require the same assembly steps, so it would be difficult to support all lawnmower models in a traditional assembly line layout. By using a cellular layout, process steps could be adjusted according to each lawnmower, and cross-trained workers would keep the cell in balance.

JIT and Inventory

Perhaps the biggest waste of all is excess inventory, which is often a result of overproduction and is a mask which potentially covers many other problems.

As represented in the graphic above, lowering the water (reducing inventory) exposes problems and waste that a company can fix or eliminate (scrap, long setup times, poor quality, supplier issues, design issues, etc.)

The JIT philosophy teaches of the evils of excess inventory and advocates the reduction of inventory in order to expose, and then fix, problems. Reducing inventory—much like repentance—is not easy, but it is exceedingly better than doing nothing. Great companies possess the individual and organizational humility, courage, confidence, and strength to confront the difficult brutal facts of their reality and develop long-term solutions to their problems, thereby capitalizing on many opportunities.

Question: What is a "pull" system and how does it work?

The "pull" system was developed in contrast to the MRP "push" system. Whether for production, material control, or distribution, a "pull" system requires a pull signal to be received from a "downstream" operation or customer in order to authorize the launch of production or movement of material. In a pure pull system, the end customer initiates the action by placing an order, which in turn causes more "pull" signals to be sent to "upstream" operations or inventory points.

A **Subway sandwich shop** is an example of a pull production system (similar to the graphic below). What happens when a customer orders a sandwich? Production commences as inventory is "pulled" from the point of use—containers at the sandwich counter. When containers are empty they become pull signals to issue more containers from central storage (fridge, etc.). When items (in central storage) hit their reorder point, pull signals are sent to Subway's distribution center or suppliers, authorizing replenishment materials to be sent. In summary, customer orders trigger a chain reaction of material movement all the way up the supply chain. This pull process keeps inventories low while enabling a responsive production process that can meet a great variety of customer requirements.

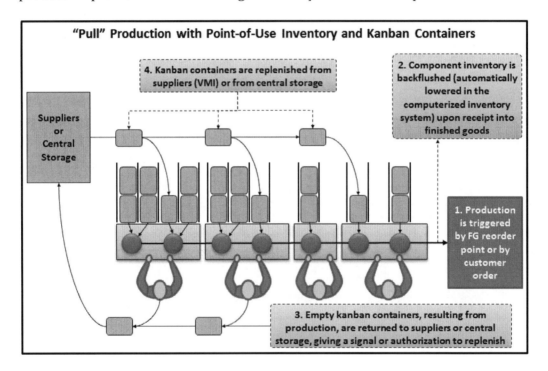

Question: What are kanbans?

Kanbans are visible cards attached to containers that authorize the movement or production of materials in response to a downstream "pull" signal. Each kanban tells you what to produce, when to produce it, and how much to produce.

Question: What is a "push" system and how does it work?

In contrast to the "pull" system is the "push" system, usually driven by master production schedules and MRP output versus actual customer orders. A pull system, with point-of-use inventory storage, works great for products made up of low-value components. However, when producing items with high-value components, it may not be a good idea to have component inventory at the point of use where it can easily disappear through shrinkage (theft). Instead, companies will launch production orders (based on MRP output) and "push" inventory kits into the production floor.

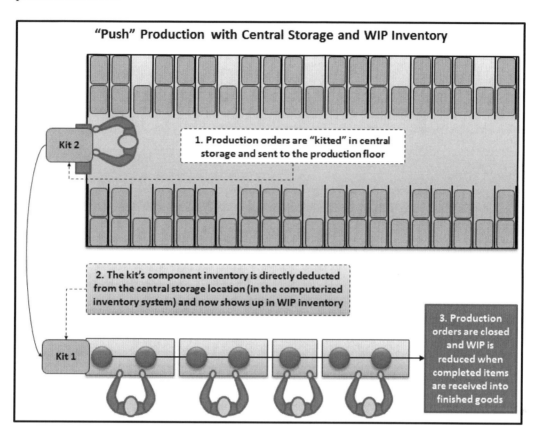

A push system, where inventory is discretely issued, makes it easier to keep track of inventory during the production process because movements of material are recorded in the computerized inventory system as they happen (called "direct-deduct" inventory transaction processing), not just at the end of production.

Question: Are JIT (pull production) and MRP (push production) mutually exclusive, or can they work together?

In reality, companies will often use a mix of "pull" and "push" production methods, along with their associated methods of tracking inventory. In such cases, part of the bill of material for an item's production (the expensive components) may be tracked via a discrete material issue to a production order kit—with a corresponding inventory transaction immediately recorded in the computerized system. Meanwhile, the low-cost components may be stored at the point of use in kanban containers, and inventory will be "automatically relieved" within the computerized inventory system, via a process called "backflushing," at the end of production.

An example of this could be an assembly line for a computer manufacturer that discretely issues CPUs or memory to production order kits from a secure central location, wanting to maintain higher visibility and stricter controls over such components. On the other hand, components like computer chassis, screws, fasteners, stickers and other low-cost items will be stored at the point of use and not tracked discretely. Rather, these low-cost components will be accounted for when the completed products are moved into finished goods and backflushing takes place in the computerized inventory system.

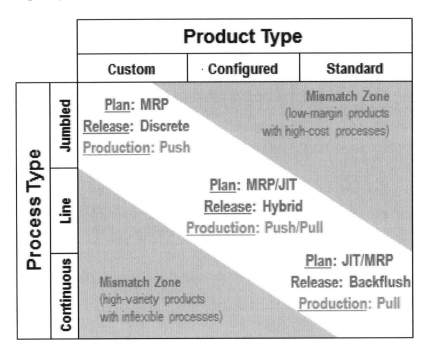

The simplified product-process diagram above shows the relationships between process type and appropriate methods for materials planning, materials release to production, and production triggers. As can be seen, even in cases where production is triggered by a "pull" signal, MRP may be used for planning purposes, to line up supplies of long lead time items; in other words, to give greater visibility into future demands of components than merely a just-in-time signal from an empty kanban container. The *difference* here is that using forecasts to drive MRP is a method for *planning materials into the future* whereas kanban is a system for *managing short-term production schedules or triggers* for execution.

The Bullwhip Effect

Push and pull systems have relevance beyond the four walls of any given company as they play an important part in inter-company coordination. Poor coordination puts companies at risk of experiencing the harmful consequences of "the bullwhip effect." (Note that a discussion on the bullwhip effect might be more relevant in the next section of this book, "Linking Supply Chains," but since JIT methods can help fight this phenomenon, the discussion is included here.)

<u>Question</u>:   What is the bullwhip effect?

The bullwhip effect is a phenomenon that occurs when a small change in demand at the end of the supply chain triggers larger and larger fluctuations in demand further up the supply chain. In a way, it's kind of like the "telephone game" where information gets exaggerated as it moves from one person to another. The resulting fluctuations in demand signals can result in the extremes of abrupt supply shortages or backorders to extreme levels of excess inventory that can take years to trim down.

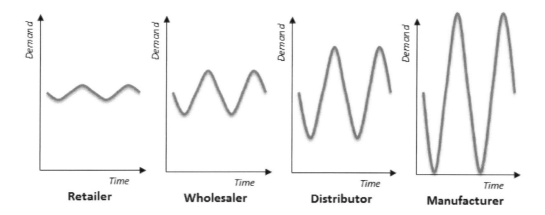

The primary causes of the bullwhip effect are the slow and serial nature of communicating demand to companies up the supply chain and the transportation delays of moving product down the chain. Other factors can exacerbate this phenomenon; things such as simple fear, short gaming,[75] promotions, quarter-end sales incentives, quantity discounts, and large production quantities.

Ways to fight the bullwhip effect include instituting every-day low prices (EDLP) instead of promotions, collaborating and sharing point-of-sale data with suppliers in order to "pull" inventory to the customer, producing in smaller batch sizes, and rationing short products based on historical demand patterns and not on inflated customer orders.

Value Stream Mapping

Value stream mapping is a lean-management method that helps organizations improve process efficiency. At Toyota this method is known as "material and information flow mapping." In value stream mapping an organization draws the "current state" of a given process and separates all events into "value-added" or "non-value-added" activities, as depicted in the lead-time ladder in the graphic below (value-added activities are measured in seconds, non-value-added activities are measured in days). Once the current state is documented the organization designs or draws a more efficient "future state" for the same process, eliminating as much waste as possible. The organization then works toward implementing or realizing this more efficient future state vision.

---

[75] Short gaming is the practice of customers inflating their demand when there is a supply shortage, hoping to receive what they really need. If many customers engage in this practice, then industry demand can be grossly overstated, further exacerbating the bullwhip effect, leading to more "shortages" and ultimately much excess inventory.

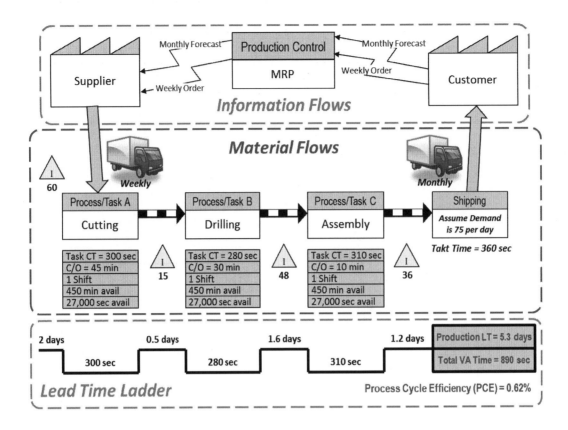

JIT-Related Calculations

Question: What is PCE (or process cycle efficiency) and how is it calculated?

Process cycle efficiency is a metric that tells how much of a process is dedicated to value-added activities. In the graphic above, where there is a total of 890 seconds of value-added activities and 5.3 days of non-value-added events, the process efficiency is 0.62%. To derive this number we'll follow these two simple steps:

1. Convert times to the same unit of measure. In this case we'll convert days into seconds. Hence, 5.3 days of non-value-added time is equal to 143,100 seconds (5.3 days x 1 shift per day x 7.5 hours per shift x 60 minutes per hour x 60 seconds per minute, for a total of 143,100 seconds).
2. Divide the value-added time by the non-value-added time: 890 ÷ 143,100 = 0.006219 or roughly 0.62%. Hence, in this example less than one percent of the production lead time is spent on value-added activities.

With this calculated PCE, along with other information on other process times (individual tasks cycle times, change-over times, available times per shift, and queue times) the organization has a clear picture of the current state and can now begin the process of brainstorming ways to eliminate waste as they design the future state for this process. This is the essence of value stream mapping.

Question: What is the **production order quantity** model (POQ), how does it relate to JIT, and how is it calculated?

The production order quantity model is used to determine the optimal size of a production run. It is similar to the EOQ model (economic order quantity, discussed in Inventory Management chapter) with one important difference. The EOQ model assumes that all inventory associated with an order will be received at the same time, like in a purchase transaction. The POQ model, on the other hand, assumes that a continuous flow of material will be received and gradually built up during the production period. The graphic below depicts this fundamental difference.

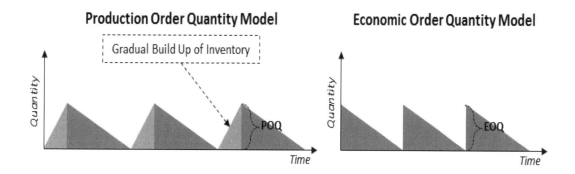

Here is the formula for calculating POQ.

$$POQ = \sqrt{\frac{2DS}{H[1 - (d/p)]}}$$

Where

D = annual demand
S = setup cost
H = holding cost per unit per year
p = daily production rate
d = daily demand or usage rate

POQ Example 1

Ernie's Engines assembles a large variety of small engines that are purchased by lawn and garden and snow-removal equipment producers. Annual demand for their most popular engine is 10,000 units per year, which translates to a daily demand rate of 40 units (assuming 250 working days per year). Setup costs are $30 and annual holding costs are $25 per unit. They are able to produce 100 units per day. Given this information, what is the optimal production order quantity?

$$POQ = \sqrt{\frac{2 \times 10,000 \times 30}{25[1 - (40/100)]}} = 200$$

Plugging this same data into Excel gives us the following formula and answer.

B9		f_x	=SQRT((2*B2*B3)/(B4*(1-(B5/B6))))		
	A	B	C	D	E
1	**Input Data**				
2	Annual demand	10,000			
3	Setup cost	$ 30			
4	Annual holding cost	$ 25			
5	Daily demand	40			
6	Daily production	100			
7					
8	**Answer**				
9	Production Order Quantity	200			

Question: Why are setup costs key to JIT production?

As discussed in the Inventory Management chapter, setup cost has a huge bearing on the economic order quantity. The larger the setup cost, the higher the economic order quantity. The same is true for production order calculations. Hence, in a JIT environment, much effort is put into lowering setup costs so that it is economical to produce in small quantities (as depicted in the graphic below).

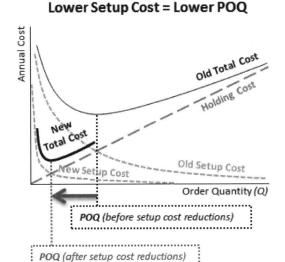

Reducing tear down and setup time reduces setup costs and make it economical for companies to produce in small batches and switch production from one item to another. To this end, Toyota pioneered the concept of "**single-minute exchange of dies**" (SMED),[76] which states that setups or production changeovers should take no more than 10 minutes. Small batches keep inventories low (hiding fewer problems) and improve flexibility—two hallmarks of JIT production. Reducing setup times is an excellent way to keep costs down and to improve productivity.

---

[76] Single-minute exchange of die is sometimes more accurately described as single-digit setup, meaning that setups should be completed within 10 minutes.

POQ Example 2

Returning to our *Ernie's Engines* example above, let's suppose one of Ernie's biggest customers, *Lenny's Lawnmowers*, wants to implement lean manufacturing in its nearby factory. As we saw in example 1, *Ernie's Engines* has an optimal production order quantity of 200 engines which currently takes 2 days. Lenny, with his new production process, would like Ernie to ship him 40 engines at a time. Assuming labor costs are $12 per hour to set up the production equipment, what does Ernie's new setup time have to be in order to economically produce engines in batches of 40 units?

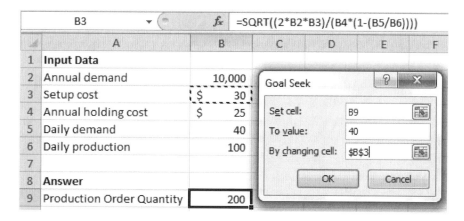

Perhaps the best way to solve the problem in this example is to use Excel's "Goal Seek" function. Even with this function this is going to take a few steps to get the right answer. (Goal Seek can be found by clicking on the "What-If" button in the "Data" tab in Excel.) We start by placing our cursor into cell B9 (the answer field for the POQ equation) and set that value to 40 (the 40 units that Lenny wants to receive with each shipment from Ernie). We also tell Goal Seek that we want to change cell B9 to a value of 40 by changing cell B3, the setup cost.

After clicking the "OK" button Excel changes the value of cell B3 to $1.20. This means that Ernie must reduce his setup costs from $30 to $1.20 if he is going to economically produce engines in batches of 40. How much time does this give them for setting up the production line? Six minutes.

$$Setup\ time = \frac{Setup\ cost}{Labor\ cost} = \frac{\$1.20}{\$12/hour} = \frac{1}{10}\ hour = 6\ minutes$$

If Ernie can find ways to reduce his setup time to six minutes, then it will be economical for him to produce and ship this engine in just-in-time quantities of 40 units as requested by Lenny.

Question: How do you calculate the required number of kanban containers?

With the above conceptual grounding in JIT production and reduced setup times, we are now ready to learn how to calculate the number of kanban containers that should be used in a given production environment. Below is the formula for determining this number.

$$y = \frac{Demand\ during\ leadtime + Safety\ stock}{Container\ size} = \frac{d \times LT + dLT(x)}{POQ} = \frac{dLT(1 + x)}{POQ}$$

Where

> y = number of kanbans (cards, containers, etc.)
> d = demand per unit of time (from downstream processes or customers)
> LT = lead time
> x = safety stock factor (a given percentage or unit of time divided by LT)
> POQ = production order quantity or size of the kanban container

Kanban Containers Example 1: Safety Stock a Percentage Buffer

The great work that *Ernie's Engines* is doing to support *Lenny's Lawnmowers* is really paying off as Lenny is seeing a sharp increase in demand due to his lower lead time and improved quality. As a result, the daily demand for Ernie's most popular engine jumps from 40 to 60 units per day. Based on these new demand numbers, Ernie wants to figure out how many kanban containers will be required to support his production and deliveries to Lenny. He is quoting a 3-day lead time and he wants to build in a 15% safety stock buffer, just in case. How many kanban containers will he need for this engine?

$$y = \frac{(60 \times 3) \times (1 + 0.15)}{40} = 5.18\ or\ 6\ kanban\ containers$$

B9		f_x	=(B2*B3*(1+B4))/B5	
	A	B	C	D
1	Assumptions			
2	Daily demand	60		
3	Production lead time (days)	3		
4	Safety stock factor	15%		
5	Kanban container size	40		
6				
7				
8	Answer			
9	Kanbans needed	5.18		

Since he cannot have a partial container, he rounds up 5.18 to the nearest whole number and determines that his kanban system will require six (6) containers. (The graphic above shows how this formula is input into Excel.)

Kanban Containers Example 2: Safety Stock a Time-Period Buffer (Days)

Let's look at this same problem again, except this time safety stock is given as a 1.5-day buffer instead of a 15% buffer. To convert this 1.5-day buffer to a percentage we must divide 1.5 days by the 3-day lead time (as seen in the graphic below). The result is a 50% safety stock buffer.

$$y = \frac{(60 \times 3) \times (1 + (1.5 \div 3))}{40} = \frac{180 \times 1.5}{40} = 6.75\ or\ 7\ kanban\ containers$$

When we apply the same formula as in the previous example—the only difference being with how we derived the safety stock percentage factor—we end up with 6.75 kanbans containers (shown below). And again, since we can't have a partial number of containers, we must round up to 7 containers.

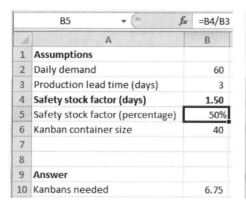

B5		f_x =B4/B3
	A	B
1	**Assumptions**	
2	Daily demand	60
3	Production lead time (days)	3
4	**Safety stock factor (days)**	1.50
5	Safety stock factor (percentage)	50%
6	Kanban container size	40
7		
8		
9	**Answer**	
10	Kanbans needed	6.75

B10		f_x =(B2*B3*(1+B5))/B6	
	A	B	C
1	**Assumptions**		
2	Daily demand	60	
3	Production lead time (days)	3	
4	**Safety stock factor (days)**	1.50	
5	Safety stock factor (percentage)	50%	
6	Kanban container size	40	
7			
8			
9	**Answer**		
10	Kanbans needed	6.75	

Chapter Summary

Below are some of the main points you should have garnered from the study of this chapter.

- **JIT, TPS, and lean production all focus on the elimination of waste**. The JIT philosophy came to its own in post-war Japan, with Toyota being the poster child for the movement. In recent decades many US corporations have implement JIT and lean production practices.
- Taiichi Ohno, a Toyota engineer and father of TPS, identified **seven major sources of waste**. Other JIT-related terms (Japanese words) and practices (5 Ss) have made it into the operations management lexicon in the US.
- **Cellular layouts** fit well with the JIT philosophies of having cross-trained employees, pull production, small batch sizes, and minimal inventory.
- **Reducing setup time (costs) is a key enabler to small-batch production**, a key tenet of JIT. Information technology makes it easier to implement multi-company JIT practices.

LINKING
SUPPLY CHAINS

Chapter 12

SUPPLY MANAGEMENT

The Lord my pasture will prepare
And feed me with a shepherd's care.
His presence will my wants supply,
And guard me with a watchful eye.
My noonday walks he will attend
And all my silent midnight hours defend.[77]

The story of Jacob in the Old Testament gives us an example of a righteous man who knew that the Lord is the ultimate, perfect supplier. Jacob acted with perfect uprightness in dealing with his unethical supplier, Laban—his uncle and the father of two of his wives.

In obedience to his father's command,[78] Jacob journeyed "to Padan-aram, to the house of Bethuel [his] mother's father"[79] to seek a wife. Upon arrival Jacob did not have much leverage, therefore he negotiated with Laban that after seven years of labor he would marry Rachel. However, he was not informed of the customs of the land, which is to say, that the eldest of the daughters must first be wed before the younger daughters may wed. Hence, because of his supplier's shiftiness, Jacob's total cost of acquisition—fourteen years versus seven years of labor, to marry Rachel—was much higher than he had anticipated. Such was life for Jacob working with an unethical supplier who had "changed [his] wages ten times"[80] over the many years of their relationship.

Without much leverage with his supplier Laban, Jacob knew that his only path to success was to rely wholly on the Lord. After 20 years of faithful and vigorous service, when it came time for him to return to Canaan, he dealt wisely and with inspiration to negotiate terms that would let him secure the best product (livestock) from his supplier (Laban). Such was Jacob's faith. No matter how difficult the supplier environment, no matter how justified he would have felt if he retaliated, Jacob knew that the Lord would make it possible for him to overcome these obstacles and have great success while remaining true to his principles.[81]

---

[77] Hymns of The Church of Jesus Christ of Latter-day Saints, #109.

[78] It's interesting to note that Jacob's mother Rebekah was instrumental in getting him to the house of Laban. In Genesis 27:43 she told him to "flee" to Laban's house and then in verse 46 she counseled with Isaac on what he should tell Jacob in their "PPI" which takes place early in the next chapter.

[79] Genesis 28:2

[80] Genesis 31:7, 41

[81] Genesis 31:8

Chapter Objectives

Ethics, negotiations, international business (local customs), acquisition costs and total cost of ownership are just a few of the important supply management concepts that Jacob learned in the process of working for and marrying Leah and Rachel. Moreover, he did not use his supplier's mercurial twists of temperament as justification for personal misconduct, but rather maintained his integrity as he learned to work and negotiate with skill and was ultimately blessed and prospered.

In this chapter we will cover some of the basic concepts and tools related to supply management. After reading this chapter you should be able to

1. Understand why purchasing is a critical part of a firm's operations.
2. Understand the process of supplier selection and compute a supplier-selection model using the factor-rating method.
3. Describe the strengths and weaknesses of the main sourcing strategies.
4. Describe the concepts of total cost of ownership.
5. Explain the importance of supplier relationship management.
6. Identify some of the leading associations for supply chain professionals.

Overview of Supply Management

Question: What is supply management?

Supply management embodies the methods and processes of modern corporate or institutional buying. This may be for the (1) purchasing of supplies for internal use referred to as indirect goods and services, (2) purchasing raw materials or components for the consumption during the manufacturing process, or (3) purchasing of goods for inventory to be resold as products in the distribution and retail process. In many organizations, acquisition or buying of services is called contracting, while that of goods is called purchasing or procurement.

Historically, supply management was not viewed as a concept of building a system of suppliers, but was based purely on cutting costs to generate a competitive advantage. Companies treated suppliers as a means to an end, and contracts were often founded solely on lowest price possible. This engendered an adversarial atmosphere, where companies would change suppliers more frequently than they typically do now. Over the past two or three decades—largely influenced by and modeled after the successes of Japanese manufacturers—American companies are placing more value on long-term relationships with fewer suppliers, where price is just one of many factors considered in a successful relationship with suppliers.

Question: What are the main components of supply management?

The supply management function of an organization is typically responsible for the following.

1. Work with personnel to identify needs for goods and services to be procured.
2. Identify potential sources of supply for the needed goods and services.

3. Evaluate and select suppliers.
4. Monitor and manage supplier performance (supplier development).
5. Streamline and make more effective the processes between the company and its suppliers (through automation, collaboration, etc.).
6. Learn about new technologies, goods and services offered by suppliers and channel that information within the company as appropriate.
7. Initiate value analyses, make-or-buy analyses, or other studies.

Question: Why is supply management so important to a company's success?

We need to look no further than the Toyota Motor Company for an example of why supply management is so important. In May 2010 Toyota paid a fine of $16.4 million to the Transportation Department because of the slow and unresponsive way in which it handled the recall of 2.3 million vehicles with sticky accelerator pedals.[82] Who made these pedals? Not Toyota, but rather, CTS, one of its key suppliers. Further investigation by Toyota revealed that many of its parts suppliers have been testing their products just once per year and not the four times per year that Toyota had thought. Perhaps better monitoring of its suppliers would have resulted in discovering the sticky accelerator pedal problem before it escalated into a recall that hurt its bottom line and its long-earned, once-unassailable reputation for outstanding product quality, reliability, and safety.

Question: How can effective supply management help a company's profits?

One simple example is through savings in purchasing. A dollar saved from reduced acquisition costs goes right to the bottom line whereas a dollar increase in revenue (from increased volume, not price increases) will only increase the bottom line in proportion to the company's net profit margin. To illustrate this point, let's look at a small retailer who has annual revenues of $20 million. The retailer spends 60% of its revenue on purchases and has a net profit margin of 4%. This retailer would like to increase its net profits and knows it can do so by lowering costs (Scenario #1 below) or raising revenue (Scenario #2 below).

Scenario #1: Reduce Purchasing Costs by 2%	
Revenue	$20,000,000
Purchasing expense percent	60%
Purchasing expense dollars	$12,000,000
Decrease to purchasing expense dollars	2%
Increased profits from reduced purchasing costs	$ 240,000

Scenario #2: Increase Sales by 10%	Base Case	w/Increase
Revenue	$20,000,000	$22,000,000
Net profit margin percent	4%	4%
Net profit margin dollars	$ 800,000	$ 880,000
Increase to net profit dollars from 10% increase to sales		$ 80,000

[82] Maynard, Micheline (2010-05-18). "Toyota Pays Its $16.4 Million Fine Over Pedals". *The New York Times*. http://www.nytimes.com/2010/05/19/business/19toyota.html.

As can be seen in the Scenario #1 table above, a 2% decrease in purchasing costs results in a savings of $240,000, all of which is added to net profits. (**Note**: to compute these savings we multiply the purchasing expense of $12 million by 2%. **We do not multiply revenue by 58%** to compute the new purchasing expense and the decrease in purchasing costs as this gives the wrong answer.)

When the retailer increases sales by 10%, as seen in the Scenario #2 table above, net profit dollars increase by 10% from $800,000 to $880,000. This increase of $80,000 in net profit dollars, resulting from a 10% increase in sales, is far short of the $240,000 increase in net profit that comes from a mere 2% decrease in purchasing costs. Again, this example shows that 100% of the dollars saved from reduced purchasing costs goes right to the bottom line (net profit) whereas increases in revenue will only increase the bottom line in proportion to the company's net profit margin.

Question: How do you compute the required increase to sales to match the increased profits that come from reduced purchasing costs?

Let's use the data from the examples above to answer this question. We know that a 10% increase in sales only netted us an additional $80,000 in profits. To compute the required dollar increase to sales that will give us $240,000 in additional profits we divide $240,000 by 4% (net profit margin percent) and we get $6,000,000 (as can be seen in the graphic below). This represents a 30% increase in sales to match a modest and realistic 2% decrease in purchasing expenses.

C20	f_x =C18/C19	
A	B	C
1		
16	**Required Increase to Sales to Match Increased Profits from Reduced Purchasing Costs**	
17	Revenue	$ 20,000,000
18	Increased profits from reduced purchasing costs	$ 240,000
19	Net profit margin percent	4%
20	Required dollar increase to sales (to match increased profits from reduced purchasing costs)	$ 6,000,000
21	Required percent increase to sales (to match increased profits from reduced purchasing costs)	30%

Real Life Example of Cost Cutting from the Financial Crisis post-2008

If you have paid attention to business and financial news since the financial crisis of 2008 you know that company profits have been very good, never higher in many cases. How can this be after such a traumatizing series of events? The answer probably has many facets, but one important contributor has been cost cutting within corporations. Demand for goods and services (especially in the United States) has largely remained flat, meaning there has been little-to-no increase to company profits from sales growth. For the most part, higher profits have come from reduced costs, and there can be no doubt that companies have focused on lowering purchasing costs as a major source of those overall savings.

Supplier Strategy and Selection

The graphic below shows a continuum of the basic sourcing options employed by most companies.

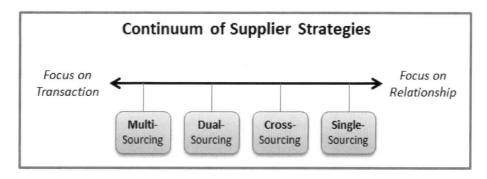

Question: Which is best, having one supplier, two suppliers, or many suppliers?

The question of using few or many suppliers is largely a function of the nature of the goods and services being sourced. In general, when the establishment and maintenance of a long-term sourcing relationship is required, then few suppliers or a single supplier is better. When price is the primary driver, and comparable goods and services are readily available from a number of suppliers, then multiple suppliers can work well. The table below contains descriptions of the **main sourcing strategies** available.

Strategy	Description	Advantages	Disadvantages
Single Sourcing	A purchased part is supplied by only one supplier, where the purchasing company often offers financial and technical help to the supplier	Enables strong relationships leading to high quality, short lead times and shared savings from process improvements	Lack of competition can lead to supplier complacency and higher costs; no backup should supplier falter
Cross Sourcing	Uses one supplier in one area of the business and a different supplier in a different area for a similar product or service	Enables strong relationships; provides a near-ready backup should a supplier falter; creates a measure of competition	Requires sufficient volume among similar business units to make it work
Dual Sourcing	Two suppliers are used for the same product or service (typically with a 70-to-30 percent split of the business)	Can leverage distinct strengths of each supplier; provides good backup; creates competition between suppliers	Can foster distrust in the relationships, sometimes becoming adversarial
Multi Sourcing	Many suppliers are used for the same product or service	Creates strong price competition among suppliers; ample supply; many backup options	Quality can suffer; may supply only preferred customers in times of shortages

An important point to consider when looking at these sourcing strategies is that most supply management professionals operate in "small worlds" where people know each other quite well; where "what goes around comes around" in one form or another. Companies that abuse their power over suppliers in a buyer's market will often face "payback" when the tables turn and they find themselves in a seller's market. Therefore, it is best to have a long-term view in all buyer-seller interactions, whether in contractual long-term relationships or when merely engaging in seemingly one-time transactions from a commodity supplier.

Question: How can the factor rating method help in the supplier selection process?

Before a company can choose a supplier, it must first have a way to evaluate potential suppliers. One common approach is the factor rating method. This simple yet powerful approach is a way to take qualitative information about suppliers and convert that information into quantitative results. Here are the basic steps.

1. Choose specific criteria that are important and valuable to the company or department making the decision. Some example criteria could be (1) price, (2) quality, (3) responsiveness, (4) technology, and (5) reputation.
2. Assign weights to the criteria to reflect the relative importance of each. (The weights typically add up to a total of 1 or 100%). If product quality is more important than price, then quality should have a higher weight than price, and so forth.
3. Rank or score the suppliers based on the criteria selected. Suppliers can be rated from best to worst or they can be scored with a simple scoring system where 4 = excellent, 3 = good, 2 = fair, 1 = poor.
4. Multiply the rankings or scores for the criteria by the weights of the same.
5. Total the weighted scores. Typically the supplier with the highest total weighted score will be selected.

	F4		f_x	=$C4*D4		
A	B	C	D	E	F	G
1						
2			**Raw Score**		**Weighted Score**	
3	Criteria	Weight	Supplier 1	Supplier 2	Supplier 1	Supplier 2
4	Price	0.20	3.00	4.00	0.60	0.80
5	Quality	0.20	3.00	3.00	0.60	0.60
6	Responsiveness	0.35	2.00	3.00	0.70	1.05
7	Technology	0.15	4.00	3.00	0.60	0.45
8	Reputation	0.10	4.00	3.00	0.40	0.30
9	**Total Weighted Score**	1.00			2.90	3.20

The example above shows how the factor rating method could be used when evaluating two different suppliers. Notice how the raw score for the criteria are multiplied by the weight for those same criteria. (An example of this is in cell F4 where Supplier 1's raw score for price, 3.00, is multiplied by the weight for price, 0.20, resulting in a weighted raw score of 0.60.) When we total up the raw scores we find that Supplier 2 has the highest total weighted score of 3.20.

Question: What is the total cost of ownership and why is it important to consider in the supplier selection process?

The total cost of ownership is the sum of all the costs associated with every activity of the supply stream. The main insight that TCO offers to the operations manager is the understanding that the acquisition cost is often a very small portion of the total cost of ownership. Additional costs such as maintenance, repair, upgrades, and additional training, to name a few, should also be considered in the selection of a supplier (and included in the factor rating analysis).

Supplier Relationship Management (SRM)

Supplier Relationship Management is a comprehensive approach to managing a firm's suppliers. Over the past three decades two trends have driven the need for more formal supplier management processes. First is the increasing number of "links" in supply chains as companies have outsourced more and more of their non-core activities to suppliers. Second is the trend toward establishing long-term relationships with a smaller base of key suppliers, thus requiring closer collaboration with supply partners to ensure business success. Recent technological breakthroughs have enabled much of the process improvements that fall under the umbrella of SRM.

Question: What is the goal of supplier relationship management?

The goal of SRM is to streamline and make more effective the processes between an enterprise and its suppliers. SRM is often associated with automating procure-to-pay business processes, e-procurement, evaluating supplier performance, and exchanging information (collaborating) with suppliers through programs and processes like VMI and EDI.

Question: What is VMI?

VMI stands for "vendor managed inventory" and is a means of optimizing supply chain performance by giving suppliers access to the customer's inventory data and having suppliers maintain the inventory level required by the customer. VMI is not appropriate for the replenishment of all items, but where demand is stable, lead times are short, and the items are inexpensive, a company can save on administration costs (ordering costs) by letting suppliers manage inventory levels.

Question: What is EDI?

EDI stands for "electronic data interchange" and is the exchange of trading documents and information, such as inventory levels, purchase orders, and shipment authorizations. In the context of this chapter, you could say that EDI is an "electronic kanban" enabler. For example, when inventory for a purchased item hits its reorder point, EDI can send an automated signal authorizing supplier replenishment. VMI, enabled by EDI, is much faster and more cost effective than having purchasing agents place discrete purchase orders.

Question: What is Supplier Development?

Supplier development can be defined as the process of giving financial and technical assistance to existing and potential suppliers to improve or expand their capabilities. An example may be teaching a supplier how to manufacture a type of item that they never manufactured before, thus giving your company the option to buy, rather than make, that item.

Question: What is a supplier scorecard?

A supplier scorecard is a tool to help companies evaluate supplier performance. Using the factor rating method (except it's used on a continual basis instead of for a one-time selection decision) a company and a supplier will agree on evaluation criteria, as well as what constitutes acceptable and non-acceptable levels of performance for the supplier. Most evaluation criteria will fit into one of these categories.

- Delivery Performance
- Quality Performance
- Cost Reduction
- Sustainable or Environmentally Friendly Practices

Over time the company will periodically rate their suppliers' performance and update their scorecards. (It would appear from the Toyota example above that there was a failure to frequently and adequately measure their suppliers' performance.) The supplier scorecard provides companies with a data-driven approach to decision making regarding its suppliers (identify areas for improvement, take corrective action, expand the relationship, search for new suppliers, etc.).

Members of The Church of Jesus Christ of Latter-day Saints are not new to the concept of evaluation. Personal Priesthood Interviews (PPIs), Temple Recommend interviews, and other meetings are forms of evaluation based on agreed upon criteria. Those who have served full-time missions engaged in similar evaluations in the form of Companionship Inventories. Just as in Companionship Inventories, business evaluations must be conducted with respect and with the mindset of improving the combined performance of both parties in the relationship.

Sustainable Sourcing

Doctrinal Foundation for Wise Stewardship of Natural Resources

The idea of "green" businesses with sustainable practices—practices that have a positive effect on the environment—should be familiar to faithful members of The Church of Jesus Christ of Latter-day Saints. Such practices date back to ancient America as evidenced by this scripture:

> And the people who were in the land northward did dwell in tents, and in houses of cement, and they did suffer whatsoever tree should spring up upon the face of the land that it should grow up, that in time they might have timber to build their

houses, yea, their cities, and their temples, and their synagogues, and their sanctuaries, and all manner of their buildings.[83]

Moreover, as the Saints gathered in Ohio in 1831 they were instructed to "act upon [the] land as for years," implying that their settlements should be done in a way that would sustain life for years, even though they would be moving on within the decade. Like the Nephites and the early Saints of this dispensation, we have an obligation to be wise stewards over the natural resources of the earth. Moreover, man was instructed to "Be fruitful, and multiply, and replenish the earth, and subdue it, and have dominion over [all animal] life."[84] Indeed, there is a "pecking order" to God's creations, and as we are wise agents who do not abuse our natural and animal resources we will see that "the earth is full, and there is enough and to spare."[85]

Sustainable Sourcing Practices

In the world "green" business practices can take many forms, and sourcing can play a vital role in these efforts. For example, companies can add sustainability metrics to their supplier scorecards by measuring such things as their suppliers' operational waste, water use, energy use, recycling, and many others. More and more, such factors are being considered in customer-supplier relationships.

Ethical Sourcing

When dealing with suppliers there is often the temptation to take personal advantage in the relationship as many suppliers are willing to tempt and accommodate unscrupulous purchasing professionals in order to win the business. The author knows of several former coworkers who were fired for unethical conduct with suppliers (taking kickbacks, golf trips, expensive dinners, other gifts whose value exceeded company guidelines, etc.).

As members of The Church of Jesus Christ of Latter-day Saints we receive countless counsel and encouragement to live by high ethical standards. Below are some representative examples from Elder Neal A. Maxwell (who quotes President Brigham Young) and from President Gordon B. Hinckley. First Elder Maxwell:

> The rising generation will determine if Latter-day Saints will continue to be known for the work ethic. Long ago, President Brigham Young advised: "I want to see our Elders so full of integrity that [their work] will be preferred....If we live our religion and are worthy [of] the name...Latter-day Saints, we are just the men that all such business can be entrusted to with perfect safety; if it can not [be] it will prove that we do not live our religion."[86]

And from President Hinckley:

---

83 Helaman 3:9.
84 Moses 2:28.
85 D&C 104:17.
86 Neal A. Maxwell, "Put Your Shoulder to the Wheel," Priesthood Session, April 1998 General Conference.

That [thirteenth] article of our faith is one of the basic declarations of our theology. We ought to reflect on it again and again. Then, whenever we might be tempted to do anything shoddy or dishonest or immoral, there would come into our minds with some force this great, all-encompassing statement of the ethics of our behavior.[87]

These encouraging and instructional words, and the example of Jacob, should give us plenty of reason and courage to do the right thing, no matter the circumstances.

Key Associations and Careers in Supply Management

In this section we will briefly discuss three different associations for supply chain management professionals (although there are several others out there): (1) the Institute for Supply Management (ISM), (2) APICS, and (3) the Council of Supply Chain Management Professionals (CSCMP). Historically, each association focused on serving the needs of professionals in different areas of supply chain management. In recent years these organizations have undergone name changes or rebranding efforts in order to broaden their appeal to professionals across all areas of supply chain management.

- **ISM** was formerly known as the National Association of Purchasing Agents (NAPA) and is "the first supply management institute in the world,"[88] founded in 1915. In 2002 NAPA changed its name to the **Institute of Supply Management** as its members, primarily purchasing professionals, were seeing an increase to the scope of their responsibilities and therefore wanted a name that would reflect this change.
- **APICS** was formerly known as The American Production and Inventory Control Society and focused its education and certification offerings on professionals who managed processes "within the four walls" of manufacturing organizations. The "APICS" name is no longer considered an acronym but is now associated with the tagline, "the leading professional association for supply chain and operations management."[89]
- **CSCMP** was formerly known as the Council of Logistics Management but changed its name in 2005 to the **Council of Supply Chain Management Professionals** due to the expanded roles of its members (beyond logistics and transportation management).

Each of these associations offers highly discounted memberships to full-time students. If you plan to pursue a career in supply chain management, you should consider joining one or more of these associations and, if you are so inclined, begin working on one or more of the professional certifications that each offers—greatly increasing your marketability.

The **Supply Chain Council** (SCC) is an association that is best known for its endorsement of the **SCOR model** (supply-chain operations reference-model). This model shows how supply chain participants engage in the same basic process blocks:

---

[87] Gordon B. Hinckley, "Fear Not to do Good," Ensign, January 2000.
[88] https://www.ism.ws/about/content.cfm?ItemNumber=4790&navItemNumber=22328
[89] www.apics.org

plan, source, make, deliver, and return. Moreover, it helps supply chain professionals "address, improve, and communicate supply chain management practices within and between all interested parties in the extended enterprise,"[90] from suppliers' suppliers to customers' customers, as depicted in the graphic below.

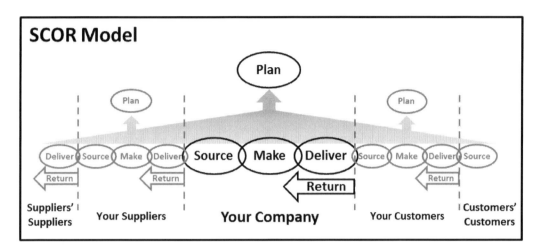

In summary, the framework and basic processes outlined in the SCOR model are intended to help professionals look beyond their immediate suppliers and customers for opportunities to improve organizational performance.

On April 30, 2014 it was announced that the Supply Chain Council would be merging with APICS. As stated in the news release, "The merger unites two industry leaders with complementary offerings to create the premier global provider of supply chain research, education and certification programs. Together, SCC and APICS offer a single-source solution for individuals and corporations looking to evaluate and improve supply chain performance."[91]

Chapter Summary

Below are some of the main points you should have garnered from the study of this chapter.

- **Supply management embodies the methods and processes of institutional buying**. Over recent decades, supply management has shifted its focus from cost cutting to managing the relationships with suppliers in order to improve supplier performance across a number of factors (technology, quality, reliability, flexibility, cost, and so forth).
- **Supplier strategies range from transactional to relational**. Each strategy has advantages and disadvantages. Proper selection of a supplier strategy is highly dependent on understanding the specific needs of the buying situation. The factor-rating method is a simple but powerful tool which can help in the supplier selection process.

[90] http://en.wikipedia.org/wiki/Supply-Chain_Operations_Reference
[91] http://www.apics.org/about/supply-chain-council-to-merge-with-apics

- The concept of **supplier relationship management (SRM)** has been driven by (1) the increasing number of "links" in supply chains and (2) the trend toward establishing relationships with suppliers. SRM embodies technology-enabled business process improvements, supplier development, and formal supplier evaluation processes (scorecards).
- **Supply management personnel often are faced with temptation and ethical dilemmas**. It goes without saying the members of The Church of Jesus Christ of Latter-day Saints should be exemplary employees when it comes to such matters.
- There are a number of **associations for supply chain professionals**. These include the ISM, APICS, and CSCMP.

Chapter 13

LOGISTICS MANAGEMENT

Let each company provide themselves with all the teams, wagons, provisions, clothing, and other necessaries for the journey, that they can.

When the companies are organized let them go to with their might, to prepare for those who are to tarry.

Let each company, with their captains and presidents, decide how many can go next spring; then choose out a sufficient number of able-bodied and expert men, to take teams, seeds, and farming utensils, to go as pioneers to prepare for putting in spring crops.

Let each company bear an equal proportion, according to the dividend of their property, in taking the poor, the widows, the fatherless, and the families of those who have gone into the army, that the cries of the widow and the fatherless come not up into the ears of the Lord against this people.

Let each company prepare houses, and fields for raising grain, for those who are to remain behind this season; and this is the will of the Lord concerning his people.

Let every man use all his influence and property to remove this people to the place where the Lord shall locate a stake of Zion.

And if ye do this with a pure heart, in all faithfulness, ye shall be blessed; you shall be blessed in your flocks, and in your herds, and in your fields, and in your houses, and in your families.

Doctrine and Covenants 136:5-11

The logistical challenges of moving tens of thousands of Latter-day Saints across a thousand miles of prairie and into a desert wilderness cannot be overstated. With good reason, the westward migration of the Saints has been called one of the greatest migrations in world history. The revelation above, given to Brigham Young, provides a framework for this great undertaking and hints at the countless details required for its successful execution.

Perhaps we take for granted the monumental work of transporting the Saints. Perhaps we think of it too narrowly, too simplistically. We know they traveled thousands of miles by boat, in wagons, pulling handcarts, and simply walking. And with this mental model it's easy and natural to focus on the exhausting exertion required to make this trip. But when we dig deeper, we see that extensive, painstaking preparation was required in order to make this westward trek possible.

Chapter Objectives

Much like our view of the Saints' westward trek, if and when we think about logistics management, we may gravitate to a simplistic transportation-centric viewpoint—moving things from point A to point B. But a deeper look at logistics helps us realize that there is great and varied effort behind the very reliable movement of goods and services which we enjoy, and probably take for granted, in our society. In this chapter we will learn about many facets of logistics management. Specifically, after studying this chapter you should be able to

1. Describe the modes, providers, and movement of inventories.
2. Describe the types and functions of warehouses.
3. Describe facilities location strategies.
4. Determine optimal locations using a variety of methods, including factor rating, total cost (break-even), and center of gravity.
5. Compute total landed cost and other supply chain inventory-related measures.

Overview of Logistics Management

Question: What is logistics management and how does it differ from supply chain management?

The Council of Supply Chain Management Professionals (CSCMP) defines logistics management as "that part of supply chain management that plans, implements, and controls the efficient, effective forward and reverse flow and storage of goods, services and related information between the point of origin and the point of consumption in order to meet customers' requirements."[92]

In some circles, the terms logistics management and supply chain management are used interchangeably. However, for the purposes of this book, we will make the following distinctions about supply chain management—items which are beyond the scope of logistics management.

- Supply chain management is a **superset** of logistics management, meaning all logistics management activities fall within the umbrella of SCM.
- Supply chain includes collaboration with channel partners—suppliers, intermediaries, and customers.
- Supply chain management personnel participate in and often lead cross-functional, intra-company activities like business process improvement initiatives, product design, and information technology implementations.

Question: How has logistics management changed in recent decades?

In the late 1970s and early 1980s the U.S. government passed a number of acts (most significantly the Motor Carrier Act and the Staggers Rail Act, both in 1980), which significantly reduced regulation in the trucking, railroad, shipping, and air

---

[92] Council of Supply Chain Management Professionals, www.cscmp.org/aboutcscmp/definitions.asp.

transportation industries. Such deregulation enabled the market to determine prices, entry and services. The resulting increase in competition gave birth to many innovations in logistics management—a true logistics renaissance.

With this overview in place, we are now ready to learn about the main areas of logistics management.

Transportation Management

Transportation management is the business function that plans and controls the activities related to mode, vendor, and movement of freight. In the United States, we enjoy unparalleled access to a great variety of products—both at retail locations and from online purchases—because of fast, flexible, and efficient transportation services. The freight transportation industry has seen tremendous growth over the past two decades. Fueled by deregulation, free-trade agreements, on-line businesses, and increased outsourcing, from "1990 to 2008, the value of U.S. international merchandise trade [all of which required transportation services] grew from $889 billion to $3.4 trillion."[93]

Question: What are the modes of transportation used for moving inventories?

The five basic modes of transportation are road, rail, air, water, and pipeline. An additional mode—intermodal—combines two or more modes and has become more popular in recent years. The table below provides the descriptions, strengths, and weaknesses of each.

Mode	Advantages	Value	Tons	Ton-miles
Road	Extensive geographic coverage, point-to-point service, fast, flexible, frequent departures, can handle all types of goods	86%	67.4%	28.7%
Rail	Low unit costs, energy efficient, high capacity, can handle wide range of products	3.7%	16.1%	36.8%
Water	Mass movement of bulk items, high capacity, very low cost, great for long-haul movement of low-value commodities	1.1%	11.1%	13.6%
Air	Fastest mode for intermediate and long movements, low damage and loss	3.2%	0.03%	0.4%
Pipeline	Mass movement of liquid and gas products, high capacity, dependable, lowest cost	1.8%	5.9%	20.5%
Multimodal	Combines advantages of more than one mode, low damage and loss	5.6%	5.5%	6.8%
Source: U.S. Department of Transportation, *National Transportation Statistics 2006* (Washington, DC: April 2006, Table 1 – 52).				

---

93 http://www.bts.gov/publications/freight_transportation/html/us_trends.html

Question: What are the legal forms of transportation in the United States?

A company that provides air, sea, or land transportation services is called a carrier. Carriers fall into two basic categories: (1) for-hire carriers and (2) private carriers. For-hire carriers are further broken down into three types: (a) common carriers, (b) contract carriers, and (c) exempt carriers. All carriers must operate under one of these legal forms. Below are further descriptions of these carriers and how they are similar and different.

1) For-hire carriers include,
   a) **Common carriers** that provide transportation to the public and without special treatment to any one party. Rates, liability, and services provided are regulated. Examples of common carriers include Southwest Airlines, Amtrak, and Greyhound.
   b) **Contract carriers** that do not serve the general public, but rather provide transportation for one or a limited number of shippers under a specific contract. Common carriers can act as contract carriers if they contract with a customer for certain services. For example, an airline may contract with a professional sports team to provide transportation for out-of-town games.
   c) **Exempt carriers** are free from regulation of services and rates if they transport certain exempt products like produce, livestock, coal, or a number of other commodities. All carriers can also act as exempt carriers when they carry specific commodities.
2) **Private carriers** are not subject to economic regulation and typically move goods for the company owning the carrier. A firm may establish its own fleet if they can achieve economies of scale or if they want to have greater flexibility and control of product movement. Wal-Mart is an example of a private carrier with its own fleet of trucks.

We should note that most carriers are second-party logistics providers (2PLs) that move items for "shippers," who are first-party entities (companies, individuals).

Question: What is a third-party logistics provider (3PL)?

A third-party logistics provider is a company that offers one or more logistics services to shippers, the most common being transportation management, freight forwarding, warehouse management, and light manufacturing. 3PLs differ from 2PLs in that they (1) offer customized versus standard services and (2) seek to establish multi-year contractual relationships (typically three to five years) versus having more of a transactional focus. Some 3PLs own no assets (no warehouses or trucks), but provide great value as intermediaries, managing complex information and relationships between a company and other logistics providers. Such non-asset based 3PLs are sometimes referred to as 4PLs or LLPs (lead logistics providers).

3PLs have seen tremendous growth since the 1980s due to deregulation (which made it possible for service providers to expand their offerings into formerly regulated areas), a general trend of companies outsourcing non-core activities, and 3PL expertise in managing increasingly complex global supply chains. There is one potential downside to contracting with a 3PL—loss of control. Shippers put themselves at the mercy of the 3PL's capabilities and potentially become one of many customers being serviced by the 3PL.

Question: What are the different types of motor carrier shipments?

There is a great variety of motor carrier shipments, where freight is constantly consolidated and broken down as carriers strive to provide an optimal service package of fast delivery and low cost.

- **Package carriers** like FedEx, UPS, and the U.S. Postal Service carry small items ranging from **letters to packages** weighing about 150 pounds and provide fast and reliable service. These companies have seen tremendous growth as they are the preferred method of transport for e-businesses such as Amazon.com and Dell. These carriers employ a variety of shipment methods (LTL, TL, zone skipping, etc.) to move items.

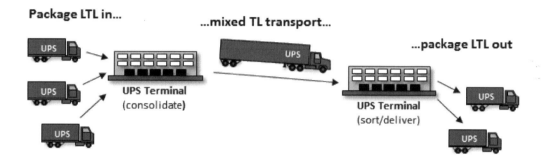

- **LTL (less-than-truckload)** is a shipment in which freight does not completely fill the truck or trailer or the shipper's freight is combined with other freight to produce a full truckload. Typically, a shipment of 10,000 pounds or more is required to qualify for a truckload discount.
- **TL (truckload)** is a shipment in which the freight completely fills the trailer.
- **Direct truck shipment** is a shipment made without any additional stops, such as for loading or changing trucks.
- A **milk run** is a consolidation technique where one truck, on a regular route, picks up mixed (LTL) loads from several suppliers, enabling more frequent, smaller deliveries from multiple suppliers.
- **Backhauling** is the return trip from the original point of destination to the point of origin. An empty backhaul trip is called a **deadhead**. Because of deregulation, carriers can contract (pick up freight) for the return trip. And in today's information-rich world, carriers are able to minimize deadheads.

Question: What is a land bridge?

The term **land bridge** refers to a practice where containers are shipped from Asia, received on the U.S. west coast, shipped by truck across the U.S., and then shipped by ocean to Europe. This process saves about two weeks' time and costs about the same as shipping directly (by boat) from Asia to Europe. Variations on land bridges include,

- A **mini land bridge** is where containers are received on one U.S. coast and then shipped by truck to a final destination on the other coast.
- A **micro land bridge** is similar to the mini land bridge, except the final destination is inland and not on the opposite coast.

Land Bridge

Question: What is reverse logistics?

The primary focus of logistics is the forward flow and storage of material toward the point of consumption. A reverse logistics system is "a complete supply chain dedicated to the reverse flow of products and materials for the purpose of returns, repair, remanufacture, and/or recycling."[94] Studies show that about 4% to 6% of all retail sales are returned.[95] Moreover, with all the talk of "sustainability" and "green business," reverse logistics is becoming more and more important. Reverse logistics systems must be flexible and designed to handle small quantities. This means they will be less cost efficient than forward-focused logistics systems.

Question: What are Incoterms?

Incoterms are a series of terms used to specify buyer and seller responsibilities for a given international commercial transaction. Each term, denoted by a three-letter code, answers questions such as

- What are the delivery points for loading and unloading the goods (seller's dock, freight forwarder, shipping dock, etc.)? Who is responsible for loading and unloading the goods at these points?
- Who pays for insurance? At which point in the transport does risk for the goods transfer from seller to buyer?
- Which party selects, arranges, and pays for the carriers? Which modes of transportation are appropriate for the given shipment?
- Which party is responsible for getting shipments cleared for export?
- Which party is responsible for clearing the goods for import? Who pays the required duties, value-added taxes, customs and other associated fees?

The 11 pre-defined Incoterms provide lots of flexibility to buyers and sellers so that negotiated agreements can be reached. They are divided into two categories—

---

94 John H. Blackstone Jr., editor, *APICS Dictionary*, 13th edition (Falls Church, VA: APICS, 2010).
95 Tom Van Riper, *Forbes Magazine*, "Reseller Sees Many Happy Returns" (December 2005).

general transport and sea and inland waterway transport—and are listed in order of least to most responsibility for the sellers, as seen in the table below.

General Transport	Sea or Inland Waterway Transport
EXW - Ex Works (*minimum seller responsibility*) - Seller makes goods available for pickup - Buyer arranges everything else	**FAS - Free Alongside Ship** (*minimum seller responsibility*) - Seller delivers goods alongside ship, cleared for export - Buyer responsible for loading goods and paying for carriage
FCA - Free Carrier - Seller delivers goods, cleared for export, to a named place - Buyer arranges and pays for everything else	**FOB - Free on Board** - Seller delivers goods on board ship, cleared for export - Buyer pays for main carriage and everything else
CPT - Carriage Paid To - Seller delivers and pays for carriage to the named place but does not pay for insurance - Buyer arranges and pays for everything else	**CFR - Cost & Freight** - Seller delivers goods on board ship, cleared for export, pays for main carriage but not insurance - Buyer arranges and pays for everything else
CIP - Carriage & Insurance Paid - Seller delivers and pays for carriage to the named place and pays for insurance - Buyer arranges and pays for everything else	**CIF - Cost, Insurance & Freight** (*maximum seller responsibility*) - Seller delivers goods on board ship, cleared for export, pays for main carriage to named port, pays for insurance - Buyer arranges and pays for everything else
DAT - Delivered at Terminal - Seller delivers goods to the named place, unloads goods, assumes all risks and costs to that point - Buyer clears goods for import and arranges and pays for everything else	
DAP - Delivered at Place - Seller delivers goods to the named place, ready to be unloaded, assumes all risks and costs to that point - Buyer clears goods for import and arranges and pays for everything else	
DDP - Delivered Duty Paid (*maximim seller responsibility*) - Seller delivers goods to the named place, ready to be unloaded, clears goods for import and pays all duties, etc. - Buyer arranges and pays for everything else	

Warehouse Management

Warehouses serve three important functions: transportation consolidation, product mixing, and customer service. It should come as no surprise that with these different functions you have different types of warehouses.

Question: What are the types of warehouses found in supply chains?

Warehouses can be defined by ownership (private or public) and function (the type of work performed). Largely due to deregulation and resulting innovations in logistics from companies like Wal-Mart, the more *passive* notion of a warehouse—a place to hold or store inventory—has given way to the more *dynamic* concept of a distribution center. Below is a list of the basic warehouse types by function.

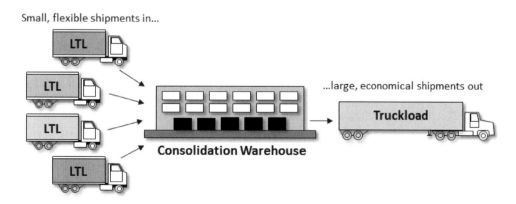

- **Consolidation warehouse**—a collection point that receives less-than-truckload (LTL) shipments from regional sources and then ships out in cargo load (CL) or truckload (TL) quantities to a manufacturing facility.

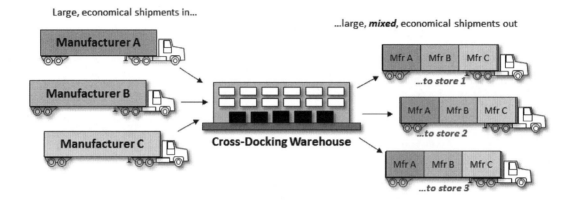

- **Cross-docking warehouse**—a facility that receives truckload quantities and sends out less-than-truckload shipments. (It is kind of the opposite of a consolidation warehouse.) Wal-Mart and Lowe's use cross-docking warehouses or distributions, with their "hub and spoke" distribution network design.
- **Postponement warehouse**—a facility that combines traditional warehouse functions with light manufacturing operations. Products shipped from such warehouses are "designed for supply chain management" or designed in such a way to allow the postponement of product differentiation until after receiving the customer order.
- **Assortment warehouse**—a facility that stores a wide variety of goods, strategically located in order to ensure short customer lead times. Perhaps a classic example of this is Amazon.com with several regional warehouses around the country.
- **Spot stock warehouse**—a facility that stores seasonal items close to the marketplace. At the end of the season the items are either liquidated or returned to a more central location for long-term storage.

Question: What are the basic processes which take place in a warehouse?

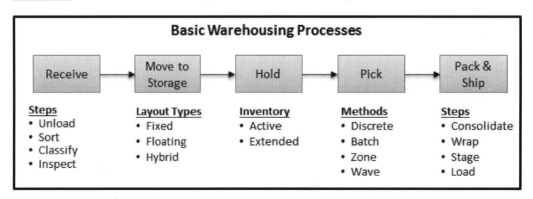

Regardless of the type of warehouse, many processes are the same. The graphic above shows the flow of the basic warehousing processes. However, these processes may differ depending upon the type of warehouse. Perhaps the most interesting and challenging—and important—step is the picking of orders. Each of the four picking methods listed below has advantages and disadvantages and must be carefully selected to meet the needs of the distribution operation.

- **Discrete order picking** calls for the picking of one order at a time (per picker) before the next order can be picked. This method works well when there are relatively few orders, each one with many case-level line items. For example, this method is used at Wal-Mart food distribution centers.
- With **batch picking** multiple orders are picked at the same time, usually with the use of a cart that holds a separate container for each order. This method cuts down on order picker walking and works well when orders are small.

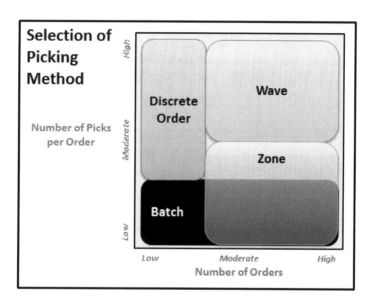

- **Zone picking** is like an assembly line for picking. The picking area is divided into zones to which order pickers are assigned. As order containers pass from zone to zone, pickers select and load items into the order container. **Pick to light** technology is often used in zone picking. This picking method cuts down on walk time and is appropriate for a moderate to high number of orders, each with a small to moderate number of items.
- **Wave picking** is a hybrid of batch and zone picking. Requirements from multiple orders are picked simultaneously in all zones. The items are later sorted and consolidated into individual orders for shipment. Orders may be picked in waves that isolate customer, carrier or destination. This method is appropriate for a moderate to high number of orders, each with a moderate to high number of line items. This is the quickest method (shortest cycle time), but sorting and consolidating the orders for shipment can be tricky.

Information technology and automated material handling systems—conveyers and automated storage and retrieval systems (ASRS)—play a major role in put-away and picking processes. Robotics is becoming more prevalent as well.

To see an amazing example of picking innovation, go to YouTube and search for "kiva systems zappos" and you will find an amazing video on robotic distribution, where Zappos.com has realized tremendous improvements to productivity and quality. You can also search for each of the picking methods listed above and find several videos that demonstrate how each is done.

Question: How are warehouse layouts organized?

The layout of a warehouse or distribution center is typically set up to optimize the tradeoff between space utilization and handling costs. The two basic layout approaches place inventory in either **fixed** locations or **floating** locations.

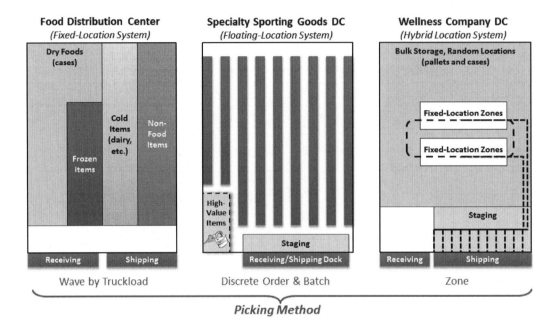

The graphic above shows three layout examples—fixed, floating, and a hybrid of the two—as well as the picking methods that are used in each environment.

- In a **fixed-location** system, a stock-keeping unit (SKU or an individual part number) is assigned a permanent location or locations, where no other items can be stored. It's kind of like having a certain place in your fridge where you always store the milk. This simple system can speed up put-away and picking times—reducing handling costs—as warehouse workers can more easily remember where certain SKUs can be found. This approach may require minimal record keeping and is appropriate when there is plenty of available space.
- A **floating-location** system randomly places SKUs in the most appropriate location, based on available space. It maximizes space or "cube" utilization, reducing costs associated with warehousing. This approach requires very accurate inventory records and is usually enabled by a warehouse management computer system (WMS) which helps optimize cube utilization and create properly sequenced pick lists.

Question: What is the role of product packaging in a logistics system?

The role of packaging in a logistics system differs from a consumer's perspective of packaging, which is driven by marketing. From a logistics standpoint, the primary focus of packaging is to protect the product and enable efficient material handling.

Individual parts or products are usually stored in bags, bins, or barrels—containers which are known as **master cartons**. When these cartons are grouped into larger units for handling purposes, the combination is referred to as **containerization** or **unitization**. Master cartons and these larger combined units are the basic handling units for logistics. The weight, cube, and degree of protection—not retail size or presentation—should be the primary focus of the master carton. These features determine transportation and materials handling requirements and have a direct bearing on the performance of the logistics system.

Logistics Decision Models

Given the volume of freight that is moved in the cost-sensitive logistics industry, it should come as no surprise that a number of quantitative methods have been developed to optimize operations. The next few pages cover some of these basic methods which focus on facility location and transportation costs.

Break-Even Analysis

A very simple method for selecting a facility location is break-even analysis. The basics of break-even analysis have already been covered in chapter 2 (Process Strategy), however the mechanics are the same, whether choosing between process options or location options. Therefore, we will not provide any further break-even examples in this chapter.

Risk Pooling and the Square Root Law of Inventory

One of the basic challenges of logistics is designing a distribution network that properly manages the tradeoff between inventory costs and transportation costs. More warehouses in a distribution network (decentralized distribution) means lower transportation costs and shorter lead times, because inventory is closer to demand centers (customers). Conversely, fewer warehouses (centralized distribution) means lower total inventory, because when demand is aggregated and pointed to fewer locations (warehouses), demand variability goes down and less network safety stock is required. This benefit to centralized distribution networks is known as risk pooling and can be demonstrated using the square root law of inventory. The formula for the square root law of inventory is as follows:

$$S_2 = \frac{\sqrt{N_2}}{\sqrt{N_1}} (S_1)$$

Where

S_1 = total system-wide inventory for N_1 number of warehouses

S_2 = total system-wide inventory for N_2 (proposed) number of warehouses

N_1 = number of warehouses in existing distribution system
N_2 = number of warehouses in proposed distribution system

Suppose a large nation-wide distributor wants to reduce its inventory costs by consolidating its warehouses. It currently has 25 regional warehouses located around the country, but they think they can make do with 4 warehouses. They currently have 300,000 units of inventory in these 25 warehouses with which they achieve a 98% service level. How many units of inventory would they need to carry in the proposed consolidated network?

$$S_2 = \frac{\sqrt{N_2}}{\sqrt{N_1}}(S_1) = \frac{\sqrt{4}}{\sqrt{25}}(300,000) = \frac{2}{5}(300,000) = 120,000 \; units$$

In this case there would be a dramatic 60% reduction in inventory, not to mention the costs savings from closing 21 warehouses. Of course, having fewer warehouses would mean that transportation costs would probably increase and may offset the inventory and operational savings from closing the warehouses. A thorough analysis of the costs and benefits must be performed before making such a decision, however, the square root law of inventory shows that there are significant inventory savings opportunities from consolidating or centralizing distribution.

Factor Rating and Location Decisions

In the Supply Management chapter we introduced the factor rating method as a tool to help with supplier selection. This same method can be applied to a number of decision-making problems, including location decisions. Factors can be considered on many levels (country, region, state, community, site). Examples include

- Political risks, currency risk, exchange rates, government incentives
- Attractiveness of the region (climate, culture, taxes, regulation)
- Infrastructure (roads, waterways, railways, energy, communications)
- Land and construction costs
- Labor talent, cost, productivity, education, attitude toward unions
- Proximity to raw materials, supplies and customers
- Zoning, regulations, environmental issues

We won't provide an example factor rating table in this chapter. To see or review how this is done, refer to the example in the Supply Management chapter.

Weighted Center of Gravity Approach

The weighted center-of-gravity approach is a method of identifying a location for a store, warehouse, factory or other facility, that represents the minimum transportation costs between that location and the demand sources. The location is expressed in (X, Y) coordinate terms, where X and Y represent coordinates on a map (onto which the X-Y grid is arbitrarily placed). The weighted center of gravity calculates the weighted average (X, Y) values for the demand locations—hence, the weighted center of gravity.

Store	Demand	X-Coor.	Y-Coor.
Chicago	600	30	120
Pittsburgh	900	90	110
New York	1,800	130	130
Atlanta	2,000	60	40

Suppose we run a warehouse, located in Atlanta, which stocks NASCAR souvenirs which are sold in four retail outlets: one each in Atlanta, Chicago, Pittsburg, and New York. The lease on our warehouse is going to expire at the end of 2011, so we must determine whether we are going to renew the lease or move to a new location. The table below contains our 2012 forecast and (X, Y) coordinates for each location. **Based on this forecast, what is the weighted center of gravity location** (and a candidate for our new warehouse location)? Below are the steps we will take to answer this question.

1. Compute the weighted (X, Y) coordinates for each location (cell range F3:G6, shown in the spreadsheet below). For example, the weighted X-coordinate for Chicago is 600 X 30 = 18,000; the weighted Y-coordinate is 600 X 120 = 72,000.
2. Sum the weighted (X, Y) coordinates for all locations (cells F7 and G7).
3. Sum the total demand (cell C7).
4. Divide the sum of the weighted (X, Y) coordinates by the sum of the total demand (cell D7—formula shown in the formula bar, and cell e7).

	D7				f_x	=F7/C7	
	A	B	C	D	E	F	G
1							
2		Store	Demand	X-Coor.	Y-Coor.	X-Coordinate Weight	Y-Coordinate Weight
3		Chicago	600	30	120	18,000	72,000
4		Pittsburgh	900	90	110	81,000	99,000
5		New York	1,800	130	130	234,000	234,000
6		Atlanta	2,000	60	40	120,000	80,000
7			5,300	85.47	91.51	453,000	485,000

Step 4 will give you the average (X, Y) coordinates for this problem—(85.47, 91.81), the weighted center of gravity.

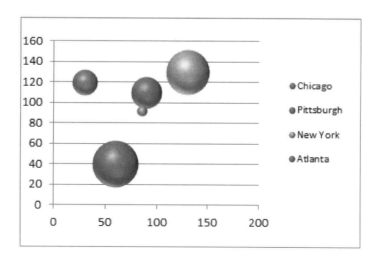

The bubble chart above gives a graphical representation of the demand centers (bigger bubbles = more demand) and the center of gravity (the small bubble on the south side of Pittsburg).

Transportation Method

The transportation method is a linear programming model concerned with minimizing the costs of meeting several geographic demand requirements from several source locations, each demand/source location combination having a different cost. To understand this method, let's look at a hypothetical problem involving a company we'll call Northwest Landscaping Materials. They produce a variety of barks, mulches, and soils in their plants located in Rexburg, ID, Tacoma, WA, and Bend, OR. The primary markets for their Gorilla Hair (mulch) product are in Seattle, Portland, Boise and Salt Lake City.

The three tables in the top-left corner of the graphic below provide given data for this problem. They contain each plant's weekly capacity, each market's weekly demand, and the shipping cost per 150 cubic yards for each demand/source combination. With this given data we can set up the remaining required tables.

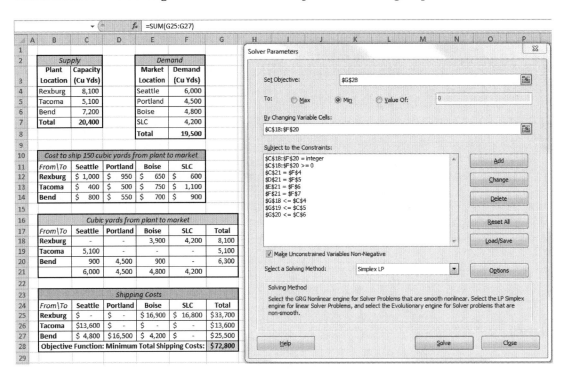

The table "Cubic yards from plant to market" shows the allocation of supply to each demand/source combination. The last table gives us the shipping cost for each combination as well as the total shipping costs. This total cost cell (G28) will become the objective function for our Solver model. The graphic also shows the Solver window. (The Solver function can be found in Excel's "Data" tab.) Take note of the "Set Objective:" cell ($G$28), the "By Changing Variable Cells:" (range $C$18:$F$20), and all nine constraints which are listed. We also set the solving method to "Simplex LP" since this is a linear model.

We should spend a few moments discussing the constraints, but first we must discuss the computation of the basic costs. Our model is set up to calculate the shipping costs for each demand/source combination. For example, the cost in cell C26 (shipping from Tacoma to Seattle) is as follows:

$$Tacoma \rightarrow Seattle\ Cost = 5{,}100 \times \frac{\$400}{150} = \$13{,}600$$

Note that in this case we divided the cost of shipping by 150 because the price for shipping ($400) is per 150 cubic yards, not per single yard. (Dividing $400 by 150 gives us a per-yard shipping cost of $2.67.) When we use this same formula for each demand/source combination we can then get a total shipping cost for the shipments from each source (Rexburg, Tacoma, and Bend). With these by-source totals, we can come up with the grand total in cell G28.

Now back to the constraints; below is the list from the snapshot above, along with some commentary on each one.

- $C$18:$F$20 = integer: this tells the model that each unit shipment must be a whole number.
- $C$18:$F$20 >= 0: the shipment numbers must be greater than zero. Solver will return a negative-number answer if we don't do this.
- The next four constraints tell the model to make sure that all the demand is completely met. For example, the total shipments to Seattle, shown in cell C21, must be equal to the demand for Seattle in cell F4. The same applies to the other markets as well.
- The last three constraints tell the model that shipments from each plant cannot exceed that plant's capacity. For example, the total shipments from Rexburg, shown in cell G18, must be less than or equal to the capacity of the Rexburg plant, as shown in cell C4.

This is a very simple transportation method example. Such Solver-based, linear programming models can be applied to a number of problems. This example gives a small taste of the type of sophisticated tools logistics companies use to make sure they are minimizing costs and maximizing profits.

Total Landed Cost

Studies have shown that the cost of logistics accounts for between 5 and 35 percent of total sales costs, which is roughly ten percent of GDP. Therefore, all costs associated with acquiring a product—including logistics and not just the unit price—should be considered in sourcing decisions. The total landed cost for an item includes all costs associated with getting a product to your customer (or getting a product from your supplier): material or unit costs, shipping costs, insurance costs, warehousing costs, and so forth.

To examine total landed costs, let's continue our example with Northwest Landscape Materials. In this case we're going to assume the Northwest has only one plant, the Rexburg plant. They want to determine the best way to get their Gorilla Hair product to the Portland market. They have two shipping options: send it by truck or send it with a multimodal solution involving rail (train) and truck. In this case, material cost is the same. It costs $950 for each direct truckload shipment, 150 cubic yards, from Rexburg to the customer in Portland. For the multimodal solution, it costs $375 per 150 cubic yards to ship by rail from Rexburg to a train terminal in Portland, $2.80 per yard to unload the product from the train and reload it onto a truck and then $125 per truckload of 150 cubic yards to make a short local delivery.

What is the total landed cost for each shipping option? The graphic below shows how this problem can be structured as well as the formula for the total cost in cell D9 (and the formula is very similar for the total cost in cell C9).

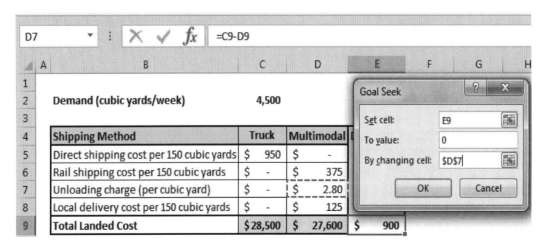

	D9	f_x	=$C2*((D5/150)+(D6/150)+(D8/150)+D7)		
	A	B	C	D	E
1					
2		Demand (cubic yards/week)	4,500		
3					
4		Shipping Method	Truck	Multimodal	Difference
5		Direct shipping cost per 150 cubic yards	$ 950	$ -	
6		Rail shipping cost per 150 cubic yards	$ -	$ 375	
7		Unloading charge (per cubic yard)	$ -	$ 2.80	
8		Local delivery cost per 150 cubic yards	$ -	$ 125	
9		Total Landed Cost	$ 28,500	$ 27,600	$ 900

Notice that our given cost data applies to ***different units of measure***: (1) a <u>per-cubic-yard</u> unloading cost and (2) a <u>per-150-cubic-yard</u> transportation cost for both truck and rail. In order to properly compute total costs we must use the same unit of measure for costs. Hence, we divide the costs for truck, rail, and local delivery by 150 to incorporate a per-cubic-yard cost in our total landed cost cells. (***Here's a tip***: *when doing homework and assessment problems, make sure you incorporate or **not** incorporate, as appropriate, unit-of-measure conversions.)* As you can see, the multimodal solution costs less, by $900.

	D7	f_x	=C9-D9					
	A	B	C	D	E	F	G	H
1								
2		Demand (cubic yards/week)	4,500					
3								
4		Shipping Method	Truck	Multimodal				
5		Direct shipping cost per 150 cubic yards	$ 950	$ -				
6		Rail shipping cost per 150 cubic yards	$ -	$ 375				
7		Unloading charge (per cubic yard)	$ -	$ 2.80				
8		Local delivery cost per 150 cubic yards	$ -	$ 125				
9		Total Landed Cost	$ 28,500	$ 27,600	$ 900			

Goal Seek
Set cell: E9
To value: 0
By changing cell: $D$7
OK   Cancel

With these baseline calculations in place, we can easily do some what-if analyses. For example, at what cost for unloading would the two shipping methods cost the same? To answer this question we can easily invoke Excel's "Goal Seek" function.

We simply set cell E9 to be equal to zero by changing the cost in cell D7 (unloading charge per cubic yard, as shown in the graphic above). After clicking "OK" we see that the break-even point between the two shipping methods occurs when the unloading costs are $3.00 per cubic yard (as seen in the graphic below).

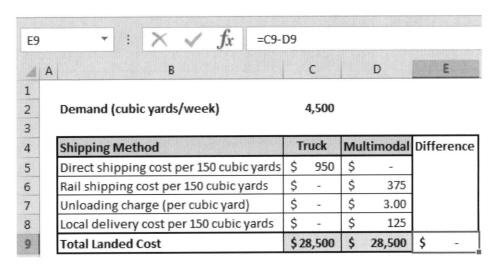

Summary Thoughts on Logistics Decision Models

The logistics decision models above provide some useful tools for making logistics-related decisions. These models, while rudimentary, provide a good conceptual framework upon which more complex and elaborate models can be built.

Chapter Summary

Below are some of the main points you should have garnered from the study of this chapter.

- **Logistics management**—often an overlooked part of supply chain management—**plans, implements, and controls** the forward and reverse flow of goods, services and information.
- **Deregulation** (late 1970s and early 1980s) and the resulting increase in competition—and new players (many 3PLs)—have resulted in a logistics renaissance the past three decades.
- **There are five basic modes of transportation**: road, rail, water, air, and pipeline. Multimodal transportation combines two or more of these basic modes to provide a greater variety of transportation services.
- The **concept of a warehouse**—a place to hold inventory—has **given way to the more dynamic concept of a distribution center**, where inventory is almost always moving (quickly being consolidated or broken down in preparation for immediate shipment). Several types of warehouses exist, and each may employ a unique mix of receiving, storing, picking, and packaging processes to meet a variety of needs.
- A number of modeling techniques exist to help with facility location and transportation routing decisions. Two of the most basic are **weighted center of gravity** and the **assignment or transportation method**.

GLOSSARY

Being able to "speak the language" is a great key to success in production and operations management. Most of the terms in this glossary (or closely related terms) appear in the chapters of this textbook. This glossary has been compiled for your easy reference.

If you are interested in a more complete dictionary of production and operations management terminology, consider joining APICS (The Association of Operations Management) and obtaining your own copy of the APICS dictionary (now on its 13th edition). Full-time students can join APICS for a mere $25 per year, and many employers will pay for APICS memberships, education, and certifications.

3PL — Abbreviation for third-party logistics.

4PL — Abbreviation for fourth-party logistics.

Acceptable quality level (AQL) — A satisfactory level of quality for acceptance sampling of successive lots.

Acceptance sampling — The process of sampling a portion of incoming or outgoing lots rather than examining entire lots. Each lot may be accepted or rejected based on the sample even though the specific units in the lot may be better or worse than the sample.

Advance ship notice (ASN) — An electronic data interchange (EDI) notification of shipment.

Advanced planning and scheduling (APS) system — A computer program that uses advanced mathematical models to optimize forecasts, production plans and schedules, distribution plans, or transportation plans and routings.

Allocation — 1) The classification of items that have been assigned to specific orders. 2) A process for distributing material in short supply. See reservation.

Anticipation inventory — Additional inventory above normal levels to cover projected trends of increasing sales due to promotions, seasonal fluctuations, plant shutdowns, and vacations.

Appraisal costs — costs associated with checking the quality within a firm, including costs of inspection, quality audits, testing, calibration, and checking time.

APICS — A leading association for operations management professionals, offering educational services and professional certifications.

APS — Acronym for advanced planning and scheduling.

AQL — Acronym for acceptable quality level.

ASN — Acronym for advance ship notice.

Assemble-to-order — A production environment where a good or service is assembled after receipt of a customer order. An ATO environment can enable a postponement strategy as a large number of end products be assembled from common components.

Assembly line — A process in which equipment and workers are laid out to follow the sequence in which raw materials and parts are assembled. See line flow, product layout, production layout.

Assignment — See allocation.

Assignment problem — See transportation method.

Associative forecast — A forecast model which uses mathematical relationships between variables to predict the future. See causal forecast.

Assortment warehousing — the storing of goods close to the customer to ensure short lead times.

ATP — Acronym for available to promise.

Available to promise (ATP) — The uncommitted portion of inventory and planned production which supports customer order promising.

Back office applications — Systems that do not deal directly with customers such as accounts payable and inventory management.

Back room — The part of the operation that is completed without direct customer contact. Service operations typically contain both back room and front room operations. See front room.

Backhaul — The process of a carrier contracting for the return trip from the original destination. Backhauling was not permitted prior to the deregulation of the 1980 Motor Carrier Act. The backhaul can be with a full, partial, or empty load. See deadhead.

Backlog — All open customer orders which have been received (from the customers) but not yet shipped.

Backorder — An unfilled past due customer order where inventory is insufficient. See stockout.

Backward pass — In a project network diagram, the process of working backward from the finish node to the start node to determine latest finish and start times and slack time. See: forward pass.

Bar coding — Using a series of alternating bars and spaces, printed or stamped on a part, which can represent encoded information for fast and accurate reading of data.

Base point pricing — A geographic-based pricing policy where customers pay no freight if they are located within a specific range from the shipping point and pay base price plus transportation when located outside that range.

Batch flow — A production process in which parts are accumulated and processed together in a lot.

Batch manufacturing — Manufacturing where parts are processed together in a lot.

Batch picking — Pulling products for multiple orders at the same time. See order picking.

Batch size — See lot size.

Benchmarking — Comparing one company's costs, products, services or processes to those of a company (or department) thought to have superior performance.

Bias — See forecast bias.

Bill of lading — A contract and receipt for freight the carrier agrees to transport from one place to another. The bill of lading is the basis for filing any freight-related claims.

Bill of material (BOM) — A listing of all the components that go into a parent assembly showing the quantity of each required to make an assembly. It is used in conjunction with the master production schedule to determine the items for which purchase requisitions and production orders must be released.

Blanket purchase order — A long-term commitment to a supplier against which

6

short-term releases are shipped, often used in conjunction with EDI.

BOM — Acronym for bill of material.

Bonded warehouse — A warehouse or part of a warehouse that is designated by the U.S. Secretary of the Treasury for storing imported merchandise, operated under U.S. Customers supervision.

Booked orders — Demand that has been confirmed with a system transaction.

Bottleneck — A resource whose capacity is less than the demand which is placed upon it or a task within a series of connected tasks that takes the longest to perform.

BPR — Acronym for business process reengineering.

Break-bulk warehousing — A special form of cross-docking in which incoming shipments are from a single source.

Buffer stock — See safety stock.

Bulk issue — Parts issued from stores to work-in-process, but not based on a job order. See point-of-use inventory, backflush.

Bulk storage — Large-scale storage of items.

Bullwhip effect — The phenomenon that occurs when small changes in product demand by the consumer at the end of the supply chain translate into wider and wider swings in demand experienced by companies further up the supply chain.

Business process reengineering (BPR) — The fundamental rethinking and radical redesign of business processes to achieve dramatic cost, quality, and speed improvements.

CAD — Acronym for computer aided design.

Can-order point — An ordering system used when multiple items are order from one supplier. If one of these items reaches its ROP, then all items purchased from this supplier can be reordered if inventory is below the can-order point (which is higher than the item's original ROP.)

Capacity — 1) The capability of a system to perform its expected function or process. 2) The expected output of a resource (machine, work center, person) over a specific amount of time.

Cargo — An item shipped in an aircraft, railroad car, ship, barge, or truck.

Carload lot — A shipment that qualifies for a reduced freight rate because it is greater than a specified weight.

Category management — A marketing organizational structure that gives managers responsibility for planning and implementing marketing for certain product lines.

Causal forecast — A type of forecast that uses cause-and-effect associations to make predictions and explain relationships between independent and dependent variables. See associative forecast.

Cause-and-effect diagram — A diagram that helps to show the main causes and subcauses leading to an effect (symptom). Also known as a fishbone diagram or Ishikawa.

Cellular layout — A hybrid layout (cross between process layout and product layout), which groups of 3 to 10 machines and cross-trained workers produce a family of products (as opposed to just one product).

Center-of-gravity approach — A method of finding a facility location which minimizes transportation costs.

Chain of customers — The sequence of customers that in turn consume the output of each other. An example might be Intel→HP→Best Buy→end user.

Changeover flexibility — See setup flexibility.

Channel integration — Strengthening the relationships up and down the supply chain, from suppliers' suppliers to customers' customers.

Channels of distribution — The specific series of companies or individuals through which the flow of goods and services passes, from producer to customers.

Chase production — A production planning method that adjusts output levels to match demand in each planning period, usually by adding or decreasing material and capacity resources.

Churn — The process of customers switching supplier preferences because they can find better or less expensive products and services elsewhere.

CIF — Acronym for cost, insurance, freight.

CNC — Acronym for computer numerical control.

COFC — Acronym for container on a flatcar.

Collaborative planning, forecasting, and replenishment (CPFR) — A concept or philosophy that aims to improve cross-company integration of supply chain planning processes.

Common carrier — A transportation provider available to the public that cannot provide special treatment to any particular party.

Computer numerical control (CNC) — The use of a computer or microprocessor to provide numerical instructions to a machine tool controller. For example, you could have a CNC drill, CNC, lathe, etc.

Computer-aided design (CAD) systems — Technology that allows engineers to develop, modify, share, and test designs in a virtual world.

Concept phase — In project management, the first phase of a project, where a broad definition of the project is created. Also known as the initiation phase.

Concurrent engineering — In the design process, the simultaneous participation of all relevant functional areas.

Configuration — The arrangement of specific components to produce an assembly.

Configurator — A software system, used in order entry, that maintains product models and allows for the complete definition of all acceptable production options with a minimum of data entry.

Conformance quality — A measure of how closely a product matches its specifications.

Consignment — The process of a supplier placing goods at a customer location without receiving payment for those goods until they are used.

Consolidation — The process of combining items from more than one supplier and then shipping the items together. See milk run.

Consolidation warehousing — A type of warehousing where items are combined to make larger outbound shipments (and reduce costs).

Constraint — An element that prevents a system from achieving its performance goal.

Consumer's risk — In acceptance sampling, the probability that a customer will accept a bad lot of goods. See type II error.

Container on a flatcar (COFC) — Transporting a shipping container on a railroad flatcar.

Containerization — A shipping method in which items are placed in containers and are not unloaded until after they arrive at their destination.

Continuous flow — A production system in which equipment is organized and sequenced according to the steps involved to produce the product. The main difference between line flow and continuous flow is in the form of the product. In a continuous flow environment, the product usually cannot be broken down until the very end of the process. For example, cheese production is an example of this, where discrete units are not created (cut) until the end of the process.

Continuous process improvement (CPI) — Making incremental, regular improvements to processes or products as opposed to making radical changes (like with BPR). Also known as continuous improvement.

Continuous review system — An inventory system where orders and on-hand balances are constantly monitored so that replenishment orders are placed whenever the reorder point is reached.

Contract carrier — A for-hire carrier that provides transportation for one or a limited number of shippers (customers).

Control chart — A graphical representation of process performance containing control limits, making it easy to detect problems with the process.

Control chart factors — A table of numbers used in the creation of mean (x-bar) and range (r) charts.

Control limits — A statistically derived line which shows the upper or lower boundary within which a normal functioning process should be performing.

Core competencies — Capabilities that enable a firm to provide value to customers in such a way that is difficult to duplicate.

Cost, insurance, freight (CIF) — A term that indicates that the seller is

responsible for the cost, the marine insurance, and the freight charges of an ocean shipment.

CPFR — Acronym for collaborative planning, forecasting, and replenishment.

CPI — Acronym for continuous process improvement.

Crashing — The practice of adding resources to critical or near-critical activities in order to shorten the duration of a project.

Critical activities — Project activities that are on the critical path.

Critical path — The longest sequence of activities through a project network diagram. It defines the project duration.

Critical Path Method — A project network planning technique which shows the elements that constrain the total time for the project.

CRM — Acronym for customer relationship management.

Cross-docking — The process of sorting incoming shipments within an intermediate warehouse and then carrying those items to outgoing vehicle docking points. In a pure cross-docking warehouse, inventory is never stored, just quickly moved from incoming vehicles to outgoing vehicles.

Cross-selling — The process of selling additional products or services to go along with the initial purchase.

Cross-sourcing — A sourcing strategy that uses one supplier in one part of the business and another supplier in a different area of the business. These suppliers can compete for future business and provide a ready backup, if necessary.

CSCMP — Acronym for the Council of Supply Chain Management Professionals.

CSR — Acronym for customer service representative.

Cube utilization — A measurement of how efficiently space is being used in a warehouse or on a vehicle.

Cubic space — A measurement of the space available in a warehouse or on a vehicle.

Customer order fulfillment process — The series of process steps required to ship to a customer, including order status reporting.

Customer relationship management (CRM) — The collection and analysis of information designed to help an organization put the customer first. It includes account management, order entry, payment processing, credit, and other functions.

Customer satisfaction — The ultimate result of delivering goods or services that meet customer requirements.

Customer service — 1) The ability of a company to meet the needs of its customers. 2) A measure of how well a company's order fulfillment process meets the customer's request date. Syn: delivery performance.

Customer service ratio — A measure of delivery performance.

Customer service representative (CSR) — Personnel who answer customer questions and provide technical support.

Customs broker — A person who handles the paperwork and tracks to movement of international shipments.

Cycle stock — One of two main concepts of inventory, along with safety stock. Cycle stock is more active than safety stock and represents the items that are depleted gradually and replenished when orders are received.

Cycle time — The time between the completion of two discrete units of production. Also, the maximum time spent on any workstation within a production line.

Cyclical — A time series component of demand.

DBR — Acronym for drum-buffer-rope.

Deadhead — The return of an empty transportation container. See backhaul.

Decision matrix — See factor-rating method.

Decision support system (DSS) — A computer system designed to help planners and managers evaluate and select an appropriate course of action.

Decision Tree — A method of analysis that uses probabilities to estimate the value of various options which are placed in a tree-like graphic.

Decision variables — The variables which will be changed to find an optimal solution. For example, variables are one of the four main components used within an Excel Solver model.

Decomposition — A method of forecasting that separates time-series data into one of three components (trend, seasonal, or cyclical) in order to identify patterns. The new forecast is made by projecting these patterns into the future.

Decoupling points — Locations in the product structure or distribution network where inventory is placed in order to create independence between process steps.

Delivery lead time — The time from the receipt of a customer order to the delivery of the product.

Delivery performance — A measure of how well a company's order fulfillment process meets the customer's request date. Syn: customer service.

Delivery policy — The company's goal for delivery lead time. Also known as the quoted lead time.

Delivery reliability — A measurement of how consistently goods and services are delivered on, or before, the promised time.

Delivery speed — A measure of how quickly a product or service can be delivered once demand is identified.

Delphi method — A qualitative forecasting method where opinions from experts are combined in a series of iterations that leads to convergence on a solution.

Demand chain management — An inventory management approach that focuses on customer pull versus supplier push.

Demand management process — The process of planning demand, communicating demand, influencing demand, and prioritizing demand in a way to better match the company's output capabilities.

Demand pull — The practice of triggering demand for a work center (or inventory stocking point) only when the downstream work center (or customer) is ready to begin the next job.

Demurrage — Carrier charges and fees when rail freight cars and ships are retained beyond the specified loading or unloading time. See detention, express.

Dependent demand — Demand that is directly derived from the bill of material structure for parent items. MRP is used to calculate demand for such items. See independent demand.

Design capacity — The theoretical maximum output of system under ideal conditions.

Design for manufacturability (DFM) — A product development approach that involves manufacturing in the early stages of product design to ensure ease of manufacture.

Detention — Carrier charges and fees when truck trailers are retained beyond the specified loading or unloading time. See demurrage, express.

DFM — Acronym for design for manufacturability.

Differentiation strategy — A business strategy that focuses on setting a product or service apart from the competition.

Direct costs — Costs which can be directly attributable to a particular job or operation. Direct material and direct labor fall into this category.

Direct material — Material that becomes part of the product.

Direct sales — Sales from the manufacturer directly to the end customer, without going through a sales channel (wholesaler, retailer, etc.).

Direct truck shipment — A truck shipment made from the shipper to the receiver, without any additional pick-up or delivery stops.

Direct-deduct inventory transaction processing — A method of inventory bookkeeping that decreases the computer's record of an item when material issued from stock. Syn: discrete issue. See backflush.

Disbursement — The physical issuance and reporting of movement of material or other items from a store room or warehouse. See issue.

Discrete issue — Syn: direct-deduct inventory transaction processing.

Discrete picking — Pulling products for a single order. See order picking.

Disintermediation — The elimination of one or more intermediate links in a supply chain (cutting out of middlemen), resulting in decreased costs and shorter cycle times.

Dispatch list — A listing of manufacturing orders in priority sequence, usually generated daily, at the work center level.

Glossary

Dispatcher — A transportation worker who directs cars, buses, trucks, railcars, and other vehicles.

Distribution — The activities associated with moving material (usually finished goods) from the manufacturer to the customer.

Distribution center — A warehouse which contains finished goods items which are usually shipped to retail locations. Also known as a branch warehouse.

Distribution channel — See channels of distribution.

Distribution cost — Costs associated with the movement and storage of finished products (like inventory costs, order processing costs, transportation costs).

Distribution inventory — Spare parts and finished goods which are in a distribution center or in transit between a warehouse and the consumer.

Distribution requirements planning (DRP) — Replenishment inventory calculations using MRP-like time-phasing techniques or other planning approaches.

Distribution system — A group of interrelated facilities (manufacturing and warehousing) which link production, storage, an consumption activities for spare parts and finished goods inventory.

Downstream — Indicates moving in the direction of the end customer.

DPM — Acronym for defects per million.

Drop ship — To have a supplier ship directly to the buyer's customer.

DRP — Acronym for distribution requirements planning.

Drum-buffer-rope (DBR) — The theory of constraints method for scheduling and managing operations that have an internal constraint or capacity-constrained resource. The "drum" is the constraint that sets the pace. The "buffer" consists of time and materials to keep the constraint fully utilized. The "rope" is the flow of information from the rope to the front of the line.

DSS — Acronym for decision support system.

Dual-sourcing — A sourcing strategy where two suppliers provide the same products or services, with the business usually split 70/30.

Dunnage — Packaging material which is used to product a product from damage during transport.

Duty-free zone — An area where semi-finished items are brought into a country for further work to be done. Duty rate is based on the value of the semi-finished item, not the finished product.

EAP — Acronym for employee assistance program.

Earliest finish time (EF) — In the critical path method, the earliest date or time at which a given activity is estimated to be completed.

Earliest start time (ES) — In the critical path method, the earliest date or time at which a given activity is estimated to begin.

Echelon — A level of supply chain nodes. For example, a supply chain with three factories, eight distribution centers, and 200 retail stores would be a supply chain with three echelons or levels.

Economic order quantity (EOQ) — A type of fixed-order quantity model that balances the tradeoff of inventory holding costs and ordering costs.

ECO — Acronym for engineering change order.

ECR — Acronym for efficient consumer response.

EDI — Acronym for electronic data interchange.

EDLP — Acronym for everyday low price.

Effective capacity (rated capacity) — The capacity a company can expect to achieve, given its product mix, maintenance, and other down time.

Effectivity date — The date on which a component is to be added or removed from the bill of material or a process operation.

Efficiency — Actual time a resource is used (to produce goods or services) divided by the effective capacity.

Efficient customer response (ECR) — A demand-driven replenishment model where production is initiated based on point-of-sale data., primarily used in the grocery industry.

Electronic data exchange (EDI) — The paperless exchange of trading documents, such as purchase orders, advanced shipment notices, invoices, etc.

Electronic product code (EPC) — A code that is used with RFID tags to carry information.

Employee assistance program (EAP) — Services provided by (larger) employers to help employees and their families with personal and work-related problems. Services might include financial counseling, substance abuse rehabilitation, and so forth.

Employee empowerment — The practice of giving non-managerial employees the responsibility and the power (normally given to staff specialists) to make decisions regarding their work — very common within Toyota's Production System (TPS).

End item — An item sold as a finished good or spare part. Syn: end product, finished good, finished product.

Engineering change order (ECO) — A revision to a design released by engineering to modify or correct a part, usually implemented on the agreed upon effectivity date. Syn: engineering change notice.

Engineer-to-order — Products whose customer specifications require unique engineering design, significant customization, or new purchased materials. Each customer order results in a unique set of part numbers, bills of material, and routings.

Enterprise resource planning (ERP) system — An integrated information system that serves all departments within an enterprise. ERP grew out of MRP systems and implies packaged software suitable for many companies versus custom software.

EPC — Acronym for electronic product code.

ERP — Acronym for enterprise resource planning.

Every day low price (EDLP) — A retail strategy to keep prices low across all products, as opposed to having certain items on sale, in order to encourage level demand and hence, more efficient supply chain operations.

Exempt carriers — A for-hire carrier that, by virtue of the type of cargo carried (often commodities like produce, livestock, or coal), is free from economic regulation.

Exploding the BOM — An essential part of the MRP process that allows the master schedule to be converted into component-level requirements.

Exponential smoothing model — A type of weighted moving average forecast that employs a smoothing constant (alpha) and can be used when little historical data exists.

Express — 1) Payment a carrier makes when ships, rail cars, or truck trailers are unloaded or loaded in less than the time allowed by contract. 2) The use of overnight or 2-day delivery for priority packages. See demurrage, detention.

External failure costs — Quality-related costs that are found after the product reaches the customer. These costs include the loss of reputation, which can be extremely high and very difficult to quantify.

Factor-rating method — A simple but effective decision-making method or tool that allows users to assign numeric values and weights to decision criteria. The output of this method is a weighted score for each decision option.

Feature — A distinctive characteristic of a product. In material planning, features are used in 2-level bills of material and typically have several options from which to choose. For example, a laptop feature could be the case, and each available color would represent the options from which to choose.

Field service — The functions of installing and maintaining a product for a customer, and usually includes help with implementation and training.

Fill rate — Syn: customer service ratio.

Final assembly — The item which is shipped to the customer and the highest level in the bill of material.

Final assembly schedule (FAS) — The schedule of end items, typically in an assemble-to-order environment, where the products are finished to the customer's specific requirements.

First-article inspection — The quality testing of a pre-production sample to determine whether the subsequent order or contract should be accepted.

Five S's — Five terms beginning with the letter "S" which encourage a clean workplace, suitable for lean production.

Five why's — The practice of asking "why" five times (or more) to get to the root cause of a problem.

Fixed costs — A cost that is not directly related to the unit volume of production.

Fixed-location storage — A method of storage where a permanent location is assigned to each item. See random-location storage.

Fixed-position layout — A factory layout that plans for the product to be in a set place; the people, machines, and tools are brought to and from the product.

Flatcar — A piece of railroad rolling stock that consists of an open, flat deck on which truck trailers and large shipping containers may be placed.

Flexibility — The ability to respond quickly, mitigating the risks of demand changes and supply variability.

Flexible manufacturing systems (FMS) — A group of numerically controlled tools which enhance operational flexibility.

Floating inventory location system — Syn: random-location storage.

Floor-ready merchandise — Items received from a supplier having all needed tags, prices, and so forth to make them ready to be placed on the retail floor.

FOB — Acronym for free on board.

FOB destination — Where the supplier pays for transportation to the buyer's location.

FOB origination — Where the buyer pays for transportation from the supplier's location.

Forecast — An estimate or prediction of future demand.

Forecast bias — The tendency for the forecast to be greater or less than actual demand. See tracking signal.

Forty-foot equivalent — A measure of a container that his equal to two 20 feet by 8 feet by 8 feet containers.

Forward buying — Purchasing materials in a quantity the current requirement.

Four M's — Four terms typically used to categorize the branches within a cause-and-effect diagram: man, machine, method, materials.

Fourth-party logistics (4PL) — A non-asset based 3PL, sometimes called the lead logistics provider.

Free on board (FOB) — The terms of sale which define where title passes to the buyer.

Freight equalization — The practice of a more distant supplier absorbing some of the freight charges in order to match the freight charges of a closer supplier.

Freight forwarder — The intermediary or "middle man" between the shipper and the carrier who often combines smaller shipments to obtain bulk shipping rates.

Front office applications — Software that faces the customer and provides functionality to take orders, configure complex products and provide service and support to customers. It includes customer relationship management (CRM), sales force automation (SFA), customer support and field service.

Front room — The place where customers come into contact with the service operation.

Functional layout — Syn: process layout.

Gantt chart — The best-known type of planning and control chart, used in project management and production scheduling.

Group technology — A manufacturing philosophy and practice that enables a cellular layout for rapid production of physically similar parts

Hedge inventory — Buffer inventory designed to protect against a labor strikes, price increases, government instability, or other events.

Heuristics — A form of problem solving where rules have been determined by experience or intuition instead of optimization.

Histogram — A graph of vertical bars representing a frequency distribution.

HOQ — Acronym for House of Quality.

House of Quality (HOQ) — A QFD tool that helps firms design product and service offerings according to customer desires. See Quality Function Deployment.

Hub-and-spoke systems — A distribution system that has a center point (hub) surrounded by the stores it services.

Incoterms — A series of terms used to specify buyer and seller responsibilities for a given international commercial transaction.

Independent demand — Demand for an item which is not related to demand for other items. Finished goods and spare parts fall into this category. See dependent demand.

Indirect costs — Costs not directly tied to production of an item, but are usually part of overhead costs.

Indirect materials — Parts and other supplies that support operations but do not become part of the product to be sold.

In-sourcing — Using the firm's internal resources to provide goods and services.

Intermodal — Syn: multimodal.

Internal failure costs — Quality-related costs before the product reaches the customer. These include rework, scrap, and process losses.

In-transit inventory — Material moving between two (or more) locations.

Inventory — Stocks of items which are used to support production, customer service, and MRO activities.

Inventory policy — The company's goals and approach to managing inventory.

Inventory pooling — See risk pooling.

ISM — Acronym for the Institute of Supply Management.

ISO 9000 — A set of international quality standards initially published in 1987 by the International Organization for Standardization (ISO).

JIT — Acronym for just in time.

Job shop — See jumbled flow.

Jumbled flow (job shop) — A manufacturing process used to produce engineer-to-order or make-to-order items. Production operations are designed to handle a wide range of product designs as material moves from one functional area to another, being processed on general-purpose equipment.

Just-in-time (JIT) — A philosophy based on the elimination of waste and improvement of productivity.

Kanban system — A production system that uses containers and cards as visual cues to "pull" material through the system.

Keiretsu — A form of cooperative relationship among companies in Japan where the companies remain legally and economically independent, but work closely in various ways such as sole sourcing and financial backing.

Lag capacity strategy — The acquisition of supply-related resources after demand is realized.

Laid-down cost — Syn: landed cost.

Landed cost — The total cost of acquiring a product, including product cost and the cost of logistics.

Latest finish time — In the critical path method, the latest date or time at which a given activity can be completed and not add to the project's duration.

Latest start time — In the critical path method, the latest date or time at which a given activity can be started and not add to the project's duration.

Law of variability — States that the more variable a process is, the less productive it will be.

LCL — Acronym for less than truckload.

Lead capacity strategy — The acquisition of supply-related resources before demand is realized.

Lean production — A philosophy that focuses on the elimination of waste and only doing those activities which add value to customers.

Less than truckload (LTL) — A small shipment that does not fill a truck and does not qualify for lower truckload (TL) rates.

Level production plan — A build plan strategy which aims to keep the production rate constant, using inventory to absorb the fluctuations in demand.

Line flow — A form of manufacturing organization in which machines and operators handle a standard, material flow (in a "product" layout). The operators generally perform the same operations for each production run, enabling mass production. This is the classic assembly line form of manufacturing.

Linear programming (LP) — Mathematical models for solving linear optimization problems subject to constraints. (Simplex LP is one of the method options within Excel's Solver function.)

Linear regression — A statistical technique used to determine the relationship between a response and one or more independent variables.

Line-haul — The direct transport of cargo from one city (or port) to another.

Load-distance analysis — A method of choosing a facility layout based on the shortest travel time.

Logistics — The art and science of obtaining, producing, and distributing material and products in the proper place and proper quantities.

Lot size — Policies regarding the quantities of purchases, production, and distribution of materials, in order to meet the organizations goals regarding cost and flexibility.

Lot tolerance percent defective (LTPD) — The poorest quality in an individual lot that should be accepted.

Lowboy — A semi-trailer with a very low deck which permits transport of taller items. For example, land-moving equipment is often transported on a lowboy.

Lower control limit (LCL) — The lower boundary above which a normal functioning process should be performing.

LTL — Acronym for less than truckload.

LTPD — Acronym for lot tolerance percent defective.

Lumper — A person who loads and unloads a semi-trailer either by hand or with a pallet jack.

MAD — Acronym for mean absolute deviation.

Maintenance, repair, and other (MRO) — Inventory items used to support general operations.

Make-or-buy decision — The act of deciding whether to produce an item internally or buy it from a supplier. Factors to consider in the decision include quality, skill requirements, proprietary knowledge, costs, capacity availability, volume, and timing.

Make-to-order (MTO) — A production environment where a good or service is made after receipt of a customer's order. The final product is usually a combination of standard items and custom-designed items to meet the specific needs of the customer.

Make-to-stock (MTS) — A production environment where products are finished before receipt of a customer order. Production is typically driven by forecasts and customer orders are filled from existing stocks.

Manufacturing order — A document (online or hard copy) which authorizes the production of specified parts. Syn: production order, work order.

MAPE — Acronym for mean absolute percentage error.

Master production schedule — The anticipated build schedule expressed in specific configurations, quantities, and dates.

Match capacity strategy — The acquisition of supply-related resources concurrent with demand increases.

Material requirements planning (MRP) — A set of techniques used to calculate requirements for materials (dependent demand items).

Materials handling system — The system that receives, moves, and delivers materials during the production and distribution process.

Mean absolute deviation (MAD) — A forecast-accuracy measure which is the average of the absolute differences of actual demand and the forecast.

Mean absolute percentage error (MAPE) — A forecast-accuracy measure which is the average of the percentage differences of actual demand and the forecast.

Mean time between failures (MTBF) — The average time interval between failures of a product.

Milk run — A regular route for pickup and consolidation of mixed loads from several suppliers.

Minimum order quantity — The minimum quantity that must be placed on a given order.

Min-max system — An order point replenishment system where the "min" is the order point and the "max" is the order-up-to level.

Mix forecast — The proportion of products that will be sold within a given product family, or the proportion of options that will be used for a given feature (in a 2-level bill of material).

Mixed manufacturing — Make-to-stock and make-to-order manufacturing using the same set of equipment.

Modular bill of material — A type of planning bill of material that is arranged in product modules or options, used to help plan requirements for products that have many optional features. See planning bill of material.

Move card — In a JIT environment, a card that indicates a specific number of units that are to be taken from a stocking point.

Moving average model — The average of a certain number of recent observations.

MRO — Acronym for maintenance, repair, and other.

MRP — Acronym for material requirements planning.

MTBF — Acronym for mean time between failures.

MTO — Acronym for make to order.

MTS — Acronym for make to stock.

Muda — The Japanese word for waste, used in a JIT or lean production environment.

Multi-factor productivity — A measure of productivity which considers two or more inputs required for a given output.

Multimodal — Transportation that combines more than one means of transportation.

Multiple regression — A regression analysis that involves more than one independent variable.

Multiple sourcing — Procurement of a good or service from more than one supplier.

Network diagram — A graphical representation of a project plan which facilitates the calculation of earliest and latest start and finish times, slack times, and the identification of the critical path.

New product introduction (NPI) — The work managing the design, prototyping and production launch of a new product.

NPI — Acronym for new product introduction.

Objective function — The goal that is to be optimized within a model.

Operating characteristic (OC) curve — A graph which is used to determine the probability of accepting lots as a function of the quality level.

Operating ratio (OR) — A measure of performance often used in the trucking industry, equal to operating expenses divided by net sales.

Operations management — The planning and controlling of all activities related to the transformation of inputs into outputs.

Optimization models — Decision support tools which solve mathematical problems based on the objective function.

Option — From a planning and scheduling standpoint, a choice that must be made when customizing the end product.

Option overplanning — The scheduling of extra quantities of options as a mix hedge for when actual demand for options differs from historical averages.

Order picking — Selecting the required quantity and specific products to be shipped. See batch picking, discrete picking, wave picking, zone picking.

Order promising — The process of assigning a delivery commit date to an order.

Order qualifiers — The minimum characteristics a company must exhibit in order to be considered a viable competitor in the market place.

Order quantity — See lot size.

Order up-to level — In a periodic replenishment system, the quantity to which materials can be ordered.

Order winners — The characteristics that cause a company's customers to choose that company's goods and services over a competitor's offerings.

Outsourcing — The process of having suppliers produce goods or services that were previously produced internally.

Outsourcing — The process of replacing internal capacity and production with that of a supplier.

P chart — An attribute control chart which monitors the proportion of the total number of units which are defective.

Packing slip — A document which provides a detailed list of the items in a particular package, carton, pallet, or container for shipment to a customer.

Panel consensus — A judgment forecasting method where a committee, sales force, or group of experts arrive at a sales estimate.

Pareto chart — A graphic tool which ranks causes from most significant to least significant, designed to focus attention on the most significant.

PCE — Acronym for process cycle efficiency.

PDCA — Acronym for plan-do-check-act.

Perfect order — An order which satisfies the "seven Rs": the right product, the right quantity, the right condition, the right place, the right time, the right customer, the right cost.

Performance — 1) The degree to which a resource output is measured against an established standard. 2) A measure of quality pertaining to the function of the product.

Periodic review system — A replenishment system where inventory levels are reviewed at regular intervals (weekly, for instance) to determine replenishment requirements.

PERT — Acronym for program evaluation and review technique.

Piggyback — Syn: trailer on a flatcar

Pipeline inventory — Syn: pipeline stock.

Pipeline stock — Inventory that is in the distribution system, including in-transit inventory.

Plan-do-check-act — A four-step process for improving quality, also known as the Deming cycle.

Planned order — A suggested, computer-generated order created by the MRP system, specifying the quantity and timing of units to be produced or purchased. Planned orders are converted into scheduled production orders or scheduled purchase orders once they are reviewed by a planner or buyer.

Planned order receipt — The planned receipt date of the MRP-created planned order.

Planned order release — The planned release date of the MRP-created planned order, equal in quantity to the planned order receipt, but offset by the lead time.

Planning and control — A process consisting of the following steps: plan, execute, measure, and control.

Planning bill of material — An artificial grouping of items used to facilitate 2-level master scheduling and material planning, where the options for each feature are expressed as percentages instead of quantities, leading to greater responsiveness to less predictable customer demand. See modular bill of material, option overplanning.

Planning horizon — The amount of time a plan extends into the future, normally far enough to cover the cumulative lead time of the longest lead time components.

Planning phase — The work of identifying, sequencing, and assigning and scheduling resources to project activities.

Planning time fence — A point in the planning horizon within which schedule changes must be approved by appropriate planners and management. Beyond this point it is usually

PO — Acronym for purchase order.

Point-of-use inventory — Inventory placed in the production process, close to where it is used.

Postponement — A product design and operations strategy that shifts product differentiation closer to the consumer by postponing distinguishing changes to the last possible supply chain location.

Postponement warehousing — A storage facility that combines traditional warehouse functions with light manufacturing operations.

Prevention costs — Costs from improvement activities aimed to reduce failure costs and appraisal costs.

Process — A planned series of operations that advances material or a procedure from one stage of completion to another.

Process capability index (Cpk) — A measurement used to see if a process is properly centered between design specifications.

Process capability ratio (Cp) — A measurement used to see if a process is capable of meeting design specifications.

Process cycle efficiency (PCE) — A metric that tells what percent of a process is dedicated to value-added activities. See value stream mapping.

Process layout (or functional layout) — A facility configuration in which operations of a similar nature (or functional departments) are grouped together (e.g., saw, lathe, mill, heat treat, press or marketing, finance, purchasing, etc.).

Process map — A diagram of the flow through a production system.

Procurement — The functions of purchase planning, buying, inventory control, traffic, receiving, incoming inspection, and salvage operations.

Producer's risk — In acceptance sampling, the probability that a customer will reject a bad lot of goods. See type I error.

Product — An end item; a good or service for sale or barter or internal use.

Product layout — Layout of equipment and human resources, arranged sequentially, based on the product's routing. See assembly line, line flow.

Product-based layout — Syn: production line.

Production card — In a JIT environment, a card that indicates items should be made or items should be removed from stock.

Production line — A series of pieces of equipment dedicated to the production of specific products or product families. See assembly line, line flow, product layout.

Productivity — A measure of output from a production process, per unit of input.

Program evaluation and review technique (PERT) — A network analysis technique which uses ranges of activity durations to come up with an estimate of project duration.

Project — Typically, a one-time endeavor with a specific objective to be met within predetermined time and dollar limitations.

Project charter — A short document that contains a statement of the scope, objectives and participants in a project.

Project phases — The four basic phases of a project are: (I) Initiation, (II) Planning, (III) Execution, and (IV) Close Out.

Pull system — The production, withdrawal, or replenishment of items only when the downstream operation or inventory point sends a replenishment signal or authorization.

Pup trailer — A short semi-trailer, usually 26 to 32 feet long, with one axle.

Purchase order (PO) — An authorization used to formalize a purchase transaction with a supplier. A purchase order, when given to a supplier, should contain the part number, description, quantity, and price of the goods or services ordered as well as the terms of payment, discounts, date of performance, and transportation and all other information related to the purchase and its execution by the supplier.

Purchase requisition — An authorization to the purchasing department to purchase specified materials in specified quantities within a specified time.

Purchasing — The term used in industry and management to denote the function of and the responsibility for procuring materials, supplies, and services.

QFD — Acronym for Quality Function Deployment.

Qualitative forecasting techniques — Forecasting methods which are based on intuition or judgment.

Quality — Conformance to requirements that result in user satisfaction, where goods or services satisfy the needs and expectations of the user.

Quality assurance — All the planned and systematic activities within an organization to provide confidence that a good or service will conform to requirement.

Quality function deployment (QFD) — A methodology designed to ensure that all major customer requirements are identified and met or exceeded through the product-design process. See House of Quality.

Quality loss function — First introduced by Genichi Taguchi, this parabolic model approximates and quantifies of a products deviation from its quality target.

Quantitative forecasting models — Forecasting methods that use historical demand data to project future demand.

R chart — A variables control chart which evaluates the stability of the variation (range) within a process. Also known as a range chart.

Randomness — A time-series component of demand.

Range (R) — The spread in a series of observations.

Rated capacity — Syn: effective capacity.

Relationship map — A diagram which shows the relationships between business functions. These maps help to show how processes are currently run, identify disconnects, and examine the benefits of proposed processes.

Reliability quality — A measure of quality dealing with the probability that a product will function properly for a specified period of time.

Reorder point system — A continuous review replenishment system. Orders are placed whenever inventory levels reach the reorder point.

Repetitive manufacturing — The repeated production of the same discrete products or product families.

Request for information (RFI) — An inquiry to a potential supplier about that supplier's product or service for potential use in the business. The inquiry can provide certain business requirements or be of a more general, exploratory nature.

Request for proposal (RFP) — A document used to solicit vendor responses when the functional requirements and features are known, but no specific product is in the RFP.

Request for quote (RFQ) — A document used to solicit vendor responses when a product has been selected and price quotes are needed from several vendors.

Reservation — The process of designating stock for a specific order. See allocation.

Responsiveness — A dimension of service quality referring to the promptness and helpfulness in providing a service.

Reverse logistics — A supply chain dedicated to the reverse flow of products and materials for the purpose of returns, repair, remanufacture, or recycling.

RFI — Acronym for request for information.

RFP — Acronym for request for proposal.

RFQ — Acronym for request for quote.

Risk pooling — Aggregating demand across locations in order to reduce overall demand variability, and hence, required safety stock.

Roadrailer — A semi-trailer that is specially equipped for rail use without the need of a flatcar.

Robust design — Design for a product or service that plans for intended performance even in the face of a harsh environment.

Rolling forecast — Moving the forecast horizon forward to new periods by adding recent historical data.

Root cause analysis — Methods to determine the core problem or problems of a process, product, organization, and so forth. See five whys.

Rough-cut capacity planning (RCCP) — The process of converting the master production schedule into requirements for key supply-related resources.

Routing — Information on the method of manufacture for a particular item, including the operations to be performed, their sequence, the work centers involved, and standard setup and run times.

RSFE — Acronym for running sum of forecast error.

Run chart — A graphical representation of how a process is running over time.

Running sum of forecast error (RSFE) — A cumulative total of the difference between actual demand and forecasts over a given period. It is used to compute the tracking signal.

Safety stock — A quantity of stock planned to be in inventory to protect against fluctuations in demand or supply.

Sales and operations planning — The cross-functional process of creating tactical plans whose output is typically at a product family (aggregate) level.

Sample mean — The average value of the sample values.

Sample — A portion of the universe of data chosen to estimate characteristics about the whole universe.

Scatter chart — A graph which shows the relationship between two variables.

Seasonality — A time-series component of demand. It describes the variations that occur at various times. A season could be certain hours in the day, days of the week, days of the month, weeks of the quarter, months of the year, and so forth.

Service level — A measure of the probability of meeting customer demand.

Serviceability — Design characteristics that facilitate ease of efficient service activities.

Setup flexibility — The ability to quickly change equipment to produce a different product.

Single period inventory system — A replenishment model used to determine the profit-maximizing quantity of a last-time purchase.

Single-factor productivity — A measure of product output from one source of input. It can be expressed using various units of measure or a monetary value.

Single-sourcing — A supply strategy that relies on only one supplier for a product or given products. This is a common practice with JIT manufacturers.

Six sigma — A methodology that focuses on the improvement of business processes by decreasing process variation and improving product quality.

Six-sigma quality — Processes that are capable of producing only 3.4 defects per million opportunities or operations.

Slack time — In the critical path method, the amount of time a given activity can be delayed and not add to the project's duration.

SPC — Acronym for statistical process control.

Spot stock warehousing — Storing seasonal items close to the marketplace in order to catch short lead time demand.

SRM — Acronym for supplier relationship management.

Standard deviation — A measure of the dispersion of data.

Statement of work — 1) A description of the products or services to be supplied under contract. 2) In project management, the first project planning document to be prepared.

Statistical process control (SPC) — The use of statistical techniques to monitor and adjust operations.

Stevedore — A firm or individual engaged in the loading or unloading of a vessel.

Stockout — A lack of components or finished goods which are needed. See backorder.

Strategic business planning — The process of creating a statement of revenue, cost, and profit objectives.

Strategic sourcing — A procurement process that continuously improves and re-evaluates the purchasing activities of a company. See: tactical buying

Supplier certification — Procedures verifying that a supplier operates,

Glossary

maintains, improves, and documents effective procedures that relate to the customer's requirements. Such requirements can include cost, quality, delivery, flexibility, maintenance, safety, and ISO quality and environmental standards.

Supplier relationship management (SRM) — A comprehensive approach to managing a company's interactions with its suppliers with the goal of streamlining cross-company operations.

Supply chain — The network used to deliver products and services from raw materials to end customers.

Supply chain management — The design, planning, execution, control, and monitoring of supply chain activities.

Support process — Activities that do not directly participate in production (accounting, information systems) but are nonetheless essential to effective company operations.

Sustainable sourcing — The practice of selecting and managing suppliers in a way that has positive effects (or minimal negative effects) on the environment.

Tactical buying — A purchasing process focused on nonstrategic, standard materials which can be sourced from many suppliers.

Tactical buying — The purchasing process focused on transactions and nonstrategic buying. The characteristics for items purchased through tactical buying include stable, standard specifications, noncritical to production, no delivery issues, and high reliability very little concern for rejects. See: strategic sourcing

Takt time — The available production time divided by the required output rate, representing the maximum allowable time between the completion of successive units. It sets the pace of production to match the rate of demand.

TEU — Acronym for twenty-foot equivalent unit.

Theory of constraints (TOC) — A holistic management philosophy developed by Dr. Eliyahu M. Goldratt (author of *The Goal*). The five steps of this philosophy include: 1) identify the constraint, 2) exploit the constraint, 3) subordinate all processes to the constraint, 4) elevate the constraint, and 5) return to step 1. See drum-buffer-rope.

Third-party logistics (3PL) — A company that offers one or more logistics services to shippers, the most common being transportation management, freight forwarding, warehouse management, and light manufacturing.

Throughput — The rate at which the system generates output units, expressed for a given time period.

Time series — A set of data that is distributed over time. For forecasting purposes, patterns of demand can be considered in time series analysis. The four components of times series are seasonal, trend, cyclical, and random.

TL — Acronym for truckload.

TOC — Acronym for the theory of constraints.

TOFC — Acronym for trailer on a flatcar.

Total cost of ownership (TC) — The total cost of ownership of the supply delivery system is the sum of all the costs associated with every activity of the supply stream. Personnel must realize that acquisition is just one of many costs associated with a supply relationship. Other costs include maintenance, repair, training, and so forth.

Total quality management (TQM) — A management approach to long-term success through customer satisfaction. TQM is based on the participation of all members of an organization in improving processes, goods, services, and the culture in which they work

TQM — Acronym for total quality management.

Tracking Signal — A measure of the forecast bias, computed by dividing RSFE by MAD (for the same period).

Traffic — A department charged with the arranging the method of shipment for both incoming and outgoing materials and products.

Trailer on a flatcar (TOFC) — Transporting a semi-trailer on a railroad flatcar.

Transportation inventory — Inventory that is intransit from one location to another.

Transportation method — A linear programming model used to minimize the costs of supplying requirements to several locations from several sources, with each demand/source combination having a different cost.

Trend — A time-series component of demand.

Truckload (TL) — A road shipment of sufficient quantity to fill an entire semi-trailer. TL shipments fewer stops, less handling, and lower shipping rates than LTL shipments.

Twenty-foot equivalent unit (TEU) — A measure of cargo capacity equivalent to a standard container (20 feet long, 8 feet wide, and 8 feet high).

Type I error — An incorrect decision to reject something that is good (like a lot or shipment from a supplier). See producer's risk.

Type II error — An incorrect decision to accept something that is bad (like a lot or shipment from a supplier). See consumer's risk.

UCL — Acronym for upper control limit.

Unitization — In warehousing, the consolidation of several units into larger units for fewer handlings

Upper control limit (UCL) — The upper boundary below which a normal functioning process should be performing.

Upstream — Indicates moving in the direction of the beginning supplier in a supply chain.

Utilization — Actual time a resource is used (to produce goods or services) divided by total design capacity.

Value stream mapping — A lean-management method that helps organizations improve process efficiency by identifying and eliminating sources of waste within a process. See process cycle efficiency.

Variable costs — An operating cost that varies with a change with each unit of production.

Vendor-managed inventory (VMI) — A means of optimizing supply chain performance by having the supplier maintain the inventory level required by the customer. This works well when demand is stable and volume is high.

VMI — Acronym for vendor-managed inventory.

Volume flexibility — The ability to quickly accommodate large variations in production levels.

Warehousing — The activities related to receiving, storing, and shipping materials to and from production or distribution locations.

Wave picking — A picking technique that is a hybrid of batch picking and zone picking. See order picking.

Waybill — A document containing a list of goods with shipping instructions related to a shipment.

Weighted center of gravity method — See center of gravity method.

Weighted moving average model — An averaging method in which the data

Glossary

to be averaged are given different weights according to their importance. See moving average.

WIP — Acronym for work in process.

WMS — Acronym for warehouse management system.

Work breakdown structure — The output from the process of identifying all the assignable tasks that must be completed as part of a project.

Work cell — The grouping of dissimilar machines into a production unit to produce a family of parts having similar routings.

Work center — A specific production area consisting of people and/or machines with similar capabilities, that can be considered as one unit for purposes of capacity requirements planning and detailed scheduling.

Work in process (WIP) — A good or goods in various stages of completion throughout the production area.

x-bar chart — A variables control chart which evaluates the stability of the mean (average) output of a process. Also known as a mean chart.

Yield — The amount of acceptable material available after the completion of a process, usually computed as the final output amount divided by the initial input amount, converted to a decimal or percentage.

Yield management — The process of anticipating and influencing consumer behavior in order to maximize yield or profits from a fixed, perishable resource (such as airline seats or hotel room reservations).

Zone picking — An assembly-line picking technique where the picking area is divided into zones and orders pass through each zone to be picked. See order picking.

Zone skipping — The use of LTL carriers to transport parcels to a parcel carrier's hub near the load's final destination instead of relying on the parcel carrier for end-to-end delivery. This allows the shipper to avoid charges incurred by the parcels crossing multiple zones en route from the shipper to the final destination.

Made in the USA
Middletown, DE
23 September 2023

39170328R00130